RELIGION
and SPIRITUALITY
in the Life Cycle

STUDIES IN
EDUCATION
& SPIRITUALITY

Peter Laurence and Victor Kazanjian
General Editors

Vol. 9

PETER LANG
New York • Washington, D.C./Baltimore • Bern
Frankfurt am Main • Berlin • Brussels • Vienna • Oxford

JAMES GOLLNICK

RELIGION
and SPIRITUALITY
in the Life Cycle

PETER LANG
New York • Washington, D.C./Baltimore • Bern
Frankfurt am Main • Berlin • Brussels • Vienna • Oxford

Library of Congress Cataloging-in-Publication Data

Gollnick, James.
Religion and spirituality in the life cycle / James Gollnick.
p. cm. — (Studies in education and spirituality; v. 9)
Includes bibliographical references and index.
1. Faith development. 2. Developmental psychology.
3. Life cycle, Human. 4. Meaning (Philosophy). I. Title. II. Series.
BV4637.G64   204'.01'9—dc22   2004020883
ISBN 0-8204-7411-8
ISSN 1527-8247

Bibliographic information published by **Die Deutsche Bibliothek**.
Die Deutsche Bibliothek lists this publication in the "Deutsche
Nationalbibliografie"; detailed bibliographic data is available
on the Internet at http://dnb.ddb.de/.

Cover design by Lisa Barfield

The paper in this book meets the guidelines for permanence and durability
of the Committee on Production Guidelines for Book Longevity
of the Council of Library Resources.

Printed in the United States of America

To the memory of
Isabelle Alice Murphy
and
Albert Jakob Gollnick,
My Mother and Father

TABLE OF CONTENTS

❧

LIST OF TABLES AND DIAGRAMS

————————— ⁊⬥ —————————

ACKNOWLEDGMENTS AND CREDITS

————————— ❧ —————————

I am grateful to David Seljak, Susan Bryant, Arlene Sleno, Paul Koop, Doreen Armbruster, Steve Izma, Peter Laurence, and Heidi Burns for their assistance in preparing this manuscript.

Some material in this book previously appeared in *Implicit Religion: Journal of the Centre for the Study of Implicit Religion and Contemporary Spirituality*.

Material from "Implicit Religion in the Psychology of Religion," *Implicit Religion*, 5(2) (2002), 81–92, is reprinted by permission of Maney Publishing Ltd.

Material from "Implicit Religion Highlights Religion in Childhood," *Implicit Religion*, 6(2) (2003), 70–85; "Is Implicit Religion Spirituality in Disguise?" *Implicit Religion*, 6(3) (2003), 146–160; and "Religion, Spirituality, and Implicit Religion in Psychotherapy," *Implicit Religion*, 7(2), (2004), 116–138, is reprinted by permission of Equinox Publishing Ltd.

INTRODUCTION

———————— ❧ ————————

All the world's a stage,
And all the men and women merely players. . . .
And one man in his time plays many parts,
His acts being seven ages.
At first the infant, mewling and puking in the nurse's arms;
Then the whining schoolboy, with his satchel and shining
morning face . . .
And then the lover, sighing like furnace, with a woeful bal-
lad . . .
Then a soldier, full of strange oaths, and bearded . . .
And then the justice, in fair round belly with good capon
lined . . .
The sixth age shifts into the lean and slippered pantaloon,
With spectacles on nose and pouch on side . . .
Last scene of all, that ends this strange eventful history,
In second childishness, and mere oblivion . . .
                          — William Shakespeare, *As You Like It*

In the above passage from Shakespeare, the end of the life cycle
appears to be about the same as the beginning, only with a shorter
future. Second childishness and oblivion seem to be all we can look forward to after we have played out the many roles of our lives. This book
challenges such a view by tracing the religious and spiritual dimensions
of our movement through the life cycle. Although religion is one of the
oldest concerns of humanity, in recent years there have been profound changes in the way people have come to view religion and its
place in the life cycle. Spirituality, which has always been considered an
essential part of religion, has for many people begun to emerge as an

interest no longer necessarily tied to organized religion. Increasingly, people discover or cultivate their spirituality by watching movies and television talk shows and by shopping at self-help, recovery, and New Age bookstores. Psychologist David Elkins (1998, p. 9) characterizes this recent divorce of spirituality from its traditional link to religion as "one of the major sociological changes of our time." This book will explore this shift and its implications for the role of religion and spirituality in the life cycle, a task that has not been carried out before.

Religion and Spirituality in the Life Cycle will also draw upon the concept of implicit religion in an effort to trace where the less obvious aspects of religion are at work in the development of personality through the course of life. Implicit religion refers to whatever functions like a religion, even though it does not seem to be religion in the conventional sense of the term. Hitherto, implicit religion has been applied in the sociology of religion primarily to study social phenomena and organizations. I propose to expand its use by focusing on the psychological dimensions of implicit religion. These elements will help us get at the less easily observed and measurable aspects of religion which nonetheless reveal how religion influences personality development. Such an application of implicit religion in a psychological direction has not been done before.

There are a number of reasons this work has not been carried out previously. First, the emergence of a humanistic spirituality separate from religious traditions is a relatively recent phenomenon. The same can be said for the concept of implicit religion, which has been applied by sociologists of religion only within the last two decades. Then too, mainline psychology has tended either to ignore or denigrate religion. Even psychologists interested in religion find it difficult to investigate the elusive qualities of spirituality and implicit religion because most of them are empirically oriented. This book is directed toward those people who are interested in this newly emerging spirituality and its changing relationship to religion, to help them be more rigorous in their thinking about spirituality and root it in concrete existence, in the body as well as the human mind.

This book is also addressed to psychologists who want to take religion seriously and to those who already see the importance of spirituality for how people move through life in modern Western societies. Some psychologists have, from the beginning of the discipline, struggled to see how the spirit and the body come together, how spirituality is rooted in the flesh and blood experience of life. We shall draw upon their perspectives as we seek to understand how spirituality and religion help shape the human personality throughout the life cycle. While this study recognizes the enormous role that society, economics, and technology play in the unfolding of the individual life cycle, it draws primarily upon psychology and psychotherapy to show that as people age, they can learn to transcend the ego, adopt universal values, and expand their worldview to experience the interconnectedness of all things. This spiritual development does not occur automatically or in all people, but it is in line with what various psychologists and psychotherapists see as healthy growth.

The plan of this book is straightforward: first, to set out the major terms guiding this exploration in chapter one, and then, in subsequent chapters, to examine the place of religion and spirituality in the major stages of life, namely, childhood, adolescence, early adulthood, midlife, and late adulthood.

THE SHIFTING RELIGIOUS AND SPIRITUAL LANDSCAPE

Several important studies since the early 1990s have documented important changes in the religious and spiritual landscape of North America. In *Megatrends 2000,* John Naisbitt (1990) speaks of a religious revival in characterizing changing patterns of religion in the United States. He cites statistics showing marked declines in the membership of mainline churches such as the United Methodist, Presbyterian, Episcopal, Lutheran, and Disciples of Christ and notes that the numbers of priests and nuns in the Catholic Church have declined dramatically. Mainline churches fare well in stable eras, observes Naisbitt, but decline in times of great change, such as the closing decades of the twentieth century. He calls attention to the striking contrast between declining mainline church attendance and the rising interest in spirituality during the same period and refers to this growing preoccupation with spirituality as one of the ten megatrends in contemporary American society.

On the Canadian scene, sociologist Reginald Bibby describes parallel changes, using extensive survey research and census data. In *Fragmented Gods: The Poverty and Potential of Religion in Canada* (1987), he documents a sharp decline in Canadian commitment to the Christian churches. Bibby comments that Canadians increasingly make use of the Christian churches and clergy selectively for particular occasions such as weddings and funerals, but are less likely to attend weekly services regularly or be active church members. *Unknown Gods: The Ongoing Story of Religion in Canada* (1993) updates this trend of decline in church involvement, but at the same time calls attention to a strong and growing interest in aspects of spirituality such as searching for the meaning of life, struggling with questions about life after death, and exploring ways to integrate various strands of personal and social life. In his study of some 4,000 young people and adults, *Restless Gods: The Renaissance of Religion in Canada* (2002), Bibby maintains that at the turn of the millennium, the prior trend of the last decades of declining attendance among mainline Protestant churches is slowly turning around, but adds that there is a strong hunger for spirituality that is not reflected in church attendance.

Various studies (Elkins, 1998; Paloutzian, 1996; Zinnbauer et al., 1999) call attention to an increased concern with personal spiritual development at the same time as involvement with mainline organized religion declines. A Gallup poll shows that 94 percent of Americans surveyed believe in God; 88 percent pray; and 53 percent say that religion is a very important part of their lives. Wade Roof's influential study *A Generation of Seekers* (1993) draws on a survey of 1,600 baby boomers to show that a large number of those who dropped out of organized religion in the 1960s and 1970s remain unaffiliated with religious institutions but deeply interested in such forms of spirituality as meditation, Native American traditions, mythology, Jungian psychology, New Age philosophies, shamanic practices, and yoga. Hood et al. (1996) report the development of an estimated 400 new spiritual/religious associations in the late 1980s alone, with evidence of the trend continuing.

PSYCHOLOGY'S CHANGING ATTITUDE TOWARD RELIGION

Certain areas of modern psychology increasingly recognize the importance of religion and spirituality, a situation very different from the early days of psychology when it aspired to be like the natural sciences, accounting for human thought and behavior strictly in terms of observable forces and clearly defined laws. The earliest psychological accounts of the dynamics and goals of human functioning were seen as an alternative to traditional, religious explanations of human meaning and values. Some people of that time even believed that psychology sought to replace religion. William James, who established one of the first psychology laboratories in North America at Harvard University toward the end of the nineteenth century, was an outstanding exception to this trend with his deep concern for spirituality and religious experience. On the whole, though, psychology did much to marginalize religious and spiritual interpretations of the human being in modern intellectual life.

Spiritual and religious views were excluded from, or even attacked by, mainstream psychology, psychiatry, and psychotherapy for nearly a century (Richards et al., 1999). Direct spiritual experiences such as visions of light, a sense of divine energy streaming through the body, death-rebirth experiences, and feelings of unity with the cosmos were considered pathological by all but a few. Generally, psychiatry would not attack religious beliefs as pathological only so long as those beliefs were shared by a large group of people. Carl Jung's Analytical Psychology and Roberto Assagioli's Psychosynthesis countered this trend of neglecting or denigrating the religious and spiritual dimensions of the psyche, but they were marginal and did not have a serious impact on academic psychology. Abraham Maslow's research on peak experiences represents the first significant recognition in mainstream psychology that extraordinary experiences such as ecstacy and egoless fusion with the world could be interpreted as signs of health rather than pathology.

Humanistic psychology's emphasis on healthy psychological functioning and transpersonal psychology's focus on extraordinary states of consciousness gradually extended psychology's parameters to include religious and spiritual aspects of the personality (Bergin, 1980). Transpersonal psychology in particular represented a revolutionary development in the field of psychology by making spirituality a significant focus of psychological theory and research. It opened modern psychology to a greatly expanded universe of realities and recognized aspects of religion and spirituality as essential foundations of psychological health and healing (Tarnas, 2001). In contrast to the positivism and reductionism that had previously dominated psychology, transpersonal theorists maintained that spiritual phenomena provide important and valid knowledge about human existence and the world (Ferrer, 2002).

Over the last few decades, psychology of religion has accumulated a vast amount of empirical research about how people's religion affects their attitudes, development, and response to crucial experiences of life. Many of these findings are summarized in the major textbooks on the psychology of religion such as Batson et al. (1993), Hood et al. (1996), Paloutzian (1996), Pargament (1997), and Wulff (1996). By and large these works have focused on the quantifiable aspects of religion, such as attendance at religious services, frequency of prayer, as well as financial contributions to, and affiliation with, religious institutions. However, there is a growing awareness of the limitations of these more measurable elements of religion and the increasing importance of the inner spiritual search. Unfortunately, the spiritual quest is more difficult to define, measure, and evaluate. Even so, a focus on spirituality pushes the psychology of religion to broaden its view of religion and thus its sphere of research. Zinnbauer et al. (1999) argue that the emergence of spirituality as a primary construct in the psychology of religion forces researchers to investigate alternative pathways to the sacred, such as meditation, twelve-step programs, new religious movements, healing groups, dance, music, and social action.

Recent editions of three major textbooks in the psychology of religion (Hood et al., 1996; Paloutzian, 1996; Wulff, 1996) reflect this change in the religious landscape when they recognize that even where religion may not be visible in the structure and development of the personality, it has an influence in less obvious but not less significant ways. These textbooks have included in their latest editions references to spirituality, although they readily admit the difficulties in defining and assessing this growing interest in spiritual matters. Zinnbauer et al. (1997, p. 551) observe that "the religious and spiritual landscape has undergone changes in recent history, and it appears as if researchers' conceptualizations of religiousness and spirituality have not caught up." In a related article, Zinnbauer et al. (1999) emphasize that this increasing distance between social scientists and questionnaire respondents concerning the meaning of religiousness and spirituality makes empirical research ever more complicated and may even endanger the psychology of religion as a field that seems to be losing its focus. Spilka (1993) has criticized the concept of spirituality as imprecise and fuzzy and therefore difficult to research in measurement-based studies. Whereas one can count members in a religious organization and determine elements of expressed belief (e.g., a belief in God, spirits, or an afterlife), it is unclear what measures might be used to assess the presence or degree of a person's spirituality. We shall discuss this problem of defining and researching spirituality in chapter one.

Still other psychologists, especially those treating psychological problems, insist that spirituality is too crucial an issue to be left aside no matter how difficult it is to arrive at precise definition and measurement. Clinical psychologist David Elkins and his associates have developed the Spiritual Orientation Inventory in an effort to assess this elusive dimension of human experience. While this research instrument has not yet generated much empirical data, it is a promising attempt to introduce the measurement-based study of spirituality. In the therapeutic context, the most recent diagnostic and statistical manual (*DSM IV*) recognizes for the first time religious and spiritual problems which are no longer considered simply pathological but rather among the difficulties normal people encounter in the course of life. Such disturbances frequently involve value conflicts, guilt, self-acceptance, and forgiveness.

Miller (1999) observes that standard training in clinical psychology has not really caught up to the gradual recognition of these crucial treatment areas. He notes that texts currently used in clinical training rarely cite the term *spirituality* in the index, and religion, if considered at all, continues to be viewed in relation to pathologies such as obsessional-compulsive disorder. Nevertheless, he insists that all health care providers should know something about their clients' spirituality in order to obtain a comprehensive understanding of their troubles and decide on effective treatment plans. Recognizing how a person's spirituality influences his or her personality functioning does not require the therapist or psychologist to share the particular worldview or values that are part of a client's spirituality. This caveat is especially noteworthy because psychologists, physicians, and scientists are not representative of the populations they serve in regard to spiritual and religious beliefs. Studies show that these health care workers tend to be considerably less "religious" than their patients and clients (Pargament, 1997, pp. 38–39). We shall deal with factors of religion and spirituality in the therapeutic context in the chapters on the adult stages of the life cycle.

LIFE CYCLE RESEARCH

The orienting framework for this study is the idea of the life cycle. Philosophical and literary precursors of this idea in psychology can be found dating to antiquity. All societies have recognized and rationalized certain basic phases of the life cycle with regard to differences between children, adults, and the aged (Neugarten, 1985). We shall consider two of the typical life-cycle schemes from antiquity in chapter one. Dan Blazer (1998) maintains that the life-cycle approach is particularly valuable because it forces investigators to integrate various perspectives in the study of human development. In his view, an understanding of the life cycle must include biological, psychological, sociological, and environmental perspectives, but the life-cycle idea was not appreciated in mainstream psychology for many decades. Most studies in developmental psychology before World War II focused on descriptive observations of infants and children, without reference to the other ages of life (Youngman, 1999).

Psychoanalytic writers such as Carl Jung and Erik Erikson have been especially influential in bringing the life-cycle notion to the larger public. Jung's essay "Stages of Life" (1930) points out the broad tendencies that mark the major transitions in life. He describes the two major divisions of the life cycle as the morning and afternoon of life. According to Jung, the primary psychological task of the morning of life is to develop a stable ego and adapt to the external world, while the main task in the afternoon of life is to experience fully and reflect on the inner world of the psyche, especially as presented in dreams and intuitions. In describing these two general periods in the life cycle, Jung calls attention to the crucial midlife transition where people begin to shift from an external to a more internal orientation. This typical midlife development is termed a midlife crisis when it is accompanied by psychological disorientation, anxiety, restlessness, and/or depression.

Erik Erikson's (1985) perspective on the life cycle is shaped by psychoanalysis and the conviction that the clinical worker should form a conception of the course of life and the sequence of generations that guides clinical work with patients. The life-cycle framework provides a total orientation for both analyst and patient, even if verification of the life-cycle idea is not possible. Erikson identifies eight ages of the human life cycle which unfold according to a regular sequence. In his view, there is a main task for each of the eight ages, and the strengths developed in each age lay the basis for managing the challenges of successive ages. For Erikson, the term "life cycle" has the advantage of underlining two important tendencies in human development: first, the individual life seeks to "round itself out" as a coherent experience; and, second, individuals seek to realize the links between generations and a connection to their ancestors (p. 36).

A significant change seems to have occurred over a recent twenty-year period in the way people think about the life cycle. This shift can be seen in the different attitudes represented in the 1970s by Gail Sheehy's *Passages: Predictable Crises of Adult Life* (1978), where there is a clear idea of the life cycle and its stages, and in the 1990s by Mary Catherine Bateson's *Composing a Life*, where the notion of following a prescribed life cycle has disappeared (Shotter, 1993, p. 5). The more recent view sees less of a life-cycle pattern than a constant need to adjust to change and discontinuity in our daily lives. Sheehy's more recent book, *New Passages: Mapping Your Life Across Time* (1996), recognizes how various forces have altered our sense of the life cycle and agrees that the idea of a standard life cycle has changed. In this later book she speaks of a ten-year shift in the timing of key components of the life-cycle idea, such as marriage, middle age, retirement, and life expectancy. Although Sheehy modifies the life-cycle framework, she does not abandon it.

In contrast to Jung, Erikson, and Sheehy, there are some social scientists who consider the life-cycle idea to have outlived its usefulness. Settersten (2003, p. 16) argues that the term "life cycle" is problematic because it has been associated with a fixed sequence of irreversible stages and implies that life movement is cyclical, with patterns repeating themselves from one generation to the next. He cites family-life-cycle models that construe family life as a sequence of stages as evidence of the inadequacy of the life cycle as a description of human development. He points to the many changes in personal and social patterns that call into question the appropriateness of fixed sequence life-cycle models: shrinking family size, nontraditional forms of family, divorce in record numbers, children returning to reoccupy the empty nest, and the lengthening of life expectancy. Such models leave little room for deviation and ignore the great variation in the way life is lived today, according to Settersten. He prefers the terms "life span," used in developmental psychology to emphasize interior phenomena, and "life course," used in sociology to highlight external, social forces.

Elder et al. (2003) point out that both the life-span approach in developmental psychology and the life-course perspective in sociology emerged in the 1970s largely as an effort to see the relationship between different stages of life, to understand how lives are socially organized and evolve over time, and to recognize the links between social influences, psychological development, and changes in society. They stress that both of these approaches were committed to intellectual breadth beyond any sharp disciplinary boundaries, although in practice there have been limits to their multidisciplinary (using insights from various disciplines without attempting to integrate them) or interdisciplinary (integrating insights from different disciplines) character. Mussen et al. (1979) explain that the life-span approach in psychology did not occur until the 1970s because, until then, the primary concern was with early development. Many earlier theories in developmental psychology held that development stopped with physical maturity, and adolescence was seen as the end of development (Fitzgerald, 1986). In the 1970s an increase in research into adolescence, adulthood, and aging began to emphasize the whole picture of the human being and to place child development within the context of the entire life span.

For Anthony Giddens (1991), the life-cycle idea applies more correctly to nonmodern societies and is not very appropriate in a modern society where the links between individual lives and the cycle of generations are no longer apparent. He believes the life cycle carries connotations of renewal as each generation rediscovers and relives the ways of life of its predecessors. The cycle of generations has less meaning in modern societies where practices are repeated only to the degree they have current rational grounds. Others counter Gidden's view of the outmoded character of the life-cycle idea, emphasizing that there remain in contemporary Western life forces that continue to connect the individual to the experiences of previous generations, such as Western assumptions about child rearing and the community's care for the elderly, norms for career development, as well as sexual and recreational practices (Coupland et al., 1993).

Although it is important to recognize the limitations of the life-cycle perspective, especially in regard to the need for a more flexible way of understanding sequence and variation in life's unfolding, it appears that the life-cycle idea remains an effective way to underscore the larger contexts of a person's religious or spiritual development. The notion of life cycle places in the foreground the important influence of past generations on our experience of life and the links in common values, ideas, and attitudes between generations. The life-cycle idea continues to remind us that our individual development should not be seen in isolation from the timeless aspirations of the human race. Erikson (1977) puts our search for an adequate model to track developments in religion and spirituality in proper perspective. He readily admits the limitations of all our theoretical frameworks when he urges us to take our theoretical models of development with a kind of serious playfulness or playful seriousness.

STANDPOINT OF THIS BOOK

I shall briefly sketch relevant aspects of my professional and personal background that influence my perspective in this book, since our dispositions, intentions, and experience all help to shape our understanding and interpretation of things. Today, there is an increasing recognition of how important it is to make explicit one's subjective standpoint in the social sciences. Even in the natural sciences, there is an awareness of the subjective element in inquiring and knowing. Michael Novak (1971) speaks of this subjectivity as a personal standpoint which plays an essential role in exploring areas of religion and spirituality. For him, a standpoint is a complex of experiences, images, expectations, and presuppositions which represent a person's sense of reality. Psychologist David Elkind (1996) points out that social sciences cannot ignore the subjective influence of personal standpoint in theory and research. He states that the social sciences in general, and psychology in particular, cannot be objective in the same way that the physical sciences are because there is no clear separation of subject from object. Social scientists are both subject and object and never completely overcome this dual position. Hans-Georg Gadamer (1989) emphasizes the inevitability of subjective influence and interpretation in *all* the sciences. For him, this fundamental prejudice is part of our historical reality and cannot be overcome by critical reason and scientific methods. In the human sciences in particular, present history, culture, and language motivate and determine themes and areas of research. Gadamer recognizes that this mediated and interpreted character of knowing is not an obstacle to be regretted but the very means that allows us to participate in the self-disclosure of the world.

Sam Keen (1978) suggests that the insights of modern physics regarding the influence of the inquiring subject on the object studied are directly applicable to the exploration of personal development. He asserts that to look at a phenomenon such as the life cycle is to influence it, distort it, and filter it through the prejudices of our own peculiar modes of perception. Franz and Stewart (1994) insist that researchers in the social sciences must always analyze their own role or position as it influences the research process. They, like many feminist social scientists, believe that it is impossible to leave demographic or ideological characteristics completely outside of research and interpretation. Carol Gilligan (1982, p. 5) represents this critical perspective when she argues that most life-cycle conceptions are presented from the male viewpoint:

> Conceptions of the human life cycle represent attempts to order and make coherent the unfolding experiences and perceptions, the changing wishes and realities of everyday life. But the nature of such conceptions depends in part on the position of the observer.

Our emotional life too is a factor in the subjective standpoint from which we examine and evaluate a topic. Goleman (1995) has presented a convincing case for the crucial role of emotions in shaping our perception at all levels of experience. His conclusions are supported by over a quarter century of feminist social science which has demonstrated the inescapable and crucial role of subjectivity and emotions in human enquiry (Ferrer, 2002, p. 59).

The discipline of transpersonal psychology in particular has reflected on appropriate methodology for studying religious experience and spirituality. Christopher Bache (2000) maintains that there is inevitably an autobiographical component to transpersonal studies. He insists that a deep knowledge of spirituality comes from taking the inner journey and reflecting on that experience. To have only a secondhand knowledge of these states, says Bache, is to labor under a great disadvantage. He adds that we are unlikely to take seriously the implications of these experiences for our understanding of the human being and the world unless we are convinced that certain kinds of religious and spiritual experiences actually do occur.

Ken Wilber (1995) asserts that transpersonal psychology requires training in the spiritual disciplines in order to understand spiritual matters. He believes that long practice may be required to open a person to experiences at what he calls the psychic, subtle, and higher levels of consciousness. He speaks of these regions as a "worldspace in which new data disclose themselves" (p. 276). According to Wilber, such data can then be checked against the experiences of others within the larger spiritual community in order to confirm the validity of such experiences and the view of reality they disclose. Wilber is influenced here by Charles Tart's notion of state-specific research and sciences. Tart (1975) proposes that knowledge derived from altered states of consciousness such as meditation, hypnosis, dreams, and mystical experience can be tested according to the basic principles of the scientific method, namely,

- observation,
- public comparisons of observations,
- logical theorizing, and
- testing the theory by observable inner and outer consequences.

According to Tart, state-specific knowledge is validated through the intersubjective agreement of adequately trained observers.

Now to my own background. My formal training in the study of religion and spirituality is based in three disciplines: the psychology of religion, psychotherapy, and dream analysis. These disciplines have shaped my approach to understanding religion and spirituality in the life cycle. From the beginning of my graduate studies at the University of Toronto in the late 1960s, I have been interested in the historical roots of religious experience. At that time I immersed myself in the life and work of Anselm of Canterbury, one of the great mystics of the Christian tradition. I have long been intrigued by the remarkable blend of reason, emotion, and will at the heart of his religious and spiritual quest. I was struck too by his psychological insights into the dynamics of religious experience.

At the same time, I studied modern psychological perspectives on religious experience. I found myself drawn to the works of Carl Jung and William James with their keen appreciation of the value of spirituality and religion for psychological health. James's approach to understanding religious experience and spirituality has been the foundation for the psychology of religion for over a century now. I find myself returning again and again to his classic book, *The Varieties of Religious Experience* (1961), in my teaching and writing. Following Jung's work led me to the Jung Institute in Zurich and the training program for Jungian analysts, a process which I continued in the form of a three-year analysis with the late Fraser Boa, Canada's first Jungian analyst. Eventually I completed my training in psychotherapy at the Gestalt Institute of Toronto and had a private practice in psychotherapy for a decade.

My research in the area of dream analysis is closely connected to my experience of, and training in, psychotherapy. Both the Jungian and Gestalt approaches to psychotherapy place dreams in the forefront of clinical work. I have been amazed at the striking way dreams are able to dramatize our psychological conflicts and preoccupations. Over the last thirty years I have catalogued over 5,000 of my own dreams and have studied thousands of other people's dreams. I have observed in this considerable body of dreams how frequently they express and wrestle with religious and spiritual concerns. This experience has convinced me of the importance of spirituality in psychological functioning throughout the life cycle and guides my discussion of the issues dealt with in this book. Where appropriate, I shall introduce dream material to illustrate certain points.

My spiritual practice has been in the areas of mental prayer, yoga, and meditation. During my mid-teens I was introduced to forms of mental prayer through retreats and friends. The Spiritual Exercises of Ignatius of Loyola is one particular method I encountered as it was used at retreats in our church. The general plan of mental prayer in the Roman Catholic tradition is to use the intellect, imagination, will, and emotions to experience what it means to be Christian. Most methods consider a scene from the life of Christ as described in the Scriptures, reflect on the meaning of the words and actions in the passage, and apply any spiritual and practical implications for contemporary life. I continued this practice for many years and found it instrumental in shaping my values and heightening my sense of the meaning of life.

In my second year of graduate school, I came down with mononucleosis, which took a heavy toll on my health. The illness lasted months, and the residual weakness made it difficult for me to concentrate on course work. I lost a lot of weight during this period and was worried that I would be unable to continue my studies. At this point, a friend suggested that I look into yoga and meditation as a way to deal with the stress and regain my ability to work and study effectively. I took this advice seriously and began doing hatha yoga, the school of yoga that focuses on mastery of the body to reach a state in which the mind withdraws from the external world. As I worked systematically with various *asanas* (bodily postures), I found that I was able to relax, become more aware of my body's rhythms, and restore trust in my body's own wisdom. Many years of being immersed in the academic world had led me to accentuate mental effort and neglect my physical condition. Although I learned that the underlying object of hatha yoga is ultimately to awaken the dormant energy that is concealed behind the human frame, I was content with the more immediate goals of paying greater attention to my body and developing confidence in its capacity for healthy functioning.

Shortly after I began doing hatha yoga, I wanted to explore meditation. Transcendental meditation (TM) was very much in the news at that time as it spread from India to Europe and North America. This form of meditation was easy to learn and promised deep relaxation and inner joy. After reading early studies on the physiological effects of TM, I decided to become initiated at a center in Toronto. Maharishi (1963) presents TM as a practical science that draws upon the teachings and wisdom of Indian spiritual traditions over the centuries, although he insists that the effectiveness of TM does not depend on knowing or subscribing to the doctrines of Indian spirituality that underlie the technique. My experience of TM was very positive as I found it helped me to relax, to concentrate, and to become more centered. I have continued this form of meditation over the last thirty years and find that it has increased my awareness of how psychological processes relate to spirituality and religion.

These spiritual practices, as well as my clinical and academic training, cause me to lean in a clinical and historical direction that recognizes the importance of religion and spirituality in the life cycle. These factors shape my standpoint and will guide our exploration through therapeutic perspectives, which often are not taken into account in academic psychology but which have a relatively long history of dealing with dimensions of spirituality. As we begin exploring religion and spirituality in the life cycle, we shall take a careful look at the meaning of our basic terms of investigation: religion, implicit religion, and spirituality.

CHAPTER ONE

STARTING POINTS

———————— ঽ৶ ————————

> It appears that spirituality is one of those subjects whose
> meaning everyone claims to know until they have to define
> it.   — Philip Sheldrake, *Spirituality and History*

This chapter looks carefully at the basic terms treated throughout the
book. It can be deflating to realize that even among scholars of religion, there is little agreement on how to define and study religion and
spirituality. For this reason, it is all the more important at the outset to
see the broad range of ways people use these terms and to specify how
the definitions used in this book relate to them.

WHAT IS RELIGION?

The scientific study of religion customarily approaches the meaning of
the word by distinguishing between, first, substantive and, second,
functional types of definition. The substantive definitions (sometimes
also called "formal" or "essential" definitions) focus on some element
of religion which is thought to be the essence of all religions. Typically,
scholars have posited a belief in God or the gods as such a fundamental
aspect of religion. Others have argued that a core experience such as a
profound experience of the holy or the sacred is the essential characteristic of religion. Critics of this approach challenge the universality of
such definitions by showing that there are exceptions to these hypothetical core elements, such as forms of Buddhism or Taoism which lack a
God concept or the many religious adherents around the world who
have never claimed to have had a transforming experience of the holy.

The other type of scientific definition of religion is the functional one (often called "operational"), which considers what psychological or sociological function religion may perform. For example, religion may function to relieve anxiety, loneliness, or guilt in human beings. Religion may also provide meaning in life for some people or offset social isolation for others. One problem with these definitions is that other things may perform the identical function, and so we have not arrived at a uniquely religious function which might serve to distinguish religion from other areas of life. Peter Berger (1974, p. 125) maintains that another problem with the functional definitions is that they legitimize the "avoidance of transcendence" in our secularized Zeitgeist. He argues that by focusing on psychological or sociological functions of religion which can be understood without reference to transcendence, religion is "flattened out" and simply equated with other phenomena. Such a view renders all manifestations of transcendence as meaningless. To counter this tendency, Berger advocates a scientific method that ensures that the meaning of a phenomenon must be understood "from within," from the perspective of those who adhere to it. This approach would go beyond reducing religion to whatever psychological or sociological functions it might perform.

In the course of our study, we shall consider a number of definitions, both substantive and functional, as they help to focus our attention on ways to think about how religion relates to the life cycle. Following Berger's lead, we shall attempt to include those phenomenological and clinical approaches which try to get at what religion or a life stage means to the person experiencing it, even as we attempt to understand how religion contributes to psychological processes in various stages of the life cycle.

Considering the etymology of the word *religion* provides further understanding of its meaning. Many texts in religious studies follow St. Augustine's view that the word *religion* stems from the Latin verb *religare*, which means to reconnect or fasten, while others follow Cicero's view that the origin is found in the verb *relegere*, which means to gather, study, read, pay attention to, or even give care to. W. C. Smith (1963) discusses these diverse origins and interpretations at length and concludes that the definition based on *religare* appears to emphasize the objective element, some power which obligates certain behavior, whereas *relegere* focuses on the subjective element, a feeling or attitude toward that power.

Even this distinction is not hard and fast. For example, Michael Novak (1971) interprets *religare* in a subjective fashion when he defines religion as the drive to make sense of all the diffuse actions of a person's life, i.e., to tie one's life together. Paloutzian (1996), also basing his understanding of the word religion on *religare*, points out it is not entirely obvious from considering the word itself with what we are connected or reconnected. Is it God, nature, a state of mind, a cosmic force, other individuals, or a community? Jung (1935a, p. 8) is the most notable psychologist to believe *relegere* to be the origin of the word religion:

> Religion appears to me to be a peculiar attitude of mind which could be formulated in accordance with the original use of the word *religio*, which means a careful consideration and observation of certain dynamic factors that are conceived as "powers."

Jung appreciates the subjective orientation of the word and argues that "to take account of or observe" better suits the psychological findings about how religion functions. Religion as carefully considering the divine (*relegere*) emphasizes the importance of the subjective attitude in religion.

These traditional approaches to the definition of religion indicate the complexity of determining exactly what we are trying to do when we wish to track the place of religion in personality structure and development. As Berger rightly points out, definitions are always designed to serve a cognitive purpose. Religion as connection or reconnection (*religare*) helps to understand how religion is related to the personality. It suggests that there may be an underlying link to a possible divine source in the psyche and its psychological functions. Psychologists have commented on the possible psychological locations of this proposed link, citing crucial religious experiences and psychological reactions to them as the key. They have suggested what psychological experiences might well have motivated the origin of religious beliefs, ethics, and myths.

Table 1 summarizes the wide range of definitions various psychologists have given to religion, showing how religion contributes to or relates to psychological functioning in terms of their personality theories. We shall consider many of these ideas in greater detail as we proceed to study various phases of the life cycle. Here, I merely want to highlight the remarkable diversity in how psychologists understand and evaluate the role of religion in the human life cycle. Sigmund Freud (1927) focuses on the experience of human vulnerability with its concomitant fears (of death, injustice, and injury) and wishes to be protected, while Erik Erikson (1950) considers the earliest relationship of trust to be foundational. Harry Guntrip (1971) believes the sense of personal connectedness to the universe grounds religion, whereas Ian

Table 1: How Psychologists View Religion

Introspective Psychology
William James

Religion is
- the feelings, acts, and experiences of individuals in their solitude, so far as they apprehend themselves to stand in relation to whatever they may consider divine;
- a person's total reaction to life.

Behaviorism
John Watson & B. F. Skinner

Religion is a traditional means of controlling behavior.

Psychoanalysis
Sigmund Freud

Religion is
- an illusion (ideas based on wishes);
- regression to the earliest stage of life (primary narcissism);
- a means of social control.

Interpersonal Relations Theory
Erich Fromm

Religion is
- any system of thought and action shared by a group which gives the individual a frame of orientation and an object of devotion;
- humanistic religion promotes human self-realization;
- authoritarian religion hinders human development.

Object Relations Theory
Ian Suttie

Religion is
- a system of psychotherapy;
- a way to better our affective relationships with others.

Harry Guntrip

Religion is a fundamental sense of personal connectedness to, and personal validation by, the universe and ultimate reality.

Donald Winnicot

Religion is a transitional space which helps people meet challenges of the external world.

Table 1 (continued)

Ego Psychology Erik Erikson	Religion is the principle means by which people acquire or reaffirm their basic trust in life.
Analytical Psychology Carl Jung	Religion is • an attitude of attention to the numinous as it emerges in the environment and the unconscious; • a defense against experience of the divine.
Logotherapy Victor Frankl	Religion is the search for ultimate meaning.
Developmental Psychology Jean Piaget	Religion is an attitude that corresponds to and reflects our early relationship with adults.
James Fowler	Religion (faith) is a way of moving into life and giving meaning to it.
Transpersonal Psychology Ken Wilber	Religion (as meditation) is a way to facilitate the movement to higher stages of consciousness.

Suttie (1935) sees its origins in our emotional relationships. Carl Jung (1938) and Victor Frankl (1975) find the need for meaning in life to be at the heart of religion. All of these experiences and the thoughts, feelings, and attitudes generated by them can be the point where religion manifests itself in the human personality. In the chapters to follow, we shall see how these various psychological views of religion illuminate its many roles in the life cycle. Now we turn to another aspect of religion, implicit religion, that can further help us to understand how religion influences our journey through life.

IMPLICIT RELIGION

The concept of implicit religion has gained increasing currency over the last two decades. Implicit religion refers to whatever functions like a religion, even though it does not appear to be a religion as conventionally understood (Hamilton, 2001). Thus, implicit religion stands in contrast to explicit religion which refers to the conventional elements of religion as expressed in religious experiences, institutions, doctrines, communities, ethical systems, myths, and rituals. Its main application in North American social science has been in the sociology of religion where it has been used to examine a broad range of social phenomena, movements, and organizations, including technology, consumerism, environmentalism, democracy, sports, animal rights, and violence in Western culture. Sociologist of religion William Swatos (1997), chronicling how this term has worked its way into general usage in the social-scientific study of religion, observes that debates in the late 1960s and 1970s over concepts of civil religion, invisible religion, civic religion, and popular religion paved the way for appreciating the value of this new interdisciplinary concept.

Edward Bailey (1990, 1997, 1998, 2000), the person most responsible for advancing usage of the concept, defines implicit religion in three primary ways: first, commitment, second, integrating foci, and, third, intensive concerns with extensive effects. For Bailey (1998, p. 10) *commitment* implies that implicit religion in contemporary society is concerned with what is usually seen as secular rather than conventionally religious. The main point in implicit religion is where individuals place their life energy, whether or not they are aware of it. Bailey suggests that commitment "nicely begs the question as to the degree of consciousness that is involved" and so it emphasizes how implicit religion includes the whole continuum from conscious to unconscious. An example of commitment would be a life devoted to preserving the environment. *Integrating foci* brings out the idea that there may be various ways people integrate their experience. Bailey (1998, p. 10) believes that the plural form "foci" precludes the assumption that an individual or body will have only one religion, thereby recognizing that a person or people may use different religions for different purposes depending on the context. For instance, a person may be dedicated to animal rights and be a devoted consumer at the same time. These various foci help individuals to make sense of, and find meaning in, their life experiences.

According to Bailey, *intensive concerns with extensive effects* calls attention to the prime locus of implicit religion, namely, the relationship between the religious and the secular. This definition of implicit religion resembles the theologian Paul Tillich's view that our ultimate concern indicates where the divine is for us, whether we view that concern as sacred or not. Implicit religion is particularly valuable for exploring the realm of "the ordinary," between the extremes of sacred and profane. Bailey (1998, p. 11) holds that most human experience and consciousness "is not very profane or very sacred, neither particularly religious nor particularly irreligious, just rather ordinary. Outwardly, it often appears neutral, rather than sacred or profane, so its 'magnetic pole' has to be deduced from its inner orientation." For example, what for one sports fan may be a casual hobby can for another person provide the meaning of life. This aspect of implicit religion highlights the nebulous boundary between our secular and sacred selves (Campbell, 2001, p. 17).

In a similar vein, Donald Horder (1973, p. 9) argues that implicit religion is an effective concept for dealing with religious and moral education in a pluralistic setting because it considers "the religious questions which are implicit in ordinary secular experience—the mystery in which our lives are set." I believe that implicit religion is not only an effective concept in the sociological and educational contexts, but also in the psychological approach to the life cycle. Implicit religion is able to get at the inner processes central to the psychological understanding of religion. It penetrates to another level of religion than conventional measures such as religious membership, professed belief in God, doctrines, frequency of prayer, attendance at religious services, or financial contributions to religious organizations. The latter can be more easily observed and quantified but may not reflect the strongest motivations and commitments around which people organize their mental and spiritual lives. A number of writers find worldview, meaning, values, and identity central to the notion of implicit religion (Gollnick, 2002; Loukes, 1965; Nesti, 1990; Stahl, 1999). These aspects of implicit religion will help us to trace religion and spirituality in the life cycle because they focus on the less obvious and less conventional aspects of religion.

William James (1961, p. 45) offers a helpful vantage point for appreciating how implicit religion contributes to our understanding of religion and spirituality in the life cycle: "Religion, whatever it is, is a man's [sic] total reaction upon life, so why not say that any total reaction upon life is a religion." He maintains that such total reactions to life include fundamental attitudes that "go behind the foreground of existence and reach down to that curious sense of the whole residual cosmos." These attitudes ground a person's worldview, sense of self, values, and meaning of life. James (1961, p. 45) asks: "Why then not call these reactions our religion, no matter what specific character they may have? Nonreligious as some of these reactions may be in one sense of the word 'religious,' nevertheless they belong to the general sphere of the religious life, and so should generically be classed as religious reactions."

In *The Varieties of Religious Experience,* James employs a phenomenological approach in which he strives to understand what a religious
experience means to the person having it. He holds that the spiritual
judgment, which involves weighing the inner meaning and consequences of an experience, determines if it is truly a religious experience. We can conclude from examining the extraordinary variety of
experiences discussed in James's classic book that almost any experience could be considered a religious experience, depending on what it
means to the person and what the consequences are. This conclusion
closely parallels Bailey's (1998, p. 13) insistence that anything can be
implicit religion, depending on our attitude toward it, which is not to
say that everything is implicit religion.

The psychoanalytic and psychotherapeutic traditions shed further
light on the definition and value of the implicit religion concept. Carl
Jung's view that meaning is crucial to maintaining a healthy psyche is
central to the psychological dimension of implicit religion. As we shall
see in greater detail in the chapter devoted to religion and spirituality
in the midlife period, he maintains that most psychological complaints
in the first half of life deal with problems of adjusting to external reality, while in the second half of life they are concerned with meaning in
life. Jung (1930) observes that a "religious outlook" is essential to
maintaining or recovering mental health and a sense of meaning in the
afternoon of life:

> It is safe to say that every one of them [his patients in the second half of life]
> fell ill because he [*sic*] had lost that which the living religions of every age
> have given to their followers, and none of them has been really healed who
> did not regain his religious outlook. This of course has nothing whatever to
> do with a particular creed or membership in a church. (p. 229)

The religious outlook is, in Jung's view, essentially an attitude of attention to the inner life and the "numinous" which emerges in the
unconscious, especially through dreams. Jung borrows the term "numinous" from Rudolf Otto to express the holy or sacred dimension in
human experience. Jung believes that the numinous is the essential
healing element for those suffering from loss of meaning, and he
insists this link is not confined to, or even necessarily connected with,
doctrinal and institutional dimensions of traditional religion.

Victor Frankl, another important figure in the psychoanalytic tradition, employs the term "unconscious religiousness," a concept close to
implicit religion, to highlight the crucial role of meaning in psychological health. He defines religion as "the search for ultimate meaning"

(1975, p. 13) and insists that there is an unconscious religiousness inherent in everyone, but unfortunately it is repressed for many in our society. This repression results in what he calls an "existential vacuum" characterized by meaninglessness and depression. Frankl (1975) argues that people have a "will to meaning" in life which is mainly satisfied by transcendent goals. While such goals are frequently associated with the notion of a transcendent God, they are not always connected to explicit religion. Thus Frankl underscores the importance of finding a specific concrete meaning in one's experience rather than searching for an abstract answer to the meaning of life.

Frankl's (1962) horrendous concentration camp experience is the source of his insight into therapeutic methods directed toward the need for purpose and meaning. There, he discovered a fundamental principle which grounds his philosophy, namely, that the ability to survive requires finding a meaning that points toward the future. This requirement applies to both the individual and society as a whole. Frankl believes that our collective human survival depends on the human race finding a meaning directed towards the future and recognizing humankind's oneness. This view echoes Bailey's (1990, p. 495) conclusion that the emerging implicit religion in contemporary society might be described as a commitment to the human.

Further psychological background for understanding implicit religion can be found in Abraham Maslow's view of religion as being dissociated from anything supernatural. He calls this "small 'r' religion." Maslow seeks a suitably broadened understanding of both religion and science which will permit the science of psychology in particular to deal with important religious questions and spiritual values. He sees this as a further development in the evolving relationship between religion and science. Just as the sciences were once part of organized religion and then became independent, so now matters of values, ethics, and spirituality are also becoming independent of institutional religion. Maslow (1964, pp. 11–12) believes that this new development is positive and undermines organized religions' claims to be "the sole arbiters of all questions of faith and morals."

Maslow recognizes that this enlarged science he proposes must search for adequate terminology to describe the religious and spiritual territory to be studied. He regrets that it is almost impossible to speak of spiritual matters without using a traditional religious vocabulary because a satisfactory scientific language is not yet available. Maslow (1964) expresses his uneasiness about redefining traditional religious language and then using it in a very different way. Although Maslow

(1964, p. 5) employs such words as *sacred, divine, holy, salvation, transcendence,* and *spiritual* to describe extraordinary subjective experiences, he does not wish to imply that these are supernatural events. He believes that his own terms such as *peak experience, self-actualization, metamotivation, metahumanness, Being-values (B-values), Being-cognition (B-cognition),* and *plateau experience* deal more adequately and less ambiguously with these important aspects of psychological and spiritual development.

James, Jung, Frankl, and Maslow have all contributed to our appreciation of the importance of understanding implicit religion if we are to go beyond people's religious affiliations and proclaimed beliefs to track religion and spirituality in the way people actually live. We shall find the psychologically oriented categories of implicit religion, i.e., worldview, values, sense of self, and meaning of life, to be particularly useful in tracing religion and spirituality in the life cycle. Now we come to the final term we shall use to study religion in the life cycle, namely, spirituality.

DEFINING SPIRITUALITY

As with religion, most studies of spirituality admit a lack of consensus on the meaning of the term. Defining spirituality appears to be at least as daunting a task as defining religion, because its usage in twentieth-century discourse is complex and at times muddled (Copley, 2000). Bernard Spilka (1993, p. 1) refers to spirituality as a "fuzzy concept" that "embraces obscurity with passion." He has serious doubts about the usefulness of this term for designing empirical research because it lacks clear definition. Hood et al. (1996) also appreciate the difficulty of conducting research on such an elusive subject as spirituality: "Spirituality is a very popular word, but its meaning is extremely obscure. Efforts to clarify the concept point vaguely toward a holistic relational perspective, which appealing as it is, has not proven useful for empirical research" (p. 115).

This ambiguity surrounding the term "spirituality" has caused some in the psychology of religion to abandon the term as being insufficiently precise for measurement-based research (Gorsuch & Miller, 1999, p. 47). On the other hand, a number of researchers consider the subject so important that they are willing to tolerate the obstacles and limitations involved in investigating spirituality. For example, sociologist of religion Wade Roof agrees that spirituality is a somewhat vague concept; nevertheless, he finds it adequately defined for his own research agenda. William Miller (1999) judges the term spirituality to have sufficient interpersonal meaning to be useful for treating many disorders in the clinical setting.

A brief look at the origins of the word will provide some historical context for the current confusion surrounding the word's meaning. Walter Principe (1983) states that the Latin word *spiritualitas* (the source of our word *spirituality*) attempts to translate the Greek word for spirit (*pneuma*) in the Pauline letters of the Christian scriptures. In those letters, spirit (pneuma) refers to the spirit of God, standing in contrast to whatever opposes God. Only in the twelfth century did spirituality acquire a new meaning, wherein it is seen to stand in contrast to the body, a shift that influenced many later spiritual movements in the direction of disdain for the body. Philip Sheldrake (1991) notes that the word has gained a variety of particular nuances and meanings throughout the course of history following the medieval period. This variety suggests that the notion of spirituality has been in flux for over a thousand years, and various connotations have grown up around the word in the last few centuries. No wonder researchers have such difficulty pinning down the meaning and role of spirituality. Here, we shall briefly consider how social scientists and people in general understand this multifaceted term today.

Sociologist Reginald Bibby (1993) observes that in a national survey of almost 2000 Canadians, more than half said that they had "spiritual needs." About half of those defined spirituality in typically religious terms such as believing in God, praying, or attending church services. The remainder characterized spirituality in less conventional terms, such as awareness, meditation, concern with the human spirit, and a sense of oneness or wholeness. Roof (1999) uses surveys and interviews to trace the resurgence of spirituality in the 1980s and 1990s. In his studies he employs the category "highly active seekers" to refer to those seeking a vital spirituality. He describes the late twentieth-century search for wholeness as the expression of a "spiritual quest culture" which associates religion with religious institutions and spirituality with an inner search for meaning. Roof (1999) finds a connection between this burgeoning spirituality and William James's notion of firsthand religion (religion based on one's own experience), and he adds that James's approach to religion and spirituality establishes an affinity with the ordinary mysticism that is so prevalent in American life. Roof believes that the flourishing self-help movement is for many an important link between the spiritual and the psychological. He cites the works of psychiatrist Scott Peck as an example of this popular blend of the psychological and the spiritual. He points out that Peck's best-seller *The Road*

Less Traveled (1978, p. 11) expresses the view that spiritual growth and mental or psychological growth are one and the same thing.

Roof argues that the tremendous growth of movements such as Alcoholics Anonymous (AA), Alanon, and a variety of other twelve-step programs is an important sign of this renewed interest in spirituality. From its founding in 1935, AA, the first and largest twelve-step program, had swollen to a membership of some two million worldwide by the year 2000. Other twelve-step programs include Alanon (for those who have significant others with alcohol problems), Gamblers Anonymous, Narcotics Anonymous, Overeaters Anonymous, Adult Children of Alcoholics, and Emotions Anonymous. Tonigan et al. (1999) indicate how these programs offer a spiritual plan for recovery and cite correlational research that demonstrates their effectiveness. Roof (1993, p. 69) believes that such programs have become a vehicle for an emerging form of religiousness because they portray individuals in a one-to-one relationship with God, or a higher power, and individuals come to see themselves on a spiritual journey. Roof calls the type of spiritual interest exhibited in the self-help movement and the twelve-step programs "psychological spirituality."

SPIRITUALITY AND RELIGION

Zinnbauer et al. (1997, p. 550) point out that traditionally the study of religiousness has been broad enough to include both spirituality and institutional beliefs and activities. However, as spirituality becomes increasingly differentiated from religion, definitions of religiousness have become narrower and less inclusive, now encompassing the institutional, theological, and ritual aspects of religion, while spirituality has recently acquired a specific positive connotation of the personal experience of transcendence (p. 531). They believe that this relatively recent distinction between spirituality and religion arose with the growth of secularism in the twentieth century and a popular disillusionment with religious institutions increasingly seen as hindering personal experience of the sacred. Psychologist of religion David Wulff (1996) notes that the key metaphors employed in the "new spirituality" are journey (or quest) and growth. He believes that the shift to people describing themselves as spiritual rather than religious indicates a heightened focus on inner processes and attitudes. Wulff finds two novel aspects about this emerging spirituality: first, its separation from religious traditions and, second, the frequent absence of an explicit transcendent object outside the self.

David Elkins's *Beyond Religion* (1998) traces the "first crack in the solidarity of religion and spirituality" to the Protestant Reformation, when the reformers held that a person's spirituality should not be under the control of the institutional church. He finds further roots of a spirituality separate from religious institutions in the Renaissance, with its focus on the freedom of the individual. Elkins identifies the most recent developments of this separation of spirituality from religion as three waves of change: first, the human potential movement of the 1960s, second, the New Age movement of the 1980s, and, third, the movement toward the soul in the 1990s. A brief description of these three waves of change follows.

Abraham Maslow, one of the founders of the human potential movement, helped to usher in the first wave of change. Drawing on research indicating that peak experiences and other such extraordinary phenomena might be important signs of personal development and health, he concludes that spirituality is a major element in normal psychological growth. Maslow does not believe that spirituality is restricted to those who are affiliated with organized religion because ethical values and experiences of transcendence are important for all who reach a certain level of human development, whether or not they have any religious affiliation. As we have already observed, Maslow maintains that a suitably enlarged science should study spiritual values in personality functioning without having to rely on religious or supernatural concepts to validate them. This idea lays the groundwork for a spirituality which may have no overt connection to traditional religious beliefs and practices.

The second wave of change occurred in the 1980s as millions became intrigued by spiritual healing, reincarnation, past-lives therapy, channeling, crystals, and New Age music. Elkins (1998) admits that this movement was in many ways a "spiritual collage and a smorgasbord of spirituality imported from many lands and traditions" (p. 17). Nevertheless, he finds that it opened up a number of opportunities for people to explore alternative spiritualities. According to Elkins, a barometer of this movement is the growth in circulation of the *New Age Journal* from 50,000 at its inception in 1983 to almost 200,000 by the end of the decade. The third wave of change Elkins describes begins in the early 1990s with the publication and popularity of Thomas Moore's best-selling book *Care of the Soul* and the ensuing flood of books, tapes, workshops, and conferences on the subject of soul. Elkins (1998, p. 17) writes: "The word soul, which until then had been associated primarily with religion or the blues, moved out from these confines and was used to describe everything from inspirational stories to intimate relationships."

Moore's and Elkins's own works draw heavily on the influential writing of James Hillman (1975), the originator of post-Jungian "archetypal psychology," who argues cogently that psychology must be revisioned from the perspective of soul if it is to be true to its calling.

Elkins describes psychology itself as a vehicle for spiritual growth and one of the major alternative paths to the sacred. He regards Carl Jung as a major influence in recognizing that spirituality is at the heart of the psychotherapeutic process. Elkins et al. (1988) have developed a research instrument to measure alternative spiritualities. The factors Elkins attempts to measure as central to spirituality are meaning, purpose, transcendence, and values such as life, altruism, and idealism. His goal is to clarify and describe the humanistic spirituality that is emerging so that future researchers will be able to judge more accurately the extent and impact of spirituality. Elkins (1998, p. 9) believes the development of a spirituality separated from religious traditions is "at the heart of the greatest spiritual revolution in the West since the Protestant Reformation."

Where Elkins views this development as both historic and liberating, others see dangers. Robert Bellah (1985) believes that it reflects an unhealthy individualism in American society. He describes the spirituality of a young nurse, Sheila Larson, as "Sheilaism" to underscore the personal and private character of faith today. Zinnbauer et al. (1999) warn of the increasing polarization which has occurred as spirituality has become separated from institutional religion. Three of the most notable polarizations they cite are:

- organized religion versus personal spirituality;
- substantive religion versus functional spirituality; and
- mundane harmful religion versus lofty helpful spirituality.

This last polarization captures the essence of what the authors find objectionable about how these two constructs are being redefined and divided. Put simply, spirituality is seen as good and religion as bad. They believe that this restrictive and narrow definition of both terms is misleading and overly simplistic. For one thing, it overlooks the fact that spirituality does not exist in a social vacuum and the search for the sacred is never purely personal or devoid of social context.

Then, too, this sharp distinction overlooks what some psychologists have observed in the past, namely, that religion has both positive and negative potential. For example, Erich Fromm (1950) recognizes the value of a humanistic religion which promotes a person's strengths and leads to self-realization while he criticizes an authoritarian religion based on guilt and obedience. Gordon Allport's (1966) distinction between intrinsic religion (where a person lives according to religious beliefs and values) and extrinsic religion (where a person uses religion for primarily self-interested goals) further demonstrates the ambiguity involved in religion. Recent distinctions between religion and spirituality seem to overlook the wisdom of Fromm's and Allport's view, that both religion and spirituality are ambiguous and both can be manifested in healthy as well as unhealthy ways (Hill et al., 2000).

Zinnbauer et al. (1997) have carried out empirical research on how people define their religousness and spirituality. Their study shows that religiousness correlates with higher levels of authoritarianism, religious orthodoxy, intrinsic religion, self-righteousness, and church attendance, while spirituality correlates with mystical experience, New Age beliefs and practices, higher income, and experiences of being hurt by the clergy (p. 561). Their results also indicate that this group of subjects define religion and spirituality along the same lines as recent scholarly writings in that spirituality is considered to mean something personal and experiential, while religion denotes primarily institutional practices, church attendance, and attachment to the beliefs of organized religion. It is interesting that most of the people in this study (74 percent) consider themselves both spiritual and religious, which means that they are somehow able to integrate their spirituality with traditional religious beliefs and practices. The authors note that most people's ability to harmonize their spiritual needs with traditional religion sets them apart from mental health workers, who, as a group, are less likely to integrate spirituality and religion than the majority of believers.

Psychologist of religion Ralph Hood (2000) comes to similar conclusions as Zinnbauer and his colleagues regarding the way people understand religion and spirituality. In his detailed review of the empirical data in the United States on the relationship between spirituality and religion, he concludes that most people identify themselves as both religious and spiritual, although a significant minority identify themselves as spiritual but not religious because, for one reason or another, they object to aspects of traditional religion. Hood found that those who consider themselves as spiritual, whether religious or not, rate significantly higher on his mysticism scale than others. He adds that, like spirituality, this mysticism is found both within and outside of religious traditions. Hood differentiates between what he calls a "spiritual mysticism" (existing outside of religious traditions) and a "religious mysticism" (existing within religious traditions). He believes that those in the spiritual-mysticism category increasingly seek independent justification from psychology and can be seen as a significant new social force. Finally, Hood notes that scientists in general and psychologists in particular tend to identify themselves as spiritual but not religious, which means they would be in the spiritual-mysticism or nontraditional-spirituality category.

Robert Fuller's *Spiritual but Not Religious* (2001) explores the philosophical and religious roots of the phenomenon that Hood associates with "spiritual mysticism" in the United States. Fuller estimates that as many as 20 percent of the American population probably fall into the "spiritual but not religious" category. He traces this nonreligious spirituality to the influence of Thomas Jefferson, Ralph Waldo Emerson, Henry David Thoreau, the Freemasons (represented by fifty-two of the fifty-six signers of the Declaration of Independence), the Unitarians, and the Universalists. Above all, Fuller maintains that William James personifies what it means to be "spiritual but not religious" with his insistence that the essence of religion is found in experiences of the divine and that religious doctrines are attempts to translate these experiences into words. According to Fuller (2001, pp. 75–76), those who see themselves as "spiritual but not religious" rely on their own experience to substantiate their beliefs. They want to experiment and determine which ideas make a practical difference in their lives. They see spirituality as a way of perceiving and responding to the divine presence in the world, and they emphasize the self's infinite potential and inner connection to God.

Fuller strives to distinguish this nonreligious spirituality from secular interests and practices which provide meaning or identity, deal with guilt, or foster social cohesion. He maintains that, although such activities may function like a religion, they often lack a distinctively spiritual quality. Relying on William James's perspective, he cites two key elements which distinguish attitudes, ideas, lifestyles, and practices as truly spiritual: first, the visible world is viewed as part of a larger spiritual universe which provides its significance, and, second, living in harmony with this spiritual world is life's chief goal. Fuller reasons that, according to these criteria, many forms of questioning and commitment could be considered spiritual, such as wonder about where the universe comes from, why we are here, or what happens when we die, or a commitment to values such as love or beauty which seem to reveal a meaning beyond the visible world. According to these same criteria, those beliefs, interests, and activities which lack any concern with a larger reality would not be considered spiritual.

James's criteria may also help to distinguish spirituality from implicit religion. A number of writers assume a close connection between implicit religion and spirituality without being too precise about the relationship (Ashley, 2000; Papadopoulos, 1999; Swatos, 1999). Mack Goldsmith (2000), for example, uses the terms synonymously. Following James's logic, it appears that some examples of implicit religion, say, in relation to democracy, sports, consumerism, and technology, would fail to qualify as forms of spirituality because they lack the element of recognizing a wider spiritual universe and the need for harmony with that wider world. Thus, while the elements of worldview, identity, values, and meaning may be embedded in phenomena such as sports or consumerism, they do not include that wider spiritual dimension.

Just as there is a great deal of overlap between the terms *spiritual* and *religious* (most people surveyed identify themselves as both), so there can be much overlap between spirituality and implicit religion. The following diagrams might illustrate the complex relationship between these terms as they are frequently used today. Some people consider religion as a broader term than spirituality, as represented by Diagram 1:

Diagram 1: Traditional View of Relationship between Religion and Spirituality

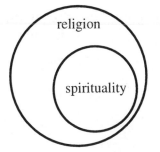

Here spirituality is seen as one of the many dimensions of religion such as the experiential, doctrinal, mythical, ritual, communal, or ethical dimensions. Others view spirituality as a broader term than religion, and one that is often not connected to religion, as in Diagram 2. In Diagram 2, spirituality is seen as the quest for the sacred (involving a person's identity, values, and worldview) which applies to many both within and outside of religious institutions. Both views, represented by Diagrams 1 and 2, recognize that spirituality and religion sometimes coincide. Diagram 1 may be thought of as a more traditional viewpoint where spirituality is connected to religion as its heart and vital inner life. Diagram 2 represents a more modern viewpoint, which acknowledges that a concern with spirituality is increasingly found in those with no ties to organized religion. These two perspectives reflect typical viewpoints in a pluralistic society that encompasses both traditional and modern attitudes.

Diagram 2: Modern View of Relationship between Religion and Spirituality

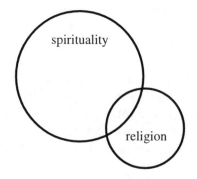

A possible way to conceptualize implicit religion in relation to the other two terms is represented by Diagram 3.

Diagram 3: Relationship between Implicit Religion, Religion, and Spirituality

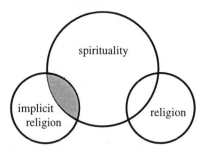

This view builds on Diagram 2 which reflects the modern view that spirituality may exist outside of religious traditions. Diagram 3 also presupposes a secular realm outside of religion where nonreligious phenomena can serve traditionally religious functions. The shaded area indicates that there can be common ground between implicit religion and spirituality, especially in the elements of identity, values, and worldview. An example would be where a person's implicit religion recognizes a wider spiritual world that gives meaning to the visible world, such as a person committed to saving the environment because she or he believes that the earth is sacred. The unshaded areas in Diagram 3 would represent those forms of implicit religion where there is no view of a wider spiritual world or where there is no conscious reflection on the elements of identity, values, and worldview that are embedded in those forms of implicit religion. Examples of nonspiritual elements in implicit religion might include peak experiences, such as sexual ecstacy or the elation of cheering for one's football team, when these experiences are not viewed as part of a larger spiritual universe.

In this book, we shall follow the trend of viewing spirituality primarily as an inner search for meaning, especially the quest for the sacred. This is not to deny the many behavioral and social implications of spirituality, but only to focus on the elements of identity, values, and worldview, which are the basic psychological structures of spirituality. These same psychological elements can be observed in implicit religion, but in that case there may or may not be self-awareness about, or reflection on, these elements. The search for the sacred may take place within or outside of religious traditions and institutions.

STAGES OF DEVELOPMENT: THEORIES OLD AND NEW

As we approach the role of religion and spirituality in the life cycle, we inevitably encounter theories that present the idea of stages of development. The metaphor of stages implies a sense of progress, sequence of development, and hierarchy. In these theories, a stage represents an identifiable structure or function that differs from previous and subsequent stages. Stages unfold in a particular sequence and build on the previous stages. The higher levels are considered more advanced or more comprehensive than the lower levels. In psychology, the most influential stage theory has been developed by Jean Piaget, who identified discrete stages in the way children's thinking develops. Piaget's theory has inspired decades of empirical research on cognitive development, much of which has refined and expanded on his descriptions of three main stages. This body of research has allowed us to understand some of the differences between the thinking of preschool children, primary school children, and adolescents. Observing these differences has helped to guide our expectations of how children think at different grade levels and what they are most likely to learn at those levels.

Following Piaget's lead, Lawrence Kohlberg has studied the development of moral reasoning. His theory too distinguishes three broad levels in the way children reason about moral dilemmas. James Fowler has extended the research of both Piaget and Kohlberg into the area of faith development to arrive at a theory of how different types of faith emerge in a more or less coherent sequence. We shall consider the particulars of Piaget's, Kohlberg's, and Fowler's theories in the next chapter. Here, I want to call attention to both the value and limitations of these theories in orienting our ideas about how important areas of religion and spirituality tend to unfold in the course of life. As prominent as these stage theories have been over the last several decades, they are not without their critics. For example, stage models are increasingly seen as being too restrictive, with their insistence that stages are irreversible, hierarchical, and universal. When such theories are applied too rigidly, they ignore important individual differences, especially when the stages seek to describe adulthood (Ryff, 1985). Owen Flanagan (1991) questions hierarchical stage models in general, and Piaget's and Kohlberg's models in particular. He argues that Piaget focuses too much on abstract, logical structures and too little on the effect of concrete content and context. He finds Kohlberg's method inadequate because it tests subjects' verbal behavior on moral dilemmas involving hypothetical cases but ignores the key factor of actual behavior. He also criticizes Kohlberg for limiting the types of moral issues tested to questions of distributive justice, a relatively small subset of ethical problems.

Howard Gardner (1983) grants that Piaget has painted a useful picture of development, but one which is limited to certain forms of thinking, and even in that domain its deficiencies are becoming increasingly recognized. Maintaining that individual stages of cognitive development are far more continuous than Piaget indicated, Gardner points to evidence that children can conserve number, classify consistently, and abandon egocentrism as early as three years old, evidence which goes against Piaget's theory. Further, contrary to Piaget's view of a whole series of abilities coalescing at approximately the same time, theoretically related abilities actually may emerge at disparate points in time (p. 21). Similarly, Fowler's work has been criticized primarily for its overemphasis on the cognitive aspects of faith and for largely ignoring the emotional and experiential dimensions of life (Fuller, 1988; Keen, 1978).

The general idea of identifiable stages in life predates these psychological theories by many centuries (Neugarten, 1985, p. 360). Two dominant perspectives, typical of these ancient views of stages in life, are the Pythagorean (in the West) and the Hindu (in the East). Unlike many of the psychological theories dealt with later, these earliest developmental theories are embedded in a religious worldview that provides people with meaning in life by connecting their lives with the cycles of nature or with a divine source of life. In the West, the Greek philosopher and mathematician Pythagoras (born c. 580 BCE) presented a theory of the four ages of the human being. A fundamental assumption undergirding his view is that numbers are the essence of all things and underlie nature, the seasons of the year, colors, the body, temperament, and personality. According to Pythagoras, the sacred number four links the stages of human life, the seasons of nature, bodily fluids (or humors) and psychological temperament. For example, childhood corresponds to the season of Spring in nature's cycle, and is the time of life when blood was thought to be the predominant bodily fluid, thus shaping a sanguine (from Latin, *sanguis* = blood) or optimistic temperament.

According to ancient Greek medical theory, health requires a balance in the four bodily fluids, namely, blood, yellow bile, black bile, and phlegm; illness occurs when that balance of fluids is disrupted and a lack or excess of one or more fluids results. Each age of the human life cycle reflects a preponderance of one of these fluids, such that excessive yellow bile in adolescence is thought to create a choleric (from Latin *cholera* = bile) or irascible temperament, excessive black bile in adulthood creates a melancholic (from Latin, *melancholia* = black bile) or gloomy temperament, and excessive phlegm in old age creates a phlegmatic (from Latin, *phlegma* = phlegm) or sluggish personality. The interrelationship of human nature, the seasons, bodily fluids, and temperaments can be summarized in the following table:

Table 2: Pythagorean Theory of the Life Cycle

Age	Seasons	Predominant Bodily Fluid	Temperament
Childhood	Spring	Blood	Sanguine
Adolescence	Summer	Yellow Bile	Choleric
Adulthood	Fall	Black Bile	Melancholic
Old Age	Winter	Phlegm	Phlegmatic

This perspective emphasizes that the human life cycle is rooted in, and reflects, nature and the body as part of nature. Both ancient Greek and Roman medicine are grounded on the view that the human being represents the microcosm, the epitome of the universe, the macrocosm. Even dream interpretation in the ancient Greek and Roman medical world relied upon this parallel, such that a dream of flooding was thought to indicate high blood pressure and dream images of drought were believed to diagnose anemia. A further dimension of Pythagoras' thought is that the human soul is immortal and migrates into another body after death, thus further linking human life to nature's cycles of birth, death, and rebirth.

In the East, the Hindu perspective sees four main stages of life. The first stage is a kind of apprenticeship which traditionally begins between the ages of eight and twelve years old and lasts for about twelve years. Students often live in the teacher's home and work there as payment for their education, which goes well beyond acquiring information to include moral training and character formation. During the second stage, which lasts some twenty to thirty years, the person's energy is devoted to his or her vocation as well as the family and community. The third stage often begins some time after the arrival of the first grandchild and entails leaving family and the home and retreating to the forest to ponder the meaning of life and human identity. This withdrawal from family life removes people from concerns with social obligations and family duties, allowing them to contemplate the deeper reality that undergirds all things. The final stage of life is that of the sage who wanders about with no fixed home, no obligations, goals or belongings, often with a begging bowl in hand. At this stage, all social and family identities give way to a realization that the human being is somehow identical with the eternal Self. The Hindu perspective on the life cycle leads relentlessly to this ultimate identity. These stages are summarized in Table 3. Zalman Schachter-Shalomi (1997) believes the idea behind this traditional Hindu model is still valuable in our times because it views life as a spiritual journey, encourages us to begin seriously cultivating a spiritual life in middle age, and looks to old age as the greatest opportunity for self-realization.

Table 3: Hindu View of the Life Cycle

Stage	Age	Type of Life	Goal
Student	c. eight to twenty years old	Apprenticeship with teacher	Moral and character training
Householder	c. twenty to fifty years old	Family and public life	Obligations to family and community
Forest Dweller	after first grandchild	Withdrawal from family and society	Contemplation of ultimate reality
Wandering Sage	old age	Wandering with no fixed home	Realization of ultimate identity

Both of these ancient developmental theories root the individual life cycle in a larger reality, whether that of nature or the divine. In these perspectives, the individual finds meaning in life by recognizing his or her relationship to the cycles of nature or by participation in the divine source of life. Carl Jung (1930) appreciates the wisdom of such theories because they provide psychological stability and a sense of great value in the everyday tasks of life. Such viewpoints furnish a solid framework of overall meaning that has been, from ancient times, an antidote for the anxiety and insecurity which often accompany human existence. Jung recognizes that we cannot simply return to a traditional worldview which places the human being at the center of the physical and psychological universe and confers personal meaning through participation in the world of nature or religion. Nevertheless, he argues that something of this earlier attitude is still crucial in our own time. In his view, finding meaning or value is the vital role that religion and spirituality play in a world which is dominated by the instrumental rationality of science and technology.

As we strive to locate the human life cycle within the growing framework of psychology and our scientific worldview, we may wonder how far our current models of science and psychology can accommodate the perennial human quest for meaning and value, a quest that is at the heart of religion and spirituality. These ancient perspectives suggest that stage models are broad and useful metaphors to orient our thinking about how life unfolds and the importance of timing in the development of significant aspects of life, such as thinking, moral reasoning, faith, religion, and spirituality.

Stages of Spiritual Development

There has been considerable debate over the degree to which stage theories apply to spiritual development. Some believe that spirituality unfolds in stages much like Piaget's theory of cognitive development, while others find such models inadequate for understanding the complexity of spiritual growth (Rothberg, 1998a). Ken Wilber, one of the major theorists in contemporary transpersonal psychology, has presented an influential stage theory of spiritual development. Wilber (1998) holds that human development is very complex and does not simply move through a few comprehensive stages to unify all areas of growth. Rather, it proceeds by way of various developmental lines, some of which may be in tension with each other, and some of which do not exhibit coherent stages. He lists a number of developmental lines, including moral, interpersonal, object relations, cognitive, self-needs, self-identity, worldview, psychosexual, and creative, believing they are loosely held together by the self-system.

Wilber (1999) argues that spirituality can, in a certain sense, be understood to unfold according to a stage developmental model. He believes there are two definitions of spirituality that suggest stages of development. This first is spirituality as the highest level of any of the developmental lines (such as cognitive, moral, interpersonal, or affective development). In Wilber's view, this definition implies that there is a stage-like unfolding. The second definition which includes a notion of stages is that of spirituality as a separate developmental line in its own right, alongside the cognitive, moral, interpersonal, and affective lines. Wilber states that many theorists, East and West, furnish evidence that at least some aspects of spirituality undergo sequential or stage-like development. He believes that meditation experiences in particular unfold according to a universal stage model, at least they manifest stage-like characteristics at what he calls a deep-structural level of analysis. We shall consider these deep structures and their sequence of unfolding when we come to the midlife period of the life cycle.

Wilber (1999) suggests that the difficulty in recognizing stages is that they are not obvious in a person's direct experience. Only by standing back and comparing experiences with others can we begin to discern common patterns. In his reading of the great religious traditions, Wilber finds that important "spiritual competencies" follow developmental stages, unfolding as increasingly subtle experiences (p. 7). He believes that there are broad hierarchical stages that he labels nature mysticism, deity mysticism, and nondual (where there is no separation of subject and object) mysticism. Wilber holds that these deep structures emerge in ascending order, with formless/nondual mysticism being the highest level. While such a reading of a progression of spiritual experiences may help to distinguish various forms and types of experience, difficulties with this hierarchical stage model appear when he uses it to rank religious and spiritual traditions.

Wilber arranges various religious traditions according to how they reflect his understanding of the universal sequence of deep structures, from psychic through subtle and causal to nondual. He believes that the highest stages of spiritual development are found in the nondualism of Advaita Vedanta's Atman-Brahman realization, Mahayana Buddhism's emptiness, and Zen's satori. The Sufi and Christian mystical union with an impersonal Godhead is judged as a less complete spirituality corresponding to the causal level. The Christian vision of God and the mysticism of the Kabbala represent the still lower subtle level of spirituality. Finally, the mystical experiences of the Mystery religions and forms of Native spirituality are relegated to the lowest transpersonal level, the psychic level, on Wilber's scale.

As Jorge Ferrer (2002, p. 105) observes, it is highly questionable that Wilber's arrangement of the deep structures of consciousness, and their representation in the world's religions, actually emerge out of a strictly impartial analysis of mystical texts and biographies. He views Wilber's model as strongly biased in favor of a nondual spirituality, of which he himself is a practitioner. In contrast, Helminiak (1996), a Christian, argues that theism ranks higher than nondualism. This seems to suggest the inevitable influence of personal and cultural biases on such hierarchical rankings. Ferrer (2002) notes that all the major religious traditions themselves have developed typologies of hierarchical gradations of spiritual traditions with the strange but not unexpected result of each tradition placing itself at the top of the hierarchy. He cites examples from Christianity, Islam, and Advaita Vedanta and adds that the Buddhist tradition contains a number of conflicting hierarchies of spiritual insights and schools (p. 160). Ferrer interprets the current discussions regarding such spiritual gradations as reflecting debates in ancient India: Wilber's attempt to persuade us that nonduality is higher and more encompassing than the dual and theistic traditions mirrors Sankara's view, while the case (represented by Helminiak) for the personal and theistic traditions as superior to a nondual and impersonal spirituality reflects Ramanuja's perspective.

Ferrer observes that, ironically, the advocates of these contradictory rankings often apply analogous criteria to establish their hierarchies. The reason these theorists come to opposite conclusions, says Ferrer, is that the criteria are vague enough to be interpreted in favor of one's own tradition. Such interpretations are rarely an objective exploration of states of consciousness, but rather are often colored by polemical and doctrinal considerations. Further, according to Ferrer, Wilber's assumption that the meditative maps found in traditional religious literature are a reliable basis for spiritual-developmental models is misguided because these maps are not so much phenomenological descriptions of meditative experiences as a blend of apologetics, scriptural commentary, and scholastic speculation. This observation is not intended to denigrate these accounts but merely to recognize that they have a different purpose from the one some transpersonal psychologists suppose. Ferrer (2002) maintains that the accounts of mystical traditions are not intended so much as descriptions of reality to be validated or falsified according to the standards of modern science as they are prescriptions for ways to transform human beings and the world. In this view, the traditional accounts of meditation are not intended to provide data to verify spiritual claims, but to express the teachings of a given religious tradition.

Donald Rothberg (1999) too questions the value of hierachically organized stages to describe transpersonal or spiritual development and wonders whether there might be more appropriate, and less misleading, metaphors for describing and facilitating spiritual development and transformation. He asks whether metaphors such as spirals, ladders, ascent, descent, paths, circles, emergence, wholeness, balance, and integration might be more valuable for understanding human development. Human beings seem to develop in vastly more complex ways than can be pictured by even a sophisticated stage-developmental model. According to Rothberg, we must hold open the possibility that people may operate from more than one stage at once in some, or all, lines of development. From a psychotherapeutic standpoint, Cortright (1997) observes that spiritual levels do not unfold according to the stages Wilber describes, and that there is no clear evidence of a single invariant sequence in the spiritual domain. In his experience, spirituality can emerge anywhere, not just at the top of the spectrum of consciousness.

Closely associated with the stages of development is the notion of lines of development. Wilber (1998, 1999) notes that because developmental lines can unfold separately, a person can be at a high spiritual stage and at the same time be at a very low psychological stage and at yet another stage in moral development. Because these lines are relatively independent, all sorts of spiritual developments can occur before, alongside of, or after various psychological developments. Rothberg (1999), too, lists multiple lines or dimensions of development, namely, cognitive, moral, emotional, interpersonal, somatic, and imaginative. He believes that it is important to counterbalance the long-standing European and North American stress on reason and cognitive development in the dominant Western models of human nature. In the last thirty years, the study of religion in children and adolescents has focused primarily on the development of religious thinking, a situation attributed mostly to Piaget's powerful influence (Hood et al., 1996; Hyde, 1990).

Daniel Goleman's *Emotional Intelligence* (1995) and Michael Murphy's *The Future of the Body* (1992) represent significant attempts to broaden our understanding of human development by giving emotional and somatic factors greater attention in our culture. Howard Gardner (1983) argues for at least seven separate lines of intelligence, including linguistic, musical, spatial, bodily, and personal. He maintains that each of these intelligences interacts with, and builds on, the others, but at the core of each line of intelligence there is an information-processing device which is unique to that particular intelligence. Knowledge about exactly what these various developmental lines look like, how they proceed in terms of conventional or transpersonal development, and how they interact is still at an early stage of articulation in both mainstream and transpersonal psychology (Rothberg, 1999).

The foregoing critique of the stage models of spiritual or religious development should give us pause in assessing the potential value and limitations of any of the theories we shall consider in our efforts to explore religion and spirituality in the life cycle. The viewpoint adopted in this book is that there are many viable spiritual paths and goals, although there may be common elements among them. The Dalai Lama and Howard Cutler (1998) maintain that some spiritual paths may be more adequate for different psychological and cultural dispositions but that does not make them inferior or superior to other spiritual traditions. Stage models are valuable in organizing certain data in various areas of human development, but they should not be generalized beyond specific evidence. Wilber's speculative efforts to organize the deep structures of transpersonal development in a clear, hierarchical sequence appear to go beyond the limited, complex, and controversial evidence furnished by mystics, meditators, and seers in the history of religion and spirituality.

While recognizing the limitations and potential dangers of stage-development models, I believe there is nevertheless value in using stages as a broad metaphor to indicate certain patterns and goals of development. Further, following the observations of Gardner (1983), Rothberg (1998a), and Wilber (1998) that there are multiple lines of development, singling out particularly those developmental lines that reflect key elements of spirituality or implicit religion can help us track their development through the life cycle. Those crucial lines of spirituality or structures of implicit religion are identity (or sense of self), values, and worldview, as we have seen in the preceding section.

At this point I want to anticipate the overall direction of religious and spiritual development in the life cycle that we shall observe throughout this book. A table showing these three fundamental structures (or streams or lines of development) indicates that each moves from the initial, largely unconscious levels in childhood, through the increasingly conscious, personal levels in late childhood and adolescence, to the more spiritual, transpersonal levels in adulthood.

**Table 4: Movement of Spirituality and Implicit Religion
as Streams of Development**

	Self-Stream	Values Stream	Worldview Stream
Transpersonal Level	Ultimate identity	Universal principles	Interconnected-ness of all things
Personal Level	Personal identity	Conscious sorting of values	Expanding world-view—peers and larger environment
Prepersonal Level	Self shaped by caretakers and early experiences	Internalizing family values	View of world from family and early experiences

Table 4 merely sketches the broad outline of religious and spiritual development. We shall observe the details of how these structures tend to unfold as we proceed through the book. Bearing in mind the limitations of the stage metaphor, we should not imagine these three general stages (prepersonal, personal, and transpersonal) as discrete and the move from one stage to another as unidirectional and once-and-for-all. This table is simply intended to show a general trend of development and allow us to track more easily the movement of religion and spirituality through the life cycle.

The stage-development metaphor is only one of the useful metaphors we can employ in trying to grasp the elusive factors of religious and spiritual development throughout life (Kelly, 1998; Rothberg, 1999). Valuable nonlinear and nonhierarchical metaphors such as the spiral, the wave, the night sky, and the seasons may capture other features of spiritual development. For example, the metaphor of seasons appeals to some because one season cannot be judged to be higher or better than another. Each season has its own characteristics and integrity, its own beauties and difficulties. Daniel Levinson's works on the seasons of a man's and a woman's life or Erik Erikson's eight ages of the human being represent the usefulness of the season metaphor. In the course of the book, we shall examine a variety of metaphors and theories to see how they illuminate the way human beings experience religion and spirituality throughout the life cycle.

TRANSPERSONAL PSYCHOLOGY

Transpersonal psychology is highly relevant for our study because it focuses directly on spiritual phenomena and insists that spirituality has a central place in our understanding of human nature and the cosmos (Ferrer, 2002). It is a recent development as a psychological science, yet its intellectual roots can be seen in the works of William James and Carl Jung. The word "transpersonal" refers, on the subjective side, to experiences in which the person's sense of identity and self goes beyond (trans) the usual sense of self to encompass wider aspects of humankind, life, psyche, and the cosmos. On the objective side, it attends to certain forces influencing human thinking, feeling, and behavior that cannot be understood strictly in terms of an individual's own personal psychology and conditioning (Walsh & Vaughn, 1993).

In the 1960s, Abraham Maslow's research on peak experiences precipitated the birth of transpersonal psychology. Maslow's (1969) thoughts about human potential and the farther reaches of human nature appeared in the inaugural issue of the *Journal of Transpersonal Psychology*. In that same inaugural issue of the journal, Anthony Sutich (1969) specified a host of experiences and forces that concern transpersonal psychology, including mystical experience, unitive consciousness, the sacralization of everyday life, ecstacy, peak experiences, ultimate values, and transcendental phenomena. Transpersonal psychology examines how such spiritual experiences influence and transform human beings. The early focus of transpersonal psychology on peak experiences and nonordinary states of consciousness gradually expanded to include exploring contemplative disciplines and integrating transpersonal states with mainstream psychology, psychotherapy, sociology, philosophy, physics, and medicine (Rothberg, 1998b).

The Transpersonal View of Human Beings and Spirituality

Transpersonal psychology provides a vision of human nature and reality that calls into question the exclusive dominance of our "everyday world" and the mechanistic or materialistic worldview that underlies much of medicine and psychology. Such a view makes room for the spiritual changes that frequently occur in midlife. Although the vast body of research growing out of the mechanistic perspective has produced significant gains, it provides only an incomplete picture of the human being and reality. From the materialistic vantage point, human beings are separate physical entities, the human body is a biological machine composed of cells, tissues, and organs, and consciousness is a function of the brain's physiological processes. This mechanistic view denies the nonmaterial aspects of reality that are not observable in ordinary states of consciousness and cannot account for the extraordinary experiences and states of consciousness investigated by transpersonal psychology.

Transpersonal experiences and nonordinary states of consciousness reveal the human-being-as-biological-machine model as a partial truth. The view emerging from the study of transpersonal experiences, such as mysticism, out-of-body experiences, near-death experiences, precognition, telepathy, and spiritual healing, shows the human being to be much more than a machine governed by space-time restrictions of matter and linear causality. From the transpersonal perspective, human beings can function as vast fields of consciousness that transcend the physical body's limitations. This does not mean that the mechanistic view of the human being is false, but only that it requires significant adjustment and expansion.

Stanislov Grof (1985) reflects on the implications of transpersonal psychology and consciousness research for a broader and more accurate model of the human being. In his view the situation in the human sciences parallels the dilemma modern physicists encounter in the wave-particle paradox regarding light and matter in subatomic processes: under certain experimental conditions, light behaves as a wave phenomenon, while under other experimental conditions it acts as a particle phenomenon. Each view has partial validity and a limited range of applicability. The experimenter and the experimental setup determine which of these two behaviors will be manifested. Niels Bohr maintains that both the wave picture and particle picture are complementary and necessary for a comprehensive understanding of this paradoxical reality. He summarizes the general principle of complementarity: "the opposite of a correct statement is an incorrect statement, but the opposite of a profound truth may well be another profound truth" (Bohr, 1958, p. 66). While Grof recognizes that there are differences between the paradoxes of subatomic physics and those involved in the human sciences, he finds Bohr's solution suggestive. Grof (1985) insists that to describe human beings in a more comprehensive fashion, we must accept the fact that they are somehow at once both biological machines and extensive fields of consciousness.

In Grof's view, the body of controversial data accumulated by the sciences of medicine, psychiatry, psychology, parapsychology, anthropology, and thanatology is now sufficient to justify the formulation of a comparable principle of complementarity in the human sciences. At the present time, the complementary model of the human being emerging from transpersonal studies has the value of recognizing the complex, and even paradoxical, reality of human nature. This new model, with its juxtaposition of two contradictory images of the human being, may be only a stepping stone to a more elegant and comprehensive theory. Grof (1985) believes that theoretical physicist David Bohm may have opened new possibilities for synthesizing and integrating the two seemingly irreconcilable images of human nature. According to Grof, the hologram may contribute to our understanding of the nature of wholeness, including human wholeness.

In particular, Grof finds Bohm's notion of reality as an unbroken and coherent whole in constant flux (the theory of "holomovement") to have revolutionary implications for understanding not only the material universe (the theory's original aim), but also the phenomena of life and consciousness. In Bohm's (1980) view, life and inanimate matter cannot be absolutely distinguished from one another. They represent an inseparable unity and cannot be explained from, or reduced to, each other. Science studies only a fraction of reality, what Bohm calls the explicate (unfolded) order. In the implicate (enfolded) order, various aspects of existence function in relation to the whole of reality.

Extending the trend of Bohm's thought, Grof (1985) suggests that everyday experiences of the material world reflect selective aspects of the explicate order, while transcendental experiences and transpersonal states can be interpreted as direct experience of the implicate order or the whole of enfolded reality. For example, the ordinary consciousness involved in the world of work and problem-solving operates at the level of the explicate order while a mystical experience of union with nature or the divine would access the implicate order. Nonordinary states of consciousness can be interpreted to mediate direct experience of the implicate order, intuiting those archetypal and mythic images that symbolize the wholeness of the universe and human reality. William James's (1961) experience with nitrous oxide illustrates how nonordinary states can access images of universal wholeness and order. He says that the altered state of consciousness induced by nitrous oxide enabled him to grasp for a time the unity of the world as described by religious mystics. Consciousness has access to both the explicate and the implicate order, at least in principle. While Grof appreciates the imaginative power of the images drawn from the research of Bohr and Bohm, he holds out the hope that even more powerful models may derive from disciplines that study human experience directly, such as psychology, psychiatry, psychotherapy, and anthropology. In Grof's view, we are approaching a major shift that will mark a radical departure from the mechanistic models that still dominate much of mainstream science.

SUMMARY

To summarize, we have observed the complexity of the terms we shall use to track religion and spirituality in the life cycle. The roots of the word *religion* suggest that it has to do with how people are connected to, and attend to, the ultimate powers of the universe or the divine. We have seen how psychologists link religion to human vulnerability, wishes, mortality, trust, behavior, relationships, and meaning in life. We shall examine those functional definitions of religion that highlight the way it works in the individual psyche and in society, without reducing religion to those functions. At each stage in the life cycle, we shall attempt to see what religion looks like "from within," what it means to those who adhere to it at a particular time in life.

Implicit religion is a category that underscores how religion is not always found in the conventional forms of doctrine, community, and ritual. It will allow us to see religious dimensions in even seemingly secular attitudes and practices of people encountering the major passages of life. Spirituality is a popular but difficult-to-define term that is most frequently used to focus on the inner processes of religion as a search for meaning and the divine. Most people surveyed consider themselves to be both spiritual and religious which means that, for them, spirituality is an inseparable aspect of religion. However, an increasing number characterize themselves as spiritual but not religious, insisting that the spiritual quest need not be attached to religious affiliation. For many, a distinguishing aspect of spirituality includes the view that the visible world is part of a larger spiritual universe which gives meaning and moral direction to the everyday world.

We have noted too that a number of human-development theorists present the movement through the life cycle as a hierarchical and invariant sequence of stages. While the metaphor of developmental stages may be suggestive of the way particular dimensions of personality unfold, we should bear in mind that human beings are far too complex to be adequately captured in even a highly sophisticated stage model. Still, ancient theories of the life cycle testify to the enduring value of stage metaphors for helping people to understand their progression from infancy to old age and death. Moreover, two such typical theories, the Pythagorean and the Hindu, illustrate how the individual life cycle is rooted in the larger reality of nature or the divine. These ancient perspectives make explicit how individuals find meaning and value in relation to the divine or the seemingly endless cycles of nature. These theories offered a religious and spiritual framework for traditional societies, just as our current scientific theories strive to provide psychological orientation for the modern and postmodern world.

So while stage metaphors may offer useful general frameworks for thinking about different lines of development, religion and spirituality, with their many components, cannot be grasped as a clear and invariant sequence of progression. Having acknowledged the limitations of any such stage model, nevertheless it is possible to recognize broad developments through the life cycle, such as the movement from the unconscious, emotional roots, through the conscious understanding, to the transpersonal experience of religion and spirituality. However, this movement through these levels is often inconsistent and cyclical, and a person can be at all three of these levels at once in regard to the different facets of religion and spirituality.

CHAPTER TWO

CHILDHOOD FOUNDATIONS OF RELIGION AND SPIRITUALITY

—————— ❧ ——————

> Our birth is but a sleep and a forgetting
> The soul that rises with us, our life's Star,
>> Hath had elsewhere its setting
>> And cometh from afar:
>> Not in entire forgetfulness,
>> And not in utter nakedness,
> But trailing clouds of glory do we come
>> From God, who is our home:
> Heaven lies about us in our infancy!
>> — William Wordsworth, "Intimations of Immortality
>>> from Recollections of Early Childhood"

This chapter focuses our examination on the role of religion and spirituality in the first period of the life cycle, childhood. Psychoanalysts and developmental psychologists have devoted a great deal of attention to this crucial phase of life and have shed light on how the foundations of religion and spirituality are established at this time. All of the psychoanalytic perspectives recognize how parents and caretakers strongly influence a child's religion and spirituality, though they differ on how this process affects personality functioning. At the same time, there is considerable difference of opinion among psychologists of religion on the degree to which religion is even present in very young children. While many psychologists of religion downplay the likelihood of genuine religion in childhood, others point to the increasing number of published accounts of childhood spiritual experiences, books such as

Robert Coles's *The Spiritual Life of Children* (1990) and Edward Robinson's *The Original Vision: A Study of the Religious Experience of Childhood* (1983), and the publication of the *International Journal of Children's Spirituality* as evidence of a significant degree of spirituality among children. We shall examine these arguments in this chapter.

PSYCHOANALYTIC PERSPECTIVES

Freud's View of the Origins of Religion in Childhood

There is little doubt about the historical significance of Sigmund Freud (1856–1939) in our growing understanding of the psyche and its development. Robert Fuller (1988) estimates that a third of all developmental theories build directly upon Freud's observations and another third define their theoretical orientation by self-consciously rejecting, and offering alternatives to, the major tenets of Freud's theories. He believes that even the third that more or less ignore Freud are at least indebted to him for having pioneered a view of human nature that stresses the significance of infancy and childhood for determining the overall structure of personality development. The theory of psychosexual development was in Freud's own estimation his most momentous and original contribution to human knowledge, next to his dream interpretation method. He views the overall direction of human development as a movement from the human infant as an irrational, pleasure-centered organism to the mature adult as a reality-oriented person. The journey along the way is long and complex, moving through well-defined though overlapping stages. It is within the context of the psychosexual stages of development that Freud's ideas about religion in childhood are given shape, so we shall consider these stages first.

Freud identifies three main stages in terms of bodily areas, called erotogenic zones, that serve as a primary source of pleasure. He labels them the oral, anal, and phallic stages. Most of the evidence for these stages grows out of reconstructions Freud and other analysts have made from adult patients, although some support comes from direct observation of children. Freud (1905) describes how the sexual instinct is developed as a complex structure and how it "comes apart" when blocked or fixated at any one of the stages of development. In this way, psychopathology reveals the components which are ordinarily part of a whole. There have been many criticisms of the legitimacy of generalizing from profoundly disturbed people to "normal" persons, but then again many people undergoing psychoanalysis are adequately functioning adults.

Oral Stage

The first stage Freud (1905) describes in the developmental sequence is the period where the mouth serves as the chief erotogenic zone. The sucking that takes place at this stage is for Freud about more than just nourishment. In "Three Essays" he observes, "No one who has seen a baby sinking back satiated from the breast and falling asleep with flushed cheeks and a blissful smile can escape the reflection that this picture persists as a prototype of the expression of sexual satisfaction in later life" (p. 182). After the child is weaned and forced to give up the mother's breast, substitutes are found, such as thumb sucking. In adulthood, forms of oral stimulation may be seen in smoking and gum chewing. Freud says that this first stage might be called the "cannibalistic" sexual orientation because the aim of the sexual instinct here is the incorporation of the object. This is the physical prototype of the psychological process which later plays a key role in development, namely, identification or internalization, as we shall see at the phallic stage. The early oral phase is sometimes referred to as the oral incorporative substage and the following period, from around six to seven months, is called the oral-sadistic subphase when the first teeth appear and the child begins to bite and chew.

According to Freud, the infant's experiences in this first stage influence the rest of his or her life. Satisfying nursing leaves behind vague unconscious memories of blissful and unbounded union with the mother and predisposes a person toward an optimistic outlook on life. Disappointment of oral needs inclines a person to become apprehensive and generally expect the worst possibilities in every situation. Abnormal indulgence at this stage may lead to a passive expectation that someone will always take care of the person. Freud himself does not speak of this stage in terms of religion or spirituality, but rather in terms of worldview. Nevertheless, given that worldview is a principal component of spirituality, the oral stage has a strong influence on this aspect of spirituality.

Experiences in the oral stage may influence character, choice of profession, and pathological symptoms. Oral character is a term that describes the lasting effect of this stage. Oral traits may be seen in oral cravings, tight-lipped stability, oral asceticism, as well as overindulgence in food, drink, or smoking. Alcoholism too has been interpreted to stem from a disturbance in the oral phase. Symptoms related to food phobias, rituals, and obesity are considered in this view to result from frustrations in the early feeding process. Karl Abraham (1924) believes that choices of profession and hobbies may be rooted in oral eroticism. Cooking and wine tasting come to mind as such examples of the influence of early oral experience on future life paths.

Anal Stage

Freud refers to the second stage of psychosexual development as the anal phase. Two sources of pleasure are associated with this phase, namely, (1) retention of fecal matter in the lower bowel and (2) expelling of fecal matter through the anal sphincter. Freud emphasizes that the child has a different attitude from the adult toward feces. He believes that the child originally experiences feces as interesting, detachable, and valuable parts of the body. Only later does disgust emerge in this regard. The toilet-training situation can be one of the child's first symbols of compliance or disobedience with the environment, and the feces are potentially a source of pleasure as well as an expression of the child's relation with caretakers. Freud (1908) states that intense anal eroticism is commonly sublimated in qualities of miserliness, obstinacy, and orderliness; he adds that sadistic cruelty is rooted in this stage of development. There are possible implications here for a person's developing worldview and sense of self, but this phase is considerably less important for spirituality than the crucial stages which precede and follow it.

The Phallic Stage

The phallic stage, sometimes referred to as the Oedipal stage, is the central influence on the formation and development of religion, in Freud's view. He believes that at about three years of age, the boy begins to desire exclusive claim on the mother's love and attention, and at the same time to feel jealousy and rage toward rivals of this love, especially the father. Over the next two years or so this rivalry continues until the boy discovers that girls don't have a penis. Freud reasons that the male child believes the girl's lack of a penis represents the possibility of castration and that consequently the boy fears that the father might castrate him if he continues to vie for exclusive possession of the mother's love.

Freud named this triangular conflict (boy-mother-father) the Oedipus complex after the story of King Oedipus, who unknowingly killed his father, Laius, and married his mother, Jocasta. The Oedipus complex is finally dissolved when the boy's ambivalence of love and hate for the father (who is loved as protector and hated as rival) finally ends when the child identifies with the father. The father as well as his authority and values are thereby internalized as the basis for a major division of the psyche, the super-ego, which becomes the child's guide to right and wrong. From this perspective, the voice of conscience is actually the voice of the parent who is internalized at a time before ego consciousness is well developed. Because this process happens at such an early age, the super-ego structure remains largely unconscious. This formation of the super-ego is the first important religious implication of the Oedipal phase.

The other crucial moment of religious significance in the phallic phase is the "creation" of the God idea, which, according to Freud (1927), grows out of the phenomenon of projection. Psychological projection is the transfer of one's own unconscious feelings, thoughts, and impressions onto external objects or persons. For example, a person who is unaware of his or her anger tends to experience others in the environment as being angry. This process follows the general dynamics of the psyche whereby what we are unconscious or unaware of is projected out onto the environment. Thus, the father, who is internalized as an unconscious structure, is subsequently projected onto the heavens as the idea of God. This projection is parallel to the way early human beings saw in the heavens the various constellations, such as the Big Dipper or the Twins, projecting onto the heavens what was in their own minds. According to Freud, this explains the origin of the religious idea that God is a heavenly Father who creates and watches over his creation. Freud finds support for this notion of God as a male parent in the traditional imagery of the patriarchal religions of Judaism, Christianity, and Islam. We shall see that some of the object-relations theorists modify Freud's ideas about the origins of religion by focusing on the influence of the mother and her role in shaping the Goddess idea in matriarchal religions.

Freud (1923a) bases most of his ideas about the stages of psychosexual development on the assumption that the psychology of women is analogous to that of men. He supposes the dissolution of the Oedipus complex is analogous in boys and girls, although he still has some doubts about how complete the parallel between male and female development might be. Freud recognizes that the female child does not have to deal with the threat of castration, so she abandons her desire for exclusive attention of the opposite-sex parent more gradually than the male child. The motivation for the female child to end the Oedipal rivalry is not castration but rather fear of losing the mother's love. This difference between the way the Oedipus complex is resolved in males and females is responsible for a difference between the male and female super-ego or conscience. Freud (1925) states that because the Oedipus complex in girls is resolved less decisively because there is no castration threat, "women are less ready to submit to the great exigencies of life" (p. 258) and "show less sense of justice than men" (p. 257). Critics of Freud such as Jean Baker Miller (1976) and Nancy Chodorow (1978) have found such ideas about the hypothesized "defects" of female moral development offensive and unsupported.

With the resolution of the Oedipus complex, children enter the latency period, which is relatively free of the sexual interests and conflicts of early childhood. According to Freud, even the memory of the Oedipus complex is repressed. Thus those crucial psychological developments which give rise to religious ideas and attitudes remain hidden in the background of personal and phylogenetic history. The latency stage ends with puberty, which in turn begins the final stage of psychosexual development, the genital stage. Sexual maturation requires subordinating the earlier stages to the primacy of genital organization. Nevertheless, traces of earlier structures remain in the unconscious, and Freud believes that a person may regress to these earlier stages in the absence of genital-stage satisfaction or in the face of difficulties.

The possibility of regression in fact accounts for one final aspect of Freud's view of religion. He considers religious experience itself, which is seen by many as the very foundation of religious traditions, to be a regression to the earliest stage of existence, to a time before the individual is differentiated from the mother or the environment. This state of undifferentiated unity he calls primary narcissism. Thus, Freud (1930) believes that when mystics report a direct experience of union with the divine, they are actually misinterpreting their experience. Freud evaluates the classical religious descriptions of union with God not as an advanced state of psychological or spiritual development but as a pathological return to the most primitive state preceding all psychological development whatsoever, the experience of oneness with the mother in the womb and immediately after birth.

Using Freud's view of the psyche, we might picture his idea of the most important aspects of religion as they shape the child's personality as shown in Diagram 4. This diagram emphasizes that religion is based on the child's experience of the parents. Two of Freud's main critiques of religion are illustrated here: First, religion tends to produce a rigid and inflexible conscience with unchanging rules, and the idea of God standing behind the conscience ensures that these rules are eternal. Second, the religious idea of God is based on the psychological mechanism of projection and the wish to have a protective parent to offset human vulnerability.

Diagram 4: Freud's View of the Origins of Religion

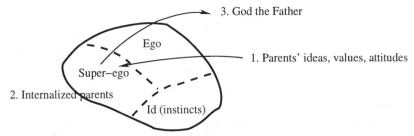

1. Parental values, ideas, and attitudes are internalized by the child.
2. This internalization establishes the super-ego, based on the parents' values and ideas. This super-ego conscience is often rigid and unable to adapt to changing circumstances, thus creating guilt and depression.
3. The idealized parental image is projected onto the heavens as the God-image.

Overall, it is clear that Freud's evaluation of religion's influence on human development is consistently negative. He sees religion as based on the dynamics of projection and wishful thinking whereby the human species "creates" a God idea to counteract the vulnerability and weakness of the human condition. Freud believes that the God idea is an attempt, albeit ultimately unsuccessful, to reduce human anxiety in the face of mortality, injustice, and the overwhelming power and immenseness of nature. For Freud, religion is essentially rooted in early childhood experience, and it retains the limitations of its unconscious origins. He sees religion as primitive and regressive, because in his view it cannot transcend the childhood situation in which it arises. Freud sees maturity as making the unconscious conscious, and this would include conscious insight into the psychological dynamics at work in the origin and maintenance of religious ideas and values. Rather than calling upon God to deal with the problems of human existence, Freud advocates accepting our lot with courage and taking responsibility for making a better world. He also believes that the God idea which stands behind the rigid super-ego conscience tends to make moral rules appear as God's laws and therefore rigid and unadaptable to changing conditions of history and society. We shall see that other theorists have used some of the insights of Freud's psychoanalysis to reach radically different conclusions about the role of religion and spirituality in human development. The first of these alternative views is represented by object-relations theory.

OBJECT-RELATIONS THEORY OF RELIGION IN CHILDHOOD

Ian Suttie (1889–1935)

Freud's view of the psyche is mainly focused on the individual person as a closed system of energy in which tensions build up and press for discharge. From this perspective, the motivation of personality is essentially instinctual drives and how they are managed by the ego and super-ego. Ian Suttie, a British psychiatrist and psychoanalyst, modifies many of Freud's views by recognizing the importance of cultural factors in psychological functioning. Where Freud sees the instincts as the mainsprings of psychological activity, Suttie considers the innate need for companionship and curiosity to be prime factors in motivation. Where Freud believes that there is an independent drive toward destruction in the human being, Suttie maintains that anger and rage are fundamentally a response to the denial of love and an attempt to restore human relationship and to avoid self-isolation.

Suttie sees the mother as having the central role in shaping the human personality. The mother is crucial because she represents the first emotional relationship to develop from the original stage of infantile solipsism, the phase where the self is not yet differentiated from the mother or environment (parallel to Freud's primary narcissism). According to Suttie, the bond of love is one of natural tenderness mediated by caresses and nurtural gratification rather than the sexual longing that Freud hypothesizes. This relationship with the mother is so central that it influences both personal and cultural development. Suttie believes that efforts to restore the love of the mother that was left behind in infancy is the ultimate source of all later social activities, including art, science, and religion. In this regard he substitutes the relationship with the mother for the key role that the Oedipus complex plays in Freud's view of the origins of art, science, religion, and civilization.

Suttie is fascinated with the history of religion and greatly modifies Freud's theory on the origins of religion. He thinks that Freud neglects the varieties of religion, especially the mother cults of antiquity. While he recognizes that Freud may be right about the general dynamics of projection and the Oedipus complex as the source of the father gods in patriarchal traditions, he holds that the prior matriarchal religions cannot be explained in this way. Instead, Suttie sees the projection of pre-Oedipal wishes, fears, and conflicts, that is, early experiences surrounding the mother, as the basis for the matriarchal religions. In this way he expands upon Freud's notion of projection as the source of the God or Goddess idea.

Suttie paves the way for a positive view of religion's effect on human development. He goes along with Freud to the extent of agreeing that certain aspects of religion may be pathological, but he does not stop there. While admitting that religion may resemble mental illness insofar as it stems from the experiences of infancy, he maintains that, in its higher forms, religion attempts to better our affective relationships with others and thus overcome the self-preoccupation and misery of mental illness (Suttie, 1935, p. 104). In this regard religion has the potential to influence development in a positive direction and act much like a system of psychotherapy.

Ronald Fairbairn (1889–1964)

Fairbairn entirely abandons classical psychoanalytic drive (instinct) theory and is the most systematic developer of the object-relations perspective. Like Suttie, he sees the roots of psychopathology in maternal deprivation and believes that aggression is not an independent instinct but a reaction to unsatisfactory relations with other human beings. While Fairbairn does not write a great deal about religion, he refers to aspects of religion in selected essays. In "The Repression and Return of Bad Objects," he states that the child deals with bad objects, especially the parents, by internalizing and then repressing them. Even if the parents are problematic, the child cannot do without them and "is possessed by them, as if by evil spirits." The task of psychotherapy is to release the bad objects from the unconscious because they are considered to be the origin of mental disorders. In this light, the psychotherapist appears to be a kind of exorcist, casting out the devils of a patient's distant past.

In a later paper, Fairbairn (1955) continues to draw upon religious metaphors to describe the psychotherapeutic process. Patients in therapy seek "salvation" from their past, from bondage to internal bad objects, from the weight of guilt, and from spiritual death. Using classical religious language, Fairbairn describes the therapeutic search for healing as corresponding in detail to the "religious quest." So the earliest stage of human development is seen as the source of malaise which motivates the quest for salvation. Thus Fairbairn focuses on what goes wrong in early development and sets forth a therapeutic perspective cast in religious language to describe the growth of personality.

Harry Guntrip (1901–1975)

Guntrip, son of a Methodist preacher and himself a Congregational minister, is strongly influenced by Fairbairn, having undergone a lengthy analysis with him. Along with other object-relations theorists, Guntrip (1969) assumes that all humans share "an absolute need to be able to relate in fully personal terms to an environment that we feel relates beneficently to us." When this basic need is not met from the early years onward, a person will suffer from a persistent state of anxiety. In Guntrip's view, religion addresses this essential need of human development by serving as a refuge for those suffering from anxiety. Religion is, for Guntrip, a fundamental sense of connectedness to, and personal validation by, the universe and ultimate reality.

Religion symbolizes the relatedness that grounds the human being and serves as an antidote to the anxiety which is epidemic in our time. Connectedness to the universe is initially mediated to the infant by other human beings, the child's earliest caretakers. In this sense, religion symbolizes those human beings who provide the affirmation and care that allow the child to feel at home in the world. As Guntrip puts it, religion stands for "the saving power of the good object relationship." Guntrip represents one of the best examples of the positive attitude of object-relations theorists toward spirituality and religion.

Donald Winnicott (1896–1971)

Winnicott was a pediatrician and psychoanalyst who studied the child's emerging awareness of being a person separate from other human beings. He observed that a devoted mother is crucial in this development because she provides a "holding environment" to contain the infant's fragmented world of experience. The mother reflects back to the child what she sees and thereby personalizes the child's early experiences. As other interests gradually occupy the mother's attention, the child must come to grips with a world that does not always respond to his or her demands. Winnicott refers to the "good enough mother" as a factor that allows the child to adjust adequately to this changing situation. Another important element in this adjustment is the "transitional object," which is often a soft blanket or a cuddly stuffed animal within the first three years of life.

The transitional object relieves the strain of separation anxiety and allows the child to bring together his or her inner world of wishes and needs with the outer world which may resist these wishes. According to Winnicott, this object, which is particularly needed at moments of crisis or anxiety, represents the breast and the child's relationship with the mother. He also believes that the transitional object is the prototype of other transitional phenomena which perform a parallel function later in life. He sees religion and art as such phenomena that allow for an intermediate area of experience, a realm of imagination between the child's omnipotent thinking and fantasy and the adult's world of sense perception and reality testing. In this regard religion is adaptive and valuable because it can help people to integrate their inner and outer worlds and cope with anxiety more effectively.

While Winnicott grants the value of religion for adapting to reality, he also recognizes its limitations should we try to force others to accept our "illusory" world of experience. He uses the word illusion (from the Latin ludere = to play) here in a positive sense to describe the role of transitional phenomena in providing a creative area of experience valuable for adaptation. His use of the word *religion* to characterize the important function transitional phenomena play in development stands in sharp contrast to Freud's use of the word in his major work on religion, *The Future of an Illusion.* There, Freud speaks of illusion as an idea based on wishful thinking, and religion is, in his view, an illusory wish for a protective parent (God) to alleviate realistic anxiety due to human vulnerability. Although Winnicott (1971) is more optimistic than Freud about the possible constructive effects of illusion, he too realizes that religion "becomes a hallmark of madness when an adult puts too powerful a claim on the credulity of others, forcing them to acknowledge a sharing of illusion that is not their own" (p. 3).

Winnicott insists that religious ideas are valuable so long as they are not intended to replace the trust that is engendered by good early relationships:

> The child who is not having good enough experiences in the early stages cannot be given the idea of a personal God as a substitute for infant care. The vitally important subtle communicating of the infant-mother kind antedates the stage at which verbal communication can be added. This is a first principle of moral education, that moral education is no substitute for love. (1965, p. 97)

Thus religion is effective as a significant affirmation of trust in the world and God only when it is supported by people who provide trustworthy relationships.

Ana-Maria Rizzuto

Rizzuto is a professor of psychiatry and a psychoanalyst who has studied both children and adults. Her work on the God-image builds on the insights of Freud and the object-relations theorists, in particular Winnicott. She distinguishes between the God concept as a product of mostly conscious thinking, what she calls the "god of theologians," and the God-image or God-representation which is based primarily on previous interpersonal experiences. Drawing upon questionnaires, interviews, and sketches of patients' families and their images of God, Rizzuto (1979) concludes that these people have not formed their God-images exclusively on the basis of one parent. The development of the God-image is, in her view, much more complex in that it is influenced not only by the father, as Freud thought, but also by the mother, grandparents, heroes, as well as by wished-for parents or feared parents of the person's own imagination.

While she recognizes Freud's contributions to our understanding of the formation of the God-image, she criticizes him for not dealing sufficiently with the God-representation in women and for focusing too exclusively on the Oedipal period as the source of the God-image. She believes that Freud did not look back far enough into early childhood for the source of the God-image. The earliest influences on shaping the God-representation are pre-Oedipal, even earlier than two years old. However, Rizzuto adds that the God-image does not get fixed in a final way at the end of the Oedipal period, as Freud thought; it is constantly being revised as our primary relationships in life change:

> This use of the God representation for regulation and modulation of object love and related self-representations begins in childhood, continues throughout life, and finds its final and critical potentialities at death, when the individual is faced with his own final self-representations at the moment of lasting separation from the world of loved and hated objects. (1979, p. 89)

The God-image is reworked at each stage in the life cycle and modified by ongoing experience throughout adulthood, even up to the point of death. The God-representation is a major element in a person's sense of self and worldview, or, to put it differently, the God-image reflects one's sense of self and worldview. Rizzuto acknowledges her debt to Heinz Kohut's research on the early development of the self. Kohut (1971) emphasizes that the need for having oneself reflected by the other is a core experience in becoming a human being. He speaks of this early experience as mirroring and explains how it is the source of self-esteem. Mirroring produces two major mental representations: first, the child's conception of him/herself, which is often an idealized, aggrandized image, and, second, a conception of the mother, which is frequently an exalted image of the mirroring mother. In Rizzuto's view, this mirroring process is the primary source for the first elaboration of a God-representation.

Rizzuto comments favorably on Freud's (1923a) idea that the father not only contributes to the formation of the God-image, but is also the source of the Devil-representation. Freud explains that the Devil and God have a common origin: the father image is split into two figures, namely, the hostile and defiant Devil and the good and paternal God. Ambivalence is at work here, as Freud believes we both love and hate our parents. We are often more conscious of one of these poles than the other, but both feelings are rooted in the unconscious. God represents a projection of our love for the father, while the Devil represents our hatred of the father. Rizzuto finds Freud's view of the Devil's image being rooted in the child's fear of the father's power as plausible, given that she has seen no female representations of the Devil.

In general, we see that the object-relations theorists recognize many of the positive aspects of religion as it emerges in childhood: Suttie sees religion as symbolizing better affective relationships and based on the effort to restore the mother's love. Fairbairn views religion as a source of therapeutic metaphors for the liberation of individuals from bondage to bad objects of early childhood. For Guntrip, religion relieves anxiety by symbolizing our connectedness to other people and the universe. Winnicott understands religion as a positive realm of the imagination which allows the person to adapt to new circumstances. Finally, Rizzuto observes that our God-image is already forming before the age of two, is based on many sources, both female and male, and is constantly reworked throughout life to reflect the changing experience of the self and the world. All of these authors see religion as making positive and lasting contributions to the formation of the child's personality. Here, religion is seen as laying crucial foundations, in contrast to Freud's idea that religion sets up obstacles that must be removed later in life by psychotherapy.

EGO PSYCHOLOGY ON RELIGION IN CHILDHOOD

After Freud's drive theory and object-relations theory, the other major psychoanalytic perspective to explore religion in childhood is that of ego psychology. A number of figures have contributed to this perspective, but none have had greater impact on our understanding of religion than Gordon Allport and Erik Erikson.

Gordon Allport (1897–1967)

Allport was one of the most important influences in making the psychological study of religion a respectable enterprise for someone aspiring to a career in psychology. After the stinging critiques of Sigmund Freud's psychoanalysis and John Watson's behaviorism, psychologists shied away from investigating religion. Allport had the stature to buck that trend and draw attention to the potential value of religion for contributing to mental health. His book *The Individual and His Religion* helped to make the study of religion an acceptable research topic in psychology, taking up where William James's *The Varieties of Religious Experience* leaves off. Like James, Allport spent his entire career teaching at Harvard University, and, like James, he attempted to weigh carefully the positive and negative features of religion.

The categories for understanding religion developed by Allport permit psychologists to make a more nuanced judgment about the psychological consequences of being religious, distinguishing between mature and immature religion. We shall consider his criteria for mature religion in the chapter on religion in adulthood. Contrary to Freud's view that religion is regressive and pathological, Allport found that only certain types of religion or particular ways of being religious have that negative effect. While Allport's distinction between mature and immature religion contributes to a more careful judgment regarding the effects of religion, it appears to lead to a negative evaluation of childhood religion.

Because Allport (1960) considers meaning and interpretation as essential aspects of religion, be believes that childhood religion has little in common with adult religion. In fact, he holds that religion is entirely lacking in infancy. While small children can imitate religious rituals, they are unable to understand their significance. Allport describes the child's religious responses as wholly social in character, imitating adult behavior such as bowing the head and folding the hands in prayer, or memorizing the words to simple prayers or hymns without understanding their meaning. He likens the child's behavior to "pointless habits" required by parents. Allport tells the story of a four-year-old child who was accustomed to saying his prayers before a religious picture. On one occasion while away from home he was told to say his prayers. Because his religious picture was not present, he set up a copy of a popular magazine he found lying on a nearby table and said his prayers. Allport concludes that the child's prayers had no more significance than nursery rhymes.

Another characteristic of childhood religion that Allport sees as immature is egocentrism, where all perception and feelings revolve around the child's growing sense of selfhood. Here Allport repeats Freud's observation that children believe that by thinking things, they make them happen. He also agrees with Piaget's view that young children sometimes believe that the sun follows them around to see whether or not they are well behaved, and, at this stage, children hear only partially, taking in just the familiar words and then weaving them into their own meaning. Anthropomorphism is a further aspect of childhood religion which Allport highlights. He cites the typical image of God as an old man, a rich man, superman, or a king, and often includes physical attributes of the child's father, though not as universally as Freud surmised. Allport notes that various disappointments in life often gradually modify the magical and egocentric aspects of childhood religion, for instance, when prayers for a sick pet or a new toy do not seem to work, or such repeated experiences may eventually cause the child to drop religion altogether.

Allport's overall contribution to understanding the place of religion and spirituality in the life cycle rests mainly on his distinction between mature and immature religion and the vast research generated by his categories of intrinsic religion (as an end in itself) and extrinsic religion (as a means to another end). His tendency to equate childhood religion with immature religion has not permitted a sufficient appreciation of religion and spirituality in childhood. Another major ego psychologist, Erik Erikson, has emphasized the religious and spiritual foundations of the child's personality.

Erik Erikson (1902–1994)

Erik Erikson has produced one of the most influential theories of the life cycle. No psychoanalytic writer has given more attention to the place of religion in psychological life than Erikson. His books on the historic figures of Martin Luther and Mohandas Gandhi in particular demonstrate his appreciation of the important role that religious values and concerns play in psychological growth. Erikson was born of Danish parents who were separated before he was born. His nordic features seemed an enigma as he grew up in Germany with his Jewish mother and stepfather. Erikson developed a great interest in art, which he studied on and off during the years he spent wandering through Germany and Italy in search of his identity. This lengthy "Bohemian" period, lasting until he was twenty-five years old, influenced him greatly. He decided to create his own name, becoming Erik Erikson, i.e., "son of Erik," indicating that he is the author of his own identity, a fitting beginning for a man who has often been called "the psychologist of identity."

In 1927 he went to Vienna to teach art to children of Freud's patients and colleagues. During this time he became intrigued by psychoanalysis and began to study at the training institute of the Vienna Psychoanalytic Society. Erikson studied with some of the major architects of psychoanalytic ego psychology, including Anna Freud, who was first a primary school teacher and then creator of a new profession, child psychoanalysis. She became his training analyst. At the same time, he was learning Montessori teaching methods, which stress the importance of giving children a creative environment in which to learn and a wide range of materials to work with.

After Erikson finished his psychoanalytic training, he moved to Boston where he became the city's first child analyst and was appointed to the Harvard Medical School. He worked with troubled children and observed how they sought to solve their mental conflicts through play. He began to recognize that what adults tend to dismiss as mere play, fun, and games, is for children themselves the very essence of life. Much of his work is designed to show what children's activity means to themselves, not to the observing adult. He emphasizes that play is the child's way to master reality through experiment and planning.

Erikson's first book, *Childhood and Society*, was immediately translated into twelve languages and is among the best-known books written by a student of Freud. In this work Erikson sets forth his ideas about the life cycle in terms of eight ages of the human being. These ages unfold according to what he calls an epigenetic ground plan, meaning that they develop after birth. Each age is characterized by a struggle between two opposing tendencies, such as basic trust versus mistrust. The positive pole he terms the syntonic element; it supports growth, expansion, and self-respect. The negative pole, the dystonic element, challenges growth. Out of this struggle a virtue or ego strength develops. These strengths or virtues have a cumulative effect in that later mental structures build on earlier ones, and ego strengths developed early in the life cycle contribute to the ability to deal with future life challenges. If certain strengths are not developed during their typical time in the life cycle, a person can still "return" to cultivate them later. In each age, a person's realization of the relevant ego strength can be understood to fall somewhere on a spectrum between the two extreme poles represented by the syntonic and dystonic elements. There is often a mixture of the two polarities, such as degrees of trust and mistrust. Erikson also recognizes that these virtues are not achieved once and for all, but continue to be challenged in other ages where they are not usually the predominant focus.

Much of Erikson's work is based on Freud's theory of psychosexual development, especially in the early stages of childhood, though Erikson focuses on the ego rather than the role of the instincts and the unconscious. This chapter considers only the childhood stages, leaving the remaining stages for later chapters.

Erikson's First Four Stages

1. Basic Trust vs. Mistrust   virtue: hope   first year of life
The child begins to gain a sense of self and feeling of goodness through the predictability, consistency, and quality of the mother's care. The trust acquired is shown in the ease of feeding, the depth of sleep, and the relaxation of the bowels. The trust developed here allows the child to deal with the frustrations of this time of life. The weaning experience can be a considerable challenge to the child's sense of trust in the mother and the world. Erikson emphasizes how the mother's and child's life cycle come together. The mother transmits her own sense of care (the virtue of the seventh age) as the life cycle is set in motion again in the child who is developing trust and hope (the virtue of the first age). This might be visualized by Diagram 5.

Diagram 5: Intersection of Mother's and Child's Life Cycle

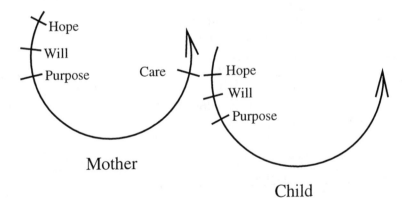

Erikson suggests that religion supports the developments of this stage. The earliest forms of religion are sacrifices and rituals to establish or restore faith (trust) in the goodness of creation and the world. Doctrines about God's creating and maintaining the world are designed to reaffirm this trust in life.

2. Autonomy vs. Shame and Doubt   virtue: will   c. 1–4 years old
The child's musculature develops during this stage. The newfound abilities to grasp things, to stand, and to walk give the child some sense of control. These new capacities must be affirmed yet limited in order to avoid danger and the shame which comes from the inability to control one's own power. Toilet training can be a focal problem during this stage where the challenge of autonomy versus shame is acutely experienced. R. Fuller (1988) observes that religious doctrines emphasizing the dangers of autonomy and self-direction may injure the valuable aspect of autonomy which is begun in this period.

3. Initiative vs. Guilt   virtue: purpose   c. 4–6 years old
The child can plan and begin to search out things or make things in this period. Erikson holds that the possibility of guilt occurs when initiative is overexercised or demands more than the child can do. Parents should maintain a balance between encouragement and regulation if the child is to avoid excessive guilt. During this time the child begins to parent him- or herself by internalizing parents and caretakers, attempting to balance unlimited exploration with self-guidance and self-punishment. Erikson recognizes this as the time when Freud's concept of the Oedipal conflict is relevant. The child's rivalry with the parent of the same sex and desire for the exclusive attention of the parent of the opposite sex may cause guilt over fantasies which cannot be realized because of the parents' dominance.

4. Industry vs. Inferiority   virtue: competence   c. 6–11 years old
At this stage the child's physical coordination allows the use of tools and learning skills. Now the child is able to devote more systematic attention to performing a task. The child learns reading, writing, and language skills as well as the rules of games and life. Erikson points out that a sense of inferiority can develop if the child is unable to do these things as well as his or her peers can.

Erikson focuses on the foundations of the ego, which are established in these early stages. He emphasizes trust and hope as the key ingredients for the gradual emergence of a healthy ego. Like the object-relations theorists, he stresses the importance of the quality of the parental relationship in the earliest stages of ego formation and the balance between autonomy and support, encouragement and guidance, initiative and regulation that are required to shape the emerging childhood ego. Erikson's approach to religion in childhood allows him to appreciate the broad contributions of religion in this period. He sees the importance of trust and hope in the formation of the sense of self and worldview, whereas Allport focuses on the later role of religion for integrating the mature ego and thereby underestimates the presence of religion and spirituality in childhood.

EMPIRICAL STUDIES

Jean Piaget (1896–1980)

Alongside the varieties of psychoanalytic perspectives we have examined so far stands a large body of research on the way children think. For more than thirty years, the study of religion in childhood has focused on the process of cognitive development, mostly building on the work of Swiss psychologist Jean Piaget. Early on, Piaget became interested in matters of religion and was particularly influenced by Henri Bergson's idea that God is identical with life itself. After completing his studies of biology and psychology, Piaget became the director of studies at the Rousseau Institute in Geneva and there helped organize a research group on the psychology of religion. While he thought that psychology cannot judge religious values, he believed it can evaluate the thought processes of deduction from these values. This interest contributed to his desire to study the way children think.

Piaget (1969) holds that children's thinking changes systematically as they proceed through childhood, and he identifies a series of stages of cognitive development through which they regularly pass. Many of his insights derive from observations of his own and other children as he watched them play games and as he questioned them about the rules of these games. He notes that there are similarities in the way children of the same age reason about these things. Here, we briefly consider each of these stages and some possible implications for thinking about religious matters.

1. Preoperational stage   c. 2–7 years old

In this stage, children are egocentric and cannot see things from another's point of view. They lack sophisticated logical reasoning and cannot grasp more than one relationship at a time. They are unable to understand that physical characteristics such as volume, mass, or length remain the same in spite of outward appearances. For example, when water is poured from a tall, thin glass into a wider glass, the young child will say that there is now less water because the level is lower in the wider glass.

2. Concrete-operational stage   c. 7–11 years old

At this stage, the child can group similar objects and behaviors into categories, such as all green objects, large or small objects. The child now understands the principle of conservation where pouring liquid from a wide container to a narrow container does not change the total amount of liquid. Children can reverse operations, for example, learning that Mary is Susan's sister means that Susan is Mary's sister. The concept of fairness begins to have meaning due to grasping the concept of reversible operations, though this notion extends only as far as concrete objects and behaviors. There is still little ability to think in terms of general principles such as kindness, goodness, or nonphysical entities such as God or heaven, so God is likely to mean a big person, a big old man in the sky, or God the Father is seen as an oversized, more powerful father similar to the child's own father. In regard to moral rules, the child begins to consider intentions when judging right and wrong.

3. Formal-operational stage   begins c. 12 years old, often fully
                                    developed by 15

Here, logic and reasoning have greatly increased. The young person can now understand abstract concepts, see interrelationships, draw high-level conclusions, and think in terms of general principles such as goodness and evil. Now it is possible to appreciate that God may not be simply like a big person or one's own parents. The older child begins to understand the limits of analogy and that metaphorical language must point beyond itself to speak about the divine and spiritual realities.

According to Piaget, children can understand and use all the earlier stages as well as their current stage of thinking. For example, when one learns to multiply, one can still add and subtract. Moving from one stage to another requires the proper inner and outer conditions. Such changes are preceded by the neurological growth necessary for reasoning at that stage (the requisite inner condition) and by appropriate experiences in the environment (the requisite outer condition). Thus, adolescents can learn calculus but will not do so unless they have learned the preparatory mathematics required.

The stages of cognitive development are basic structures applying to any area of thought. A person is rarely at a given stage in all areas of thinking. Because thinking for a particular area depends on experiences in that area, there may be no relationship between stages of several content areas. This means that thinking in moral development, mathematics, chemistry, and religious conceptualization may be at different levels, depending upon the amount of stimulation and experience in those areas. This situation has important implications for religious and spiritual education.

If children are approached with religious conceptualizations or moral reasoning at a lower level than they are functioning at in that area of thinking, they will consider the reasoning to be foolish. If they are approached at a higher level, either they will not comprehend it at all, or they will reconceptualize the ideas according to their present level. Thus, talk about God will be translated into ideas like Santa Claus or Casper the friendly ghost by children in the preoperational stage, and into ideas like an old man in the sky or a big father by children in the concrete-operational stage.

If a concept is presented only at the preoperational or concrete operational stage and not reintroduced at the formal-operational stage, the person's conceptualization may remain rather primitive. This situation can be a problem for religious groups whose children participate as part of the family and then stop in late childhood or adolescence. These children will likely continue to conceptualize religion and spirituality at an earlier level of thinking and thereby feel that religion is childish because their only contact with this area of life was in childhood. Thus, when they hear religious and moral ideas, they will tend to assume a concrete-operational-stage meaning and may not really hear what is being said. Goldman (1965) has done much to draw out the religious implications of Piaget's studies of cognitive development for religious education. Two other prominent researchers, Kohlberg and Fowler, have applied Piaget's stages to the areas of moral reasoning and faith development.

Kohlberg's Stages of Moral Reasoning

Lawrence Kohlberg has produced a stage theory of moral reasoning which builds on Piaget's levels of cognitive development. His original study is based on sixty boys between the ages of ten and sixteen. Kohlberg (1987) discerned a pattern of moral reasoning that encompasses three levels, each divided into two stages. He found that these stages unfold in an invariant sequence, with the highest stages not achieved by many people. Kohlberg has reinterviewed at three-year intervals as many of the original sixty boys as he has been able to find.

Kohlberg has created a number of stories about moral dilemmas in order to assess people's moral reasoning. He has nine stories in his questionnaire and recommends using at least four of them to obtain an adequate assessment. One of the best known of these stories is that of Heinz, whose wife is near death with cancer. The medication she requires is available but very expensive and the creator of the drug refuses to sell it for less or allow Heinz to pay for it later. Being desperate, Heinz breaks into the store and steals the drug. Following the story, Kohlberg presents questions that attempt to draw out the type of moral reasoning used to evaluate this situation. The following give an idea of the general type of questions asked:

Should Heinz have taken the drug? Was it right? Why or why not?

Is it a husband's duty to steal the drug if there is no alternative? Is it a relative's duty?

Should Heinz steal the drug if it is his best friend who is sick?

Would you steal the drug to save your wife's life or your own life?

Does the druggist have the right to charge that much and be inflexible about payment?

Should the judge send Heinz to jail for stealing or let him go free? Kohlberg (1987, p. 300) is not so much concerned with the specific answers given to these questions as with the process of reasoning used to arrive at the answers. For example, someone at stage two and another person at stage six would likely agree that Heinz should steal the drug for his dying wife, but the former would call upon practical reasons of self-interest (he needs his wife) while the latter would argue that the moral duty to save a life takes precedence over the legal duty not to steal.

Here, we shall look at the first two levels and four stages, most of which apply to children, although many adults typically share some of these stages.

Preconventional level. At this level children think in terms of cultural rules and labels of good and bad, but they interpret these in terms of the physical consequences of actions or the physical power of those who stand behind the rules and labels. This earliest level of moral reasoning is based primarily on avoiding pain and maximizing pleasure.

Stage One: Punishment and obedience orientation. Children consider the physical consequences of actions. The main concern is to avoid punishment by the authorities who enforce moral rules.

Stage Two: Instrumental relativist orientation. Children are concerned with satisfying their needs. If they take into account sharing and fairness, it is in a physical and pragmatic manner.

Conventional level. At this level, people focus on the expectations of the family, group, or country rather than on obvious consequences of actions. Here, there is both conformity with, and loyalty to, personal expectations and social order. Kohlberg finds that people at this stage actively maintain and justify the existing social order.

Stage Three: Interpersonal concordance orientation. Here, people judge the good as that which pleases others. The main focus is on conforming to stereotypical images of what is expected. A person's intention becomes a consideration in moral reasoning and being "nice" is a goal.

Stage Four: Law and order orientation. Here, attention is given to authority, the need for rules, and maintaining social order for its own sake. Doing one's duty is a priority.

While Kohlberg's (1987) attempts to assess moral reasoning have found many proponents and some reliability studies to support his theory, critics claim that his work has a cultural and gender bias. The fact that his original study was carried out with all male subjects leaves him open to the charge of male bias (Flanagan, 1991). Carol Gilligan (1982) believes that male psychologists emphasize excessively the values of autonomy and rationality over relationship and emotion. In studying the results of Kohlberg's questionnaire, she observes that women exemplify stage three on his scale, where morality is seen in interpersonal terms and the key values are helping and pleasing others. Gilligan points out that men and women approach moral problems differently: women have a more contextual and narrative approach, focusing on connections (relationships and responsibilities) while men view moral problem-solving in a formal and abstract fashion, emphasizing rights and rules. She notes that boys tend to see Kohlberg's test as a "math problem" to be solved while girls focus on relationships that extend over time when they evaluate the moral dilemmas posed (p. 18).

Fowler's Stages of Faith

James Fowler's research, based on the work of Piaget, Kohlberg, and Erikson, provides another major contribution to our understanding of the development of religion and spirituality in childhood. He attempts to bring together insights from each of these psychologists and thus may help to summarize aspects of the picture of child development we have seen so far. In *Stages of Faith* (1981) Fowler presents an imaginary dialogue among Piaget, Kohlberg, and Erikson in an effort to clarify their ideas and distinguish his contribution from theirs. Fowler focuses on how people's beliefs are organized and related to their other ideas about life rather than on what they believe. In his view, faith is a way of moving into life and giving coherence and meaning to various aspects of experience (p. 4). He emphasizes faith as a way of knowing, which makes it dependent on the cognitive structures described by Piaget and Kohlberg. While Fowler recognizes that faith goes beyond its cognitive dimensions, some criticize his concentration on the cognitive aspects of faith (Fuller, 1988; Keen, 1978). Fowler stresses that faith is not always religious, but rather a universal human concern prior to being religious or irreligious. In this sense, faith is close to the notions of spirituality and implicit religion we have considered in chapter one.

Fowler's research is based on interviews with people of all ages and various religious traditions. From these interviews, he identifies stages of faith which reflect Piaget's and Kohlberg's conclusions about cognitive development as well as Erikson's ideas on ego development. Fowler follows Erikson's pattern of identifying a characteristic strength and a potential danger at each stage. He emphasizes that people develop through these stages according to their own unique circumstances, so the ages given for each stage are merely an approximation, representing the minimum age at which a person is able to reach a particular stage. Like Kohlberg, Fowler maintains that few people actually move up to the later stages of development. In this chapter, we shall again limit the discussion to those stages that have a direct bearing on childhood.

Stage Zero: Undifferentiated   0–3 years old
Fowler describes this period of early childhood as a prelinguistic, preconceptual disposition towards the conditions of life. Object-relations theorists believe that this is the period during which the self is beginning to form into a cohesive whole. Here, the self and God-representation tend to merge, and the self begins to differentiate from the other. The foundation of basic trust which Erikson highlights is prominent at this stage.

Stage One: Intuitive-Projective   c. 4–7 years old
At this stage, logical connections between various image clusters (such as God, parents, angels, the sacred) have not yet formed. The child experiences a magical, egocentric worldview in which fact and fantasy run together. This stage is sometimes referred to as the fairy-tale stage in which God may be hard to distinguish from Santa Claus. Imagination is vivid and children appropriate religious or spiritual images and stories unpredictably. The examples and teachings of the significant adults in the child's environment play a major role in this faith stage. Fowler considers children's imagination to be the primary strength of this stage, orienting them towards ultimate reality through powerful

images. The corresponding danger is the child being overwhelmed by frightening or damaging images.

Stage Two: Mythic-Literal   c. 7–11 years old

Children at this stage can sort the real from make-believe. They are capable of thinking logically and following cause-and-effect relationships. Religious thinking at this stage is literal, realistic, and anthropomorphic, so God and angels are thought of as real, concrete persons. Parental authority still has more weight than peers' opinions, though not for long. Now the child is able to take another person's point of view and can thereby understand more complex stories. Narrative forms including myth allow the child to appropriate and conserve the community's tradition and to communicate discovered meaning. This capacity for narrative constitutes the key strength of this stage while anthropomorphic thought and a narrow moral literalism represent the corresponding danger.

We can see from this brief summary of Fowler's stages how similar they are to the models of Piaget and Kohlberg. Like them, Fowler is more concerned with the psychological structures that underlie religious and spiritual beliefs than with the content of beliefs. He is concerned primarily with the cognitive aspects of religion, how beliefs are organized and related to other ideas and aspects of life. He rarely attends to the emotional side of religion and morality or the experiential dimensions of prayer and mysticism.

The general thrust of the cognitive-developmental stream is to emphasize the gradual progression of cognitive capabilities and the limitations of young children's thinking. For those who focus on the cognitive aspects of religion or spirituality, this research trend seems to provide grounds for the view that religion and spirituality are extremely limited or even nonexistent in childhood. We have already seen that Allport dismisses childhood religiosity as imitative, unreflective, and lacking in understanding. Many psychologists of religion believe that the child's religious and spiritual life is severely limited by his or her level of cognitive and emotional development. Though Paloutzian concedes that children may be religious in some sense, he accepts the common view that there is probably no meaningful religion in young children because they are not psychologically ready for a fully developed religious life. He states: "It appears that religious development can be accounted for by stages of general psychological development, plus our understanding of the limits of childhood experience, and family and social modeling influences with their associated selective exposure to religious ideas, teaching and practices" (1996, p. 103). Hood et al. (1996, pp. 67–68) present research findings that show children's religious identity, morality, God-images, and prayer are dependent to a certain extent on the Piagetian stages of cognitive development. They summarize this trend of development as moving from early childhood, where children are unable to understand religious concepts at all, through a very egocentric period to a point where they have a limited, concrete understanding to a more abstract and complex religiousness in adolescence.

Regarding transpersonal psychology, Ken Wilber (1996) holds that there is little evidence that children have religious or spiritual experiences. In his judgment, claims for childhood religious experience are not backed by a sufficient number of credible and coherent cases. At most, he grants that such childhood experiences would be transient peak experiences that represent little real spiritual development. Stan Grof (1975) considers childhood experience primarily within the framework of psychodynamic theory, which limits the possibilities of children's spirituality, although he does believe that the perinatal experiences uncovered in regression psychotherapy are in touch with the transpersonal realm. Employing a depth-psychological perspective, Michael Washburn (1988, 1994) argues that children are cut off from transpersonal experience by a primal repression that originates in the later pre-Oedipal period and is consolidated with the resolution of the Oedipal complex, i.e., at about five or six years old. Washburn's developmental scheme does not take into account experiences that antedate or escape this hypothesized primal repression.

SPIRITUAL EXPERIENCE IN CHILDHOOD

Not all psychologists agree. Thomas Armstrong (1984) states that most transpersonal psychologists believe that transpersonal issues begin to surface when the fully mature personality begins to experience the need to transcend the limitations of personal boundaries. As a result, transpersonal psychology tends to rely on ego psychology and cognitive-developmental psychology for its understanding of childhood processes, with the regrettable consequence that childhood spirituality is minimized or overlooked. However, a number of researchers have provided a substantial body of evidence substantiating the claim that children are capable of having genuine religious and spiritual experiences. Michael Piechowski (2001) asserts that there are indeed a significant number of published accounts of childhood spiritual experiences that frequently go unrecognized. Armstrong (1984) contends that transpersonal experiences do occur, in some children at least, and coexist alongside both the prepersonal and personal stages of development described by Wilber, Washburn, and others. He states that there are three main sources supporting this contention: first, biographies and autobiographies of extraordinary individuals; second, research on contemporary adult memories of religious experience; and third, direct reports of children on their spiritual experiences. Here, we shall consider some of the available evidence.

Carl Jung was one of the first psychologists to recognize the significance of spiritual experiences in childhood, especially as they manifest themselves in children's dreams. Although Jung did not focus on child analysis, he was interested in the remarkable symbols and motifs which sometimes emerge in the dreams of even very young children. He recognized that, in certain instances, children's dream images did not simply reflect their own psychological condition but tapped into the deeper level of the psyche. Jung (1928) called these symbols that appeared throughout the ages and in various cultures the archetypes of the collective unconscious. Some of these symbols represent age-old spiritual concerns which one might not expect to occupy a young child's mind.

Jung (1961) comments on a dream series of an eight-year-old girl which he calls "the weirdest series" of dreams he ever saw. He notes that these dreams are like a sequence of philosophical problems. Nine of the twelve dreams deal with the theme of destruction and restoration. One concerns God's restitution of everything after an evil monster kills off all animals. The child had no contact with this ancient motif, and her family was entirely unaware of this theme. Jung observes that these dreams show only superficial traces of her Christian culture and much more closely resemble primitive myths. Jung states that when he first read the dreams, he had an uncanny feeling that they were a premonition of disaster. He found the contrast between the youthful age of the dreamer and her terrifying nocturnal visions of life and death to be disconcerting. Rather than reflecting the joy and exuberance of life's springtime, they seemed to express the attitude of one looking back upon life rather than forward to its unfolding. Jung maintains that the approach of death casts an anticipatory shadow over a person's dreams, and he sees this dream series as a preparation for death similar to the instruction given at primitive initiations. The girl gave the dreams to her father as a Christmas present when she was ten years old. She died unexpectedly from an infectious disease about a year later.

Jung (1936a) considers examples of spontaneous archetypal images in children's dreams as proof that they can be in touch with a wider spiritual realm than their everyday concerns. Further, he maintains that the dreams of children, especially between the ages of three and five years old, where there is little or no likelihood of any prior, direct knowledge of such symbols or motifs, provide valuable evidence of the collective unconscious. In his autobiographical *Memories, Dreams, Reflections*, Jung (1963) discusses at some length a particularly important dream of his own from when he was three or four years old. This dream influenced his entire life and helped to shape his spirituality. In the dream, he is in a meadow near his home and comes upon a rectangular, stone-lined hole. He notices a stone stairway in the hole and cautiously descends to the bottom of the stairs where he finds a doorway with a round arch covered by a heavy green curtain. He pushes the curtain aside and discovers in the dim light a rectangular chamber with a red carpet in the center of a stone floor that leads to a platform with a magnificent golden throne. On the throne he sees what appears to be a tree trunk made of skin, about fifteen feet high and two feet thick, and at the top, in a glowing light, a rounded head with a single eye gazing upward. He is terrified and cannot move. Then he hears his mother's voice from outside the chamber saying, "*This* is the man-eater." He awakens in terror, and for many nights after is afraid to fall asleep for fear he might have another such dream.

Jung says that this dream haunted him for years and only decades later did he realize it was a ritual phallus. Upon reflection, he believes the underground temple symbolizes the mysteries of the earth. For a long time he puzzled over the meaning of his mother's words in the dream, associating them with Jesus and the Christian religion. I don't want to discuss the details of Jung's associations to, and interpretation of, this powerful dream, all of which can be found in his autobiography. Here, I merely wish to indicate that Jung believes this childhood dream was crucial to his spiritual development and his attitude toward religion. For him, the ritual phallus represents a dark, mysterious, and terrifying aspect of an unnameable subterranean God which somehow balances the light and clarity surrounding Christian teachings about God. He says that throughout his youth, whenever he heard anyone speak too emphatically about the love and kindness of the Lord Jesus, the memory of this "frightful revelation" reappeared to cast its shadow over what seemed to him the one-sidedly light and positive aspects of the divinity that he encountered in Christian theology. For Jung, this early childhood dream initiated him into the secrets of the earth, his initial realization that somehow the divine contains a mystery of opposites, something nonhuman and underworldly alongside human warmth and transcendent love.

More recently, Michael Paffard (1973) describes a number of transcendental experiences in childhood derived from his study of autobiographies and hundreds of questionnaires. He defines transcendental experiences broadly as being beyond the limits of ordinary modes of consciousness, thought, feeling, or perception, whether they are religious or aesthetic. The title of his book, *Inglorious Wordsworths*, is inspired by the fact that some of the major scholars of mysticism consider the poet William Wordsworth as *the* classic example of the nature-mystic. Paffard is particularly intrigued by Wordsworth's own childhood experiences, where he seems to be one with external things, viewing them as aspects of his own nature or as something inside himself.

According to Paffard, it is a commonplace of literary criticism to observe that Wordsworth shed new light on childhood for the nineteenth century as revealingly as Freud did for the following century. People frequently interpret Wordsworth's famous lines from "Intimations of Immortality from Recollections of Early Childhood" (cited at the beginning of this chapter) as an indication of the significance Wordsworth places on spiritual experiences in childhood. Paffard explores those writings of Wordsworth which express transcendental experiences and notes that Wordsworth's mystical intuitions in childhood sometimes contain elements of fear and are not always associated with nature.

Paffard discusses other childhood spiritual experiences highlighted in autobiographies, especially those of C. S. Lewis and A. L. Rose. In *Surprised by Joy*, Lewis tells of an experience of "enormous bliss" which he had when he was seven or eight years old. He was standing beside a flowering currant bush when a memory emerged, one that seemed to arise out of the depths of centuries, of his brother bringing a toy garden into the nursery. He describes the memory as a desire for something he could not name and adds that he knew the desire was not for that toy garden itself, nor even for his past. Before he was able to identify the desire, it was gone. It was only a momentary glimpse of some forgotten world and a longing that evaporated almost as soon as it was felt. After this fleeting, magical moment, the world turned ordinary again. While the experience may seem trivial at first glance, Lewis asserts that it had a profound influence on his spiritual development and the central story of his life.

Lewis describes another such experience of intense desire from about the same age, this time stimulated by reading Beatrix Potter's

Squirrel Nutkin. He says the book awakened in him a fascination for the "Idea of Autumn." Without knowing why this experience had such a hold on him, it filled him with joy and the same sense of incalculable importance as the glimpse that occurred in the presence of the flowering currant bush. Lewis (1955, p. 22) describes this joy as something different from ordinary life or pleasure, an experience "in another dimension." Paffard explains that, for Lewis, "joy" is a kind of technical term for the ineffable, a desire for something beyond definition, something only glimpsed or hinted at in a fleeting moment rather than clearly grasped. For a time, these experiences rivaled the value Lewis placed on orthodox Christianity, which for him lacked the sense of urgency, depth, and significance of these surprising, revelatory moments. These experiences remained an important touchstone for his life, and later he would interpret them primarily as important reflections of heavenly truth.

A colleague of Lewis at Oxford, A. L. Rowse, seems to have had similar childhood experiences. In his autobiography, *A Cornish Childhood*, he describes a morning walk on his way to school in the springtime. As he looked at the apple blossoms in an orchard near a group of thatched cottages, he was suddenly overwhelmed by a sense of the transcendence of things and the fragility of human life. Time stood still for him. He says he was incapable of describing this powerful and uneasy feeling to himself or others and could only think of it as a reaching out toward perfection. Afterwards, he characterized the experience as an inner resource, a kind of revelation that became a secret touchstone of experience, a kind of religion for him. In later years when he tried to understand the power of this childhood experience, he ascribes its poignancy to this paradox: although he felt that time was standing still, another part of himself knew that it was moving, carrying him and life with it.

Paffard notes striking similarities in these childhood spiritual experiences recorded by Lewis and Rowse. For both, there is an aspect of pain or grief due to the realization that such glimpses of eternity are only transitory and one must soon return to the ordinary consciousness of everyday life. Lewis and Rowse both underscore the lifelong impact of these experiences on their sense of self. Lewis states that the central story of his entire life is really about these childhood experiences and, compared with them, everything else that happened to him was in a certain sense insignificant. Rowse says that when he reflects on his life as a whole, he thinks of these ecstatic moments as his real inner life, what he calls his "revealed religion" in which the beauty of the world is manifested.

The rest of Paffard's study is an analysis of nearly 500 questionnaires filled out by male and female students between the ages of seventeen and nineteen years old. A relatively small number of these reported experiences occurred in childhood. The vast majority happened after the age of eleven, with the peak between the ages of sixteen and seventeen. Paffard summarizes the data collected as follows: Most of these experiences occurred when the person was alone, during the evening, and out of doors. Roughly a quarter had similar experiences a number of times, and about half had them quite frequently. Fewer than half sought such experiences regularly.

EXAMPLES OF SPIRITUAL EXPERIENCES IN CHILDHOOD

Religious Experience Research Unit, Oxford

Evolutionary biologist Sir Alister Hardy set up the Religious Experience Research Unit at Oxford University (Manchester College) in 1969. This project grew out of his lifelong interest in transcendental experiences, an interest he regarded as a natural extension of his biological outlook. For some sixty years he collected firsthand accounts of such experiences in the hope that they might contribute to a perspective which would take into account not only economic and nutritional needs, but also emotional and spiritual behavior. Hardy (1979) is strongly influenced by William James's *The Varieties of Religious Experience*, and, like James, he is primarily concerned with the experiential and spiritual, rather than the doctrinal and institutional, aspects of religion. His understanding of spirituality includes a recognition of the transcendental powers controlling the universe. Among the thousands of accounts collected by the research unit, Hardy (1979) includes the following examples of spiritual experiences remembered from childhood, which I paraphrase here:

One lady recalls that from the age of six to twelve years old, she experienced states of oneness at quiet times. Frequently, this feeling of unity would suddenly pass into what she calls "tremendous exaltation" where time seemed to stand still. Another woman describes having several experiences during childhood where she felt the presence of a power surrounding her and acting on her behalf. She says that she was too young to give it a divine explanation at that time, although later she thought of these experiences as manifestations of God's presence. A man tells of an experience that occurred when he was eight years old. He was looking at a large, old pear tree filled with white blossoms.

A blackbird was singing at the top of the tree as the sun was beginning to rise. Without warning, he heard the words "that is beautiful," and the entire scene seemed to become magnified. Everything around him seemed to glow with an intense light. The grass became a vivid green and the bird's song became louder and sweeter. This experience remained a powerful memory throughout his long life.

One young lady reports an out-of-body experience that occurred at the age of twelve while she was ill. She believed she was dying as she floated up from her body. To her surprise, a remarkable feeling of liberation and joy accompanied this experience. She returned to her body gently, and since that time says she has been unafraid of death. One respondent speaks of a feeling throughout childhood that a force inside was struggling to push its way into consciousness. These were moments of great joy along with a heightened awareness of the surroundings and a sense of coming upon a great truth. While Hardy does not include a large number of childhood experiences among the examples presented in his book, those who did report such early experiences considered them to be of enduring value and vitally important in their lives. According to Hardy, the religious and spiritual experiences he studied often had their roots in early childhood.

Edward Robinson, Hardy's successor as head of the Religious Experience Research Unit, focused directly on the religious experiences of childhood. Robinson (1983) estimates that 15 percent of the 4,000 correspondents of the Oxford research center testify to the early childhood origins of their religious and spiritual experiences. He believes that the significant number of those reporting such early experiences calls into question the current cognitive-developmental view that genuine religious thought and experience do not appear before adolescence. In particular, he challenges Ronald Goldman (1965), who calls attention to the limitations of children's ability to understand religious concepts and stories. Goldman is mainly concerned with the proper timing for introducing biblical material in religious education and argues, following Piaget's approach, that religious insight first begins to appear between twelve and thirteen years of age.

Though Robinson grants the value and truth of many of Piaget's insights about cognitive development, he believes that Piaget's view of childhood is limited. His main criticism is that Piaget assumes that reality is the way adults see it, and if children do not see it that way they are inadequate and wrong. The focus of cognitive development is on how children gradually develop adult ways of perceiving, thinking, and experiencing. Robinson, on the other hand, finds that children have a natural capacity for insight, imagination, and knowing that does not require development into a higher form. In fact, he believes that the presence and continuance of these childhood foundations are often crucial for a mature religious life. Part of the problem in becoming aware of and appreciating religious experience in childhood, according to Robinson, is the dominant educational psychology, which does not find such experiences because it does not look for them. He reminds us that expectations in relationships with children, as in so many areas of life, determine what we discover.

Robinson discusses his own methodology with reference to that of Piaget and Freud. He emphasizes that all theories are limited by their presuppositions and methods. Piaget's questions are designed to show how children come to think as adults, and his method effectively demonstrates that. Freud's questions are appropriate for a doctor who wants to determine how disturbances in childhood influence later psychological health, and his psychoanalytic methods achieve this aim. According to Robinson, their inventive methods produce results by breaking down the total living situation in order to examine an isolated section of it. Robinson believes his own methods, drawn from cultural anthropology, are more holistic, attempting to return again to the total living context through biographical notes and case histories. He recognizes that memory and the passage of time may distort aspects of these reported experiences, but he believes it is important to appreciate that something significant happened for the person, and these experiences instigate a process of perceiving, questioning, and reflecting that often continues to affect that person's outlook, values, and attitudes throughout life. According to Robinson, the exact details surrounding these events are of less consequence than the psychological and spiritual seeds they plant in the developing personality. From this vantage point, childhood is viewed as a dimension of life which remains at the core of personality.

Much of Robinson's study, like that of Hardy, is devoted to presenting and analyzing the collected accounts of spiritual experience. Here, I shall describe a few of these cases:

A lady remembers an experience between four and five years of age (which she is able to determine through a dated photograph and the clothing she was wearing at that time). While she was walking with her mother in a mist, all at once the flowers which appeared here and there through the mist seemed to shine like a brilliant fire in a shimmering tissue of mist. She says she somehow understood that everything, animate and inanimate, had its own special place in this universal tissue of being. While she is aware that she did not have the words or concepts to describe the vision at that age, she says the whole impression and its total meaning were grasped mysteriously in a single instant. An intense feeling of love for the world and a certainty of ultimate good accompanied this experience and returns whenever she remembers it. She states that the vision grounds her identity, remains with her as a reservoir of strength in times of anguish, and gives her an affinity with plants, animals, and people.

A young woman recalls a revelatory experience early one summer morning when she was eleven years old. She was looking from her house window at the river, trees, and green fields nearby. As the sunlight shimmered on the leaves of the trees and on the surface of the river, she felt she was on the verge of a great revelation and about to be initiated into a mystery of indescribable significance. For a few seconds, she felt that she was part of the trees, the sunshine, and the river and that all of this belonged to some great unity. She was filled with an excitement and spiritual exultation more intense and qualitatively different from other times when she was struck by the beauty of nature. She refers to this event as one of the most memorable experiences of her life.

One woman describes a number of childhood experiences that remain vivid in her memory in which she felt tremendous joy upon encountering great beauty in nature, music, or poetry. She states that these experiences were often followed by feelings of "homesickness" and sometimes loneliness. For her, these experiences usually involved sensing the sanctity of everything in nature and usually occurred when she was alone. Another woman talks about the sharp contrast between the clarity of her religious experiences in early childhood and the frustration of having no language to express them when they occurred. She insists that the lack of words did not affect the nature of the experiences themselves.

A man tells of instances in his childhood as far back as four or five years old when he felt united with the world and had a sense of absorption in something far greater than himself, of which he was nevertheless a vital part. A deep realization of nature's beauty, especially when looking out over mist-filled valleys and woods, usually triggered these experiences in which he felt an overwhelming sense of trust and gratitude to the world. He says that at times he and the world dissolved into a vast new reality which unexpectedly revealed itself. Another man recalls that, as a boy of eight years, he was standing alone in a room wondering where he had been eight years earlier. As he thought about this, a wave of tremendous feeling swept over him and he was aware of being somebody extremely ancient and weighed down by time. Even many years later, he looks back at this moment as an important realization about his life and the nature of human existence.

A woman recollects walking home from school at about ten years of age when she stopped and stood still for some time as the realization struck her that she was not identical with her body. She thought about soon having the body of a young girl and then later of a woman and becoming aware that even her mature body will not be her, that she will always be somehow distinct from her body. Another woman reports that on her seventh birthday, she had a feeling of intense awareness that she had discovered a great secret of life. She felt that she passed out of time and became one with the world, and somehow the world was existing through her. She says this experience occurred twice in her childhood and remains a striking memory.

One of the most remarkable experiences presented in Robinson's book is that of a woman who remembers a very early childhood trance that she calls the greatest single experience of her life. She recalls crawling on the floor when she was about one year old. While she was listening to a record, she went into a trance where she felt she "touched Heaven," becoming aware of the magnificence of the power that orders the universe and a sense of complete oneness with the totality of the world. When she came out of the trance some short time later, she was painfully aware of being an isolated part of the totality she had just been aware of. Some months later, while she was learning to walk, clutching a table leg for support, she experienced where she had come from before birth and was shown in a flash her whole life in front of her. While the details of this future vision vanished, she remembers the important point was not future events but how she chose to react to them.

OTHER STUDIES OF CHILDHOOD SPIRITUALITY

Armstrong (1984) observes that accounts of childhood spiritual experiences go beyond the dominant model of religious development offered by Fowler and Goldman and Western psychology's usual stage-specific schemes of child development. In his view, these experiences transcend the accepted capacities currently attributed to various age and developmental levels. One of the autobiographical accounts he presents is from Ramakrishna, the nineteenth-century Bengali saint who reports his first spiritual ecstasy at the age of six or seven. While walking along a narrow path eating puffed rice from a basket, he noticed a beautiful, dark thundercloud. As it enveloped the whole sky, a flock of snow-white cranes flew in front of it. He was so overwhelmed by this magnificent sight that he lost consciousness and fell to the ground, with the rice flying everywhere. Later, he spoke of this experience as one of indescribable joy.

Armstrong presents another dramatic experience reported in *Autobiography of a Yogi* (1971). Yogananda was suffering from a life-threatening illness when he was eight years old. His mother told him to gaze at a photograph of a spiritual master revered by the family. As he looked at the picture, he saw a blinding light enveloping his body and the entire room. He reports that his symptoms vanished immediately and he returned to complete health. Armstrong lists a number of other historical figures who had transpersonal or spiritual experiences as children, including Dante, Blake, Gurdjieff, Black Elk, Meher Baba, Blavatsky, Shankara, and Krishnamurti.

In Armstrong's opinion, a very significant source of information concerning transpersonal experience comes from children themselves. He finds some of the material on children's dreams discussed by Jungian analyst Frances Wickes to be a clear indication of childhood spiritual experience. In the dream of one young girl, she is on the beach when a big wave washes in various things, including many starfish. One of the starfish is blue and has an eye in the middle of its body. The girl says this starfish looks at her and "knows me—me-myself," and that makes her realize it is hers and she takes it home. Wickes interprets the starfish as a symbol of wholeness, blue as the color of spirituality, and its seeing, not just me but "me-myself," as indicating contact with a deeper level of identity than the child's emerging ego (cited in Armstrong, 1984). As we saw in Jung's discussion of dreams, these dream symbols express a worldview and a deep sense of identity.

Armstrong emphasizes that not all childhood experiences are transpersonal or spiritual any more than all adult experiences are. He notes that Wilber's distinction between "prepersonal" and "transpersonal" experiences in human development is important because theorists tend to confuse the two, either reducing transpersonal experiences to prepersonal experiences or exalting prepersonal states to transpersonal realms. Armstrong insists that such a differentiation should be applied within childhood itself, so that childhood is not simply equated with the prepersonal realm. He sees this danger as repeating the error made by traditional Western psychology of frequently infantilizing or pathologizing adults' genuine spiritual experiences.

In the United Kingdom, educational researchers have shed valuable light on qualities that are central to children's spirituality. David Hay and Rebecca Nye (1996, 1998) have carried out extensive research indicating a high incidence of religious experience among schoolchildren. They describe a number of characteristics of these spiritual experiences, including the following:

- a strong sense of wider connections to others and the world;
- eagerness for terms that can deal with such powerful experiences;
- a desire to craft these terms into a spiritual worldview; and
- a search for explanations of such experiences.

Nye emphasizes that children possess valuable nonrational kinds of knowing which may be more relevant for understanding their spirituality than knowing their stage of thinking about religion (in Watts et al., 2002). Margarete Donaldson (1992) believes that the "value-sensing" mode of knowing that is a crucial part of children's spirituality is widely neglected in current education in the United Kingdom. In her view, discursive thinking gets in the way of this intuitive, value-sensing mode of knowing. This view approximates that of mysticism scholar Evelyn Underhill (1922), who insists that the roots of the spiritual faculty lie in the feelings rather than in the intellect. Hay (1982, 1990) observes that attitudes in British society present obstacles to expressing spiritual experiences, making it difficult to research this important area of life.

Psychologist Edward Hoffman (1998) concludes from his study of children's religious experiences that numerous people have undergone tremendous peak and even mystical experiences as children. He describes many different kinds of childhood peak experiences, including inspiring encounters with nature, profound insights about life and death and self-identity, spontaneous moments of bliss or ecstacy, intense prayer, near-death episodes, and unforgettable dreams. Hoffman's research is motivated by the work of Abraham Maslow. He notes that Maslow's study of peak experiences was the starting point of transpersonal psychology (the term itself popularized by Maslow). In the 1960s, Maslow researched peak experiences in college students, colleagues, and himself, and with the birth of his granddaughter Jeannie in 1968 he became particularly interested in the subject of peak experiences in childhood. He believed that children have the capacity for spiritual epiphanies and numinous moments, but they lack the vocabulary to articulate their experiences. Unfortunately, Maslow died before he had the opportunity to carry out systematic research in this area.

Wanting to follow through on Maslow's intended study, Hoffman initially interviewed children in order to learn about their spiritual experiences. However, he found this approach unproductive because the children were unable to describe their most exalted and ecstatic moments. He then turned to interviewing men and women recruited through newspapers and periodicals. Adopting a phenomenological method, he encouraged people to describe in their own words their most uplifting childhood experiences. While recognizing that adults may not always recall such experiences with complete accuracy, he believes that with sufficient material gathered from adults (over 250 accounts), a clear-enough pattern might emerge to shed significant light on this topic. Here are a few of the examples Hoffman provides:

A Canadian woman tells of an overwhelming childhood experience of the sun where it is radiantly pulsating and breathing. She says that from that day onward, she has had a new and profound appreciation of the sun and regards it and the earth as living beings. An Australian woman reports that after a near-death experience from nearly drowning as a child, her attitude to life changed drastically: She began to appreciate her surroundings more and to experience the preciousness of life. She no longer fears death and constantly strives to understand why she was given a second chance at life.

A Swiss man tells how as a young boy he was overcome by an indescribable state of happiness while walking in the forest. As he came upon a lush meadow in the clearing, the greenness of the leaves and the brilliant sunlight filled him with an intense feeling of beauty and perfection. An elderly woman remembers that, at the age of four, she was in her backyard, surrounded by large, silver-leaf poplars with black-and-white bark. Without warning, a "blazing feeling of happiness" overtook her and she became filled with an awareness of how wonderful the world was. She said that the memory of this experience remained with her throughout her entire life as a beacon of light even in times of great sadness.

A young lady describes a mystical state that she entered frequently as a child while thinking about her sense of "I" and that it would never end. In her mind she would see and experience herself going on and on, without stopping or dying, as part of an infinite process. She says she always felt renewed when she returned from this inner state. An artist speaks about a repetitive childhood dream that became the catalyst for her inner awakening. In the dream, her waking-life neighborhood is replaced by a semicircular plaza of mother-of-pearl shimmering in the sunlight. Beyond a colonnade of white marble she sees a boundless, sparkling ocean under a serene, blue sky and is filled with infinite joy and peace. She says whenever she recalls this dream image, she feels centered and is living from her higher self.

Hoffman concludes his study by stressing the preliminary nature of his findings. He believes that much research remains to be done in the area of children's peak and spiritual experiences. Hoffman observes that two thirds of the respondents to his author's query were women, which raises questions about whether girls are more likely to undergo such experiences than boys or merely more likely to report them. He asks whether such differences are related to biology, upbringing, or a combination of the two.

Michael Piechowski (2001) highlights three kinds of childhood experiences that he believes contradict the dominant developmental models of transpersonal psychology:

- when children realize on the basis of their own experience that adults around them are unaware of a spiritual realm;
- when children experience an identity that goes beyond the physical self and even beyond one lifetime; and
- when on their own, they achieve states of nonordinary consciousness.

He believes that these childhood spiritual experiences have been overlooked by mainstream transpersonal psychology because of the "unpredictability in the dissemination of knowledge." Reviewing the relevant literature, Piechowski estimates that the currently available pool of published accounts of childhood spiritual experiences numbers more than 700. In his view, this vast and growing literature clearly indicates the prevalence of childhood spiritual experiences and their importance in initiating a lifelong spiritual quest that allows people to face and endure life's difficulties and tragedies. The great majority of these childhood experiences are positive, joyous, and reassuring, according to Piechowski, although some of them are reported to be unsettling, or even frightening.

Piechowski calls attention to the variety of techniques that children use to enter a heightened state of consciousness. In some accounts, children seem to stumble upon methods that resemble classical forms of meditation, such as mental and physical withdrawal, focusing on their breathing or on a visual pattern in a window or tapestry, repeating a phrase, concentrating on infinity, or following a chain of questions about their own origin and the origin of life and the world. One person recalls that, at the age of four, repeating constantly "I am me, I am me" brought a feeling of deep peace and a strong sense of God's presence. Another reports that at the age of three or four, he was sitting quietly alone, conjuring up memories. Beyond these memories he faced blankness in his mind's eye and gradually became aware that he transcended all his memories and his true identity was larger than the boy he was, extending all the way to infinity.

Some of these children are spiritual prodigies, and we may see more prodigies in the spiritual domain when our culture begins to value and encourage excellence in that area (Feldman, 1986). However, Piechowski insists that many of the children who have spiritual experiences are not at all unusual. Drawing on his years of researching educative advancement, he states that genuine childhood spiritual experiences are neither extremely rare nor exceptional. He believes that the shortcomings of young children's conceptual capacities shown by Piaget and Kohlberg are largely the result of the verbal nature of their testing methods and the child's struggle to figure out what kind of answer the adult wants. In regard to the developmental schemes of Wilber and Washburn, he states that they do not take into account the extensive case material revealing numerous instances of children's spiritual experiences. According to Piechowski, these cognitive-developmental and transpersonal theories give only a generalized picture of development without being able to account for individual differences. He asserts that much is lost in such theoretical developmental frameworks and that they should be modified to ensure that the abstracted general picture does not veer too far from actual lived experience.

A problem encountered in trying to collect and call attention to actual cases of childhood spirituality is the taboo that surrounds the subject (Armstrong, 1984). Piechowski points out that when he presents examples of children's spiritual experiences to parents and to professional audiences at national meetings, people express relief and gratitude that someone is willing to break the silence about this topic. He concludes his study of transpersonal experiences in childhood by observing that their overall content has the same character as adults' transcendental experiences, namely, that they reveal a larger, unseen spiritual reality behind our ordinary everyday world.

Overall, it appears as though there is a great deal of religion and spirituality in childhood, so long as we do not restrict ourselves to looking for the more cognitive aspects of religion. Clearly, there are limits to the way children grasp and formulate their spiritual experiences, but that does not diminish their intuitions about the wider dimensions of themselves and the world. Many of the examples in the last section demonstrate that children's spiritual experiences penetrate to levels of emotion and trust in the universe that escape purely rational analysis.

SUMMARY

This chapter has examined a number of psychological theorists who have illuminated important aspects of childhood religion and spirituality. We have seen that various psychoanalytic perspectives differ on the value they attribute to religion, but all recognize the close relationship between religion, spirituality, and the early experiences of parents and caretakers. Freud highlights religion's early childhood origins, the influence of psychological projection on the creation of the patriarchal God-image, and the role of religion in reducing anxiety in the face of mortality, nature's immense force, and human injustice. Freud's assessment of religion's impact on human development is negative, but he calls attention to important psychological dynamics such as internalization and projection which are at work in the origins of religion.

The object-relations theorists view religion in a more positive light, seeing religion as rooted in the nourishing experience of the mother's love and connecting us to other people and the universe. They see religion as thus establishing a crucial foundation for healthy personality development. Ego psychology appreciates the contribution religion can make in establishing trust as the basis for the emerging sense of self and integrating the mature ego. Cognitive-developmental psychology has underlined the influence of growing cognitive capabilities on children's thinking about religion. They have described the different levels at which religious ideas, values, and practices are likely to be understood as children progress through the preoperational, concrete-operational, and formal-operational stages. All of these psychological vantage points have contributed to our understanding of how religion emerges in childhood and how it can influence personality development.

To the extent that developmental psychologists have studied the religious aspects of the child's life, they have concentrated on the way children think about religious beliefs and practices. The search for empirical data leads them to rely heavily on the cognitive research methods pioneered by Piaget and his followers. Unfortunately, this primary focus on the more cognitive aspects of religion tends to underestimate the presence of religion and spirituality in childhood. Consequently, a common view among psychologists of religion as they review the literature on childhood religion is that genuine religion and spirituality are either extremely limited or even absent during childhood. However, the number and quality of published examples of spiritual experiences in childhood challenge this view by testifying to the strong presence of spirituality in childhood, seen especially in the child's sense of wonder at the mysteries of life and in the feeling of trust and connection to other human beings and the world.

In childhood religion and spirituality, we observe the developing emotional and unconscious sources of religion. To return to Table 4 from chapter one, we see that the foundations of religion are largely unconscious and emotional, but this does not mean that they are without significance.

Table 5: Foundations of Implicit Religion and Spiritual Development in Childhood

	Self-Stream	Values Stream	Worldview Stream
Transpersonal Level			
Personal Level			
Prepersonal Level	Sense of self shaped by parents, caretakers, and siblings	Family values internalized	View of life formed by family and early experiences

It is on these largely unconscious and emotional prepersonal foundations that the more consciously developed aspects of religion and spirituality will be built.

CHAPTER THREE

THE ADOLESCENT QUEST FOR IDENTITY

———————— ❧ ————————

> For what was once play and pretense, in adolescence becomes rehearsal with different ways of living until the main life performance, namely the individual's lasting identity in the adult world, is established.
> — Erik Erikson, *A Way of Looking at Things*

In this chapter we shall consider the adolescent stage of the life cycle, a crucial time for the development of both religion and spirituality. A major goal of this period is the creation of identity, which lies at the heart of spirituality and the ongoing formation of the self. The many changes and pressures of adolescence move young people to wrestle with questions of values and religion as they shape their identity and worldview. A review of the empirical studies will show conflicting aspects of the role of religion in adolescence. Finally, we shall explore how identity formation and the creation of one's personal story express the main elements of adolescent spirituality and implicit religion.

ADOLESCENCE AND THE SEARCH FOR IDENTITY

The problem of identity, which frequently besets people within modernity, has been called the "spiritual problem of our time" (Langbaum, 1977, p. 353). The search for identity is essentially the quest to find overall unity and purpose in human life. This problem has preoccupied people in Western democracies for the past 200 years, though the quest for identity is not so salient for many non-Western societies that put less of a premium on articulating an autonomous self. Unlike traditional societies, modern and postmodern societies do not tell adults who they should be by way of clear roles and attitudes passed down from one generation to the next (McAdams, 1996, p. 381). Nevertheless, modern societies have the general expectation that a person should be someone who is unique, yet fits in. There is pressure on the self both to separate and to be connected at the same time. According to psychologist Dan McAdams (1997), in modern societies the quest for identity does not occur in earnest until late adolescence. Before that point, the young person does not feel the need to pattern personal experience in a unifying way. When young people reach the stage where they are expected to fashion a unified identity in contemporary society, they may find that their self-conceptions are too diverse and multifaceted to produce a coherent identity. McAdams observes that the difficulty involved in forging a unified and purposeful self increases in a society that offers an ever-greater number and variety of life possibilities and greater uncertainty about what an integrated person should look like.

Adolescence represents a transition from a high degree of dependency in childhood to greater independence from the family. A great deal of stress in adolescence can result from the relative weakness of the adolescent ego, the intensification of drives, and the rejection of parental support. Peter Blos (1979, p. 142) speaks of adolescence as a "second individuation" process; the first one, usually completed by age three, involves hatching from the symbiotic relation with the mother to become an "individuated toddler" (Mahler, 1968). In adolescence, individuation means decreasing dependency on the family and becoming a member of the larger society. In both periods there is a major development of individuality as the person separates from his or her previous environment. This internal balancing and rebalancing of the boundaries between one's self and others is a central aspect of identity formation at any time in life, but it reaches a phase of heightened activity in adolescence (Kroger, 1989).

Erik Erikson's (1950/63) work on ego identity is a landmark in understanding how the self is constructed by meshing past childhood identifications with present physical and social changes and future commitments. Erikson's work reversed a long trend wherein, at the beginning of the twentieth century, the topic of the self virtually went underground because it was not compatible with the dominant behavioristic paradigm in psychology (Ashmore & Jussim, 1997). With the ascendance of cognitive psychology, there has been much greater openness to, and interest in, the activities of the self, including the functions of ego and identity. For Erikson, identity formation in adolescence heightens processes underway since the first months of life, when the infant introjects the parents to establish the earliest sense of self. During childhood, identification with significant others serves to structure the ego. In adolescence, the ego strives to synthesize all previous significant identifications into a unique and reasonably coherent identity.

Erikson (1950/63, p. 261) believes that a key challenge of adolescence is to retain a "sense of continuity and sameness" with the self developed in the preceding childhood years. He calls attention to how the major physiological changes of puberty influence adolescent identity. The ego is radically shifted as rapid physical growth may seem to the young person like the ego is being transplanted into a different body. Young people may feel uprooted as they strive to consolidate their new body ego. The development of the primary and secondary sexual characteristics of puberty, along with hormonal shifts and growth spurts, all give a greater prominence to the body than was experienced in the childhood sense of the self. The timing of these changes depends greatly on individual differences. When the physical developments are very early, very sudden, or very extensive compared with their peers, adolescents may become self-critical and suffer a lack of confidence. These interrelated physical and social factors cause considerable fluctuations in the adolescent sense of self, and the instability of self-evaluations often reaches a peak in early adolescence (Brinthaupt & Lipka, 2002). Erikson states that childhood identification with parents, siblings, and peers helps the adolescent to retain a sense of sameness while experiencing so much physical discontinuity.

People's sense of self is inextricably intertwined with their bodies, so physical changes should be seen as changes of the self. Thus adolescents report that their physical appearance and characteristics are among their greatest problems and concerns as they strive to understand themselves (Finkenauer et al., 2002). It is less the "objective" biological changes that preoccupy adolescents than their subjective evaluation of these changes. The often unrealistic cultural and social standards of physical attractiveness enter into this subjective appraisal, so adolescents often feel low self-esteem because the size, shape, and general appearance of their bodies fall short of the cultural ideal. Biological changes such as breast development in girls and facial hair in boys also contribute to the adolescent's gender identity. Studies show that in early adolescence, parents react to the physical changes of puberty by encouraging their daughters to be dependent, affectionate, and gentle, and their sons to be assertive, competitive, and independent (Finke-nauer et al., 2002). These gender differences are also seen in adolescent peer relationships. Compared with boys, girls have more intimate friendships, more willingness to share their ideas and feelings, and tend to be more accepting and supportive. Compared with girls, boys take greater risks, behave more aggressively, prefer more active behavior, and in relationships focus on doing things. When adolescents perceive discrepancies between their experience and the gender expectations of their culture, they tend to experience anxiety, depression, and poor self-esteem.

Erikson (1968) maintains that this struggle for identity is the fundamental task of adolescence. As young people grow out of childhood, they seek to understand who they are as unique human beings separate from their place in the family. This often means sorting through their family roles (e.g., as being sons, daughters, brothers, sisters, the bright one, the slow one, the instigator, and so on) to determine to what degree such roles actually correspond to the young person's feelings, ideas, and attitudes. Moreover, as young people experience themselves in their various social roles (e.g., as students, friends of different people and groups, workers, romantic partners, or members of athletic teams), they may find these roles contradict each other. Multiple roles, with their varying expectations, may prompt young people to search for answers to basic identity questions, such as: Who am I? What values do I hold? What kind of work do I want to do? What is the meaning of my life?

In the last chapter, we saw how the child's sense of self is shaped from the earliest relationship with the parents. This formation of the self is a lifelong process that reaches a new and critical level in adolescence with the more conscious development of identity. In Erikson's (1968) view, the ego strives for meaning and experiences anxiety without that meaning. For adolescents, there can be a fairly long, often uncomfortable time when identity creation seems to be at a standstill and their meaning and place in the world are not yet clear. In technological societies where many years of preparation are necessary for entry into the adult world, there is often a delay before adolescents can settle on a meaningful identity. Erikson (1995, p. 537) calls this period an identity moratorium, "a period of seeming inadaptability in the very service of adaptation," where a positive identity is not yet consolidated. During this period, adolescents experiment with different roles and behaviors to discover a fit between their inner lives and the opportunities presented by their society.

A basic source of meaning is found in one's work, and young people try to connect the earlier developed roles, skills, and interests with the occupations that are available in a particular society. Finding a job that fits their skills and interests goes a long way toward relieving their anxiety. While a great deal of the work of shaping identity and choosing an occupation takes place at the level of consciousness, we should not underestimate the role that the unconscious can play in these matters. Some authors have pointed out that in modern societies, young people's task of creating their identity is made more difficult because these societies do not provide myths and rites of passage to guide them (Bly, 1990; Campbell, 1988; Giddens, 1991; Woodman, 1985). We know too that some traditional societies look to dreams to assist their young people in vocational choices. The vision quest among certain Native peoples is an example. In such communities, the young person goes off to a solitary place to pray and wait for a dream or vision in which an animal spirit might appear and indicate what that person's role within the community will be.

Even in modern societies where there is little general appreciation of dreams, some young people still find guidance in their dreams. Carl Jung's effort to find his work in life is a good example of how dreams can assist in occupational choice. As Jung approached the end of secondary school, he felt overwhelmed by the difficulty in settling on a suitable vocation. His father was worried about him because Carl was interested in everything imaginable but did not know what he really wanted to do in life. Jung (1963) describes the struggle within himself and how two dreams emerged to give concrete shape to his future direction and identity. In the first dream, Jung finds himself in a dark woods where he comes upon a burial mound. He begins to dig and is amazed to discover the bones of prehistoric animals. He is tremendously excited by this discovery. At that moment in the dream, he realizes he wants to know more about nature and the world around him.

The second dream too finds Jung in the woods. In a very dark place there he sees a circular pool in which a remarkable creature lies half immersed. It is a giant radiolarian, a round animal about three feet across, made up of innumerable organs shaped like tentacles. Jung is astonished that this magnificent creature is lying undisturbed in such a hidden place. He awoke from the dream filled with excitement and an intense desire for knowledge. He states that these two dreams decided him clearly in favor of a career in science. It is interesting that both dreams begin in a dark, wooded area, a common symbol of the unconscious. There he discovers his interests, namely, investigating the mysteries of the natural world around him. While these dreams did not simply tell him what to do, they allowed him to focus clearly on his deepest passion and thus avoid what Erikson calls "role confusion." Young people who are unable to settle on a suitable occupational identity may suffer from role confusion, which often leads them to compensate by overidentifying with leaders of cliques and heroes in sports or the arts. Young love may also serve to offset role confusion. Erikson argues that much of adolescent love and conversation has to do with shaping identity by projecting one's confused or diffused ego image on a romantic partner and thereby seeing it reflected and clarified.

Fidelity and Ideology

As with the other stages described by Erikson's theory, in adolescence there is an ego strength or virtue that develops as the young person strives to form a coherent identity and avoid possible role confusion. Fidelity is the primary ego strength that is cultivated in the process of identity formation. Erikson (1968) understands fidelity as the ability to maintain loyalties freely chosen despite the inevitable value conflicts involved in these choices. He stresses the importance of being able to commit oneself to beliefs and people even while struggling with value conflicts and ambiguity that result from the many forces pulling adolescents in different directions. Fidelity can be directed toward people, values, and ideas. We have observed the significant influence of peers and the adolescent desire to be loyal to them and the need to be accepted by them.

Another crucial foundation of identity is loyalty to a set of ideas about the world that Erikson terms "ideology." His notion of ideology closely approximates what we have dealt with as worldview, one of the major components of implicit religion and spirituality. Erikson (1950/63) speaks of the adolescent's "ideological mind," which often builds on certain social ideas and values to provide orientation and belonging. Young people are particularly vulnerable to the persuasive power of ideologies such as nationalism, consumerism, communism, or capitalism in their efforts to establish a clear identity and be affirmed by their peers. At the same time, ideology helps to define for the young person what is right and true; it defines what is dangerous and evil as well. Ideology not only helps to sort good from evil in the external world, but also judges various self-representations to be positive or negative.

Positive or negative social images of ethnic attributes are a part of the structure of personality which organizes the ego's identification with positive and negative drives and emotions. In this sense, identity creation involves not only an internalization of family, caretaker, and peer role models, but also an internalization of the present structure of society with its ideals, tensions, and conflicts. Thus, ideology promotes a differentiation of self/ingroup identification and anti-self/outgroup disidentification. It thereby helps the adolescent achieve self-integration at the cost of condemning and possibly persecuting an outgroup (Gregg, 1991, p. 195). This negative aspect of identity formation is not usually considered a pathological development but rather an unconscious dynamic at work even in healthy personalities.

The negative self-images are typically separated from the emerging ego identity (through repression) and then projected onto other individuals or groups. Erikson (1968, p. 58) theorized that an unconscious evil identity which the ego fears to resemble is frequently composed of images of violated or deformed bodies, ethnic outgroups, and exploited minorities. This feature of identity formation can contribute to personal and social conflict. Erikson keeps this dark side of ego identity in the foreground by analyzing the relationship of phenomena such as racism, anti-Semitism, and ethnocentrism to the creation of ego identity. From this perspective, the various "isms" that represent the social dimension of ideology are not just strongly held personal attitudes but are cultural patterns of ego synthesis (Gregg, 1991).

Identity and the Unity of the Self

McAdams (1997) explores the characteristics of selfhood that make identity problematic in modern societies:

1. The self is seen as made rather than given or conferred. People in modern societies experience their identity as a project that they are responsible for, and the self-construction of identity is a key dimension of the self in modernity (Taylor, 1989).
2. Individuals fashion the self in everyday life, within the worlds of family, work, and everyday people. In modern societies, identity creation is a task for everyone, not just for a select few such as royalty, aristocracy, or the saintly.
3. The modern self has many layers and inner depth. The project of constructing a self requires examining one's inner life in order to grasp some truth or meaning there. This exploration often leads a person to view the inner world as a source of moral authority.

4. The self develops over time. McAdams maintains that medical and nutritional advances have caused people to expect a full life cycle and consequently to see themselves as moving through regular stages of life. In this respect, developmental thinking becomes a part of their self-identity, with corresponding notions of progress and self-improvement.

5. Finally, the self seeks temporal coherence. As life is increasingly seen as a long journey, people seek to give coherence and continuity to the self in order to make sense of the great diversity of life episodes and experiences over time. Unifying the self is a process which continually synthesizes subjective experience over time.

McAdams (1997) emphasizes the unity of the self. He reminds us that in the psychoanalytic tradition the process of becoming and being a self is typically regarded as the work of the ego as it navigates between the conflicting internal forces of instinct and super-ego and the external forces of the world and society. While McAdams underscores the importance of creating a unitary identity, others place more emphasis on the experience of multiple selves. Susan Harter (1997) characterizes the problem of adolescent identity precisely as a "proliferation of selves," due to the many demands on adolescents to create various selves associated with the different roles in which they find themselves. Harter notes from her research that adolescents frequently describe their true self-behavior as the "real me inside" and "saying what you really think" in contrast to their false self-behavior as "being phony" and "saying what you think others want to hear" (p. 85).

Struggling with the distinction between the true and false self is a problem dealt with in both psychology and spirituality. Carol Gilligan (1982) adds to this picture of adolescent identity confusion by observing that girls tend to "lose their voice" (suppress their own views) in adolescence, when they seem to forget what they knew as children by hiding their feelings and refusing to express their opinions. According to Gilligan, adolescent females are influenced by the cultural stereotype of the "good woman" who is polite, pleasant, and unassertive. The considerable social pressure on girls not to focus on their own talents and interests but to attract boys further complicates identity formation in adolescent females, and many women do not reclaim their "voices" until midlife (Borysenko, 1996). This pressure can clearly aggravate the task of creating a unitary and coherent sense of identity.

In light of the multiple roles involved in identity formation, Finkenauer et al. (2002) speak of the self as a constellation of identities, each of which depends on a particular context and time frame, such as student, daughter, girlfriend, or chum. Each of these different identities adds up to form the person's overall identity, which provides a certain continuity and consistency. Adolescents may experience inner conflict about how these various identities fit together. At the same time, they may try on different roles and learn how they can manage their self-presentation and the impressions they give to others. Such adolescent explorations of identity and the accompanying confusion mean that adolescents have more acute problems and daily difficulties than people at other periods of life (Finkenauer et al., 2002).

EMPIRICAL STUDIES ON ADOLESCENT RELIGION

In the last chapter, we considered the increasingly complex mental abilities of adolescents represented by formal operational thinking as described by Piaget. This capacity for abstract thought allows us to think about a variety of possible situations and to formulate hypotheses about how to deal with them. Hypothetical thinking permits us to imagine a host of possibilities about our beliefs, attitudes, identity, and behavior. This makes it possible to conceptualize basic religious ideas and values and to compare and evaluate them. So it is no surprise that a prominent aspect of religion in adolescence is to raise questions about received family and/or religious beliefs and values. Fuller (1988) maintains that this critical attitude is coupled with an indifference to, or even rebellion against, authority associated with parents and religious institutions. He observes that adolescents are mainly concerned with social relationships, peer pressure, and financial security. According to Fuller, young people in Western societies are usually too preoccupied with interpersonal, educational, and socioeconomic matters to be very concerned with religion.

In Keen's (1978, p. 119) view, the rebel is a fitting symbol of adolescence. He sees this stage of life as diametrically opposed to the childhood stage. Where children's fundamental task is to develop trust and harmony, to say "yes," adolescents say "no" and define themselves against others. While this stage already has roots in the "terrible twos," according to Keen, it comes into prominence when a person is struggling to find an identity that is distinct from the parents. Keen sees the chief characteristics of adolescence as doubt, resistance, and rebellion, but he believes the negativity of this stage is a vital step on the way to adulthood, where a person is capable of saying both "yes" and "no."

Some of the earliest studies in the psychology of religion associated the turmoil surrounding adolescence with religious conversion. Edwin

Starbuck (1899) carried out the first empirical-statistical investigation of religious conversion and established the view that conversion most frequently occurs during adolescence. Stanley Hall (1904) too noted that most conversion experiences take place around the time of puberty with its attendant physiological changes. He argued that there is a close relation between the emergence of sexuality, love, and religious experience. Other studies over the years have supported this link between adolescence and religious conversion, though there have been divergent explanations for the correlation (Paloutzian, 1996).

Other empirical studies emphasize the decrease in religious involvement during adolescence. Hood et al. (1996) cite findings that show religiousness typically decreases during the ten-to-eighteen-year-old period for mainstream religious groups and that adolescents are less religious in general than middle-aged or older adults. Nevertheless, they caution that this does not mean that adolescents are not religious, or that religion does not affect them. Emphasizing the effect of religious socialization, they note that adolescents who abandon their family religion typically come from homes where little emphasis is placed on religion in the home, and they stress the similarity in values and attitudes between adolescents and their parents. In their view, parents often remain the most powerful factor in the adolescent's religion, even though parental impact weakens as adolescents age and become more susceptible to peer influence. Hood et al. (1996) add that some studies show mothers have a greater impact than fathers on adolescent religious beliefs and practices. Their review of the literature reveals that adolescence is a relatively stable development, in contrast to earlier conceptualizations (such as those of Fuller and Keen) of it being largely a time of turmoil and rebellion against parents and social institutions.

Paloutzian (1996) emphasizes contradictory tendencies in adolescents' approaches to religion, citing data that indicate adolescents are both religious and nonreligious. They are religious in the sense of showing a high degree of religious involvement, practice, and discussion, and nonreligious in that they doubt more and are less accepting of literal or traditional religious doctrines. He cites polls that indicate a high percentage of teens believe that organized religion is important and that teenagers attend religious services regularly. He notes that recent Gallup polls in the United States show that 95 percent of the thirteen-to-eighteen age group believe in God or some type of universal Spirit and about 75 percent say that they pray. At the same time, Paloutzian calls attention to other studies that reveal adolescence as a time of increased religious doubt, which he interprets as reflecting a general tendency to question and wonder about things. In Paloutzian's view, religion in adolescence can be seen as part of a general coping pattern to deal with the paradoxes of the young person's circumstances. Some of the typical adolescent paradoxes and conflicts he lists are the need to be independent from parents while still being dependent upon them, being careful about sexual behavior yet exploratory, believing in God yet questioning the supernatural, and subscribing to a superior ethical principle while tending toward moral relativism. In Paloutzian's judgment, religion during adolescence is shaped by reactions to these paradoxical circumstances.

Paloutzian highlights the influence of peers as a primary social factor that pushes the adolescent beyond the childhood religion shaped largely by the family and religious institutions. Peers exert a particularly strong influence during adolescence because they often represent alternative viewpoints and values. This may be the first occasion young people really experience friends who have a very different worldview or who hold new and challenging attitudes toward sexuality and the meaning of life. Peers can often exert a great deal of pressure on young people's beliefs, attitudes, and behavior, which may result in actually changing them, or at least forcing a reassessment of previously held viewpoints. Paloutzian points out that even where peers do not use direct pressure to bring about such changes, their mere presence as a comparison group invites self-reevaluation.

Brinthaupt and Lipka (2002) assert that growing social pressures can threaten the stability of the self during adolescence: Compared with childhood, peer relations become more important and intense, especially as they shape the young person's assessment of personal competence. They describe the influence of the peer relations on the formation of identity and observe that the most popular groups often have a hierarchical structure with only one or two leaders. The people who belong to these groups continually experience social uncertainty and unstable self-esteem, principally due to the pressures of the cliques' ingroup/outgroup dynamics. They cite a study of predominantly white, middle-class preadolescents in the United States that shows about a third of the students belonged to one of the large popular cliques, with about 10 percent of students striving to be included in the most popular groups. Those in this "wannabe" group experienced low self-esteem, status insecurity, and an unclear identity. Approximately half of all the students were part of smaller, independent groups of friends whose loyalty offset their exclusion from the popular cliques. Another 5 to 10 percent of the students found themselves at the lowest end of the status hierarchy, ostracized from their peers and suffering from the greatest problems of self-esteem. An adolescent's position in the social hierarchy of peers of course would have a direct bearing on central aspects of the young person's spirituality, especially her or his sense of self and identity.

Another important social factor that often modifies religion during adolescence is schooling, which works to promote questioning of accepted religious foundations. Education emphasizes the importance of scientific thinking and the naturalistic explanations of things. In Paloutzian's view, such accounts of the world may seem to undermine earlier religious explanations which use the language of God and the supernatural to account for the same things. Even when the school does not explicitly challenge religious views, language, and values, the focus on a strictly scientific approach to life may seem to challenge or even invalidate a religious perspective.

Synthetic-Conventional Faith

We have discussed Fowler's stages of faith development as they unfold in childhood. Now we shall consider his view of the typical faith stage of adolescents, what he calls synthetic-conventional faith. We should remember here that Fowler's understanding of faith is very close to our ideas about spirituality. Fowler emphasizes how a coherent faith orientation can guide young people through the various and sometimes incompatible experiences of their lives. Because the expectations and judgments shaping the person may include a variety of influences, such as parents, peers, employers, religious institutions, political parties, and the media, there may be tensions and contradictions in the adolescent's identity and values. This situation calls forth the synthetic aspect of this stage, when the person seeks to synthesize these disparate elements into a coherent identity, worldview, and set of values. The person feels deeply about his or her identity, beliefs, and values, but these are grounded in the authority of significant others or group consensus. Fowler emphasizes that the person is not critically self-aware of this identity system, which remains tacit and therefore often contains contradictory values and beliefs. The word "conventional" in the name of this stage refers to the need to conform to the expectations and judgments of others, because in many respects the person is not yet able to develop or create an independent identity and perspective on life. In Fowler's view, the moral judgment of the faith-stage-three adolescent corresponds with Kohlberg's stage three of conventional moral reasoning (interpersonal concordance orientation), but adults at this faith-stage may also exhibit the law-and-order orientation of Kohlberg's stage four.

Fowler maintains that the transition to stage-three faith occurs at the earliest at about eleven or twelve years old, and for some this stage lasts until the age of seventeen or eighteen, while for others it lasts through middle age and even into old age. Generally speaking, this stage characterizes the way most adolescents experience the world. The capacity for mutual role-taking and constructing a self-image for others are hallmarks of this stage and a direct result of applying formal operational thinking to interpersonal relationships. According to Fowler, these newly acquired sensitivities mean that people come to depend on "significant others" for creating and maintaining their sense of identity as well as for the beliefs and values which guide their actions.

According to Fowler (1981), adolescents need a variety of mirrors to reflect the rapid changes in their physical and emotional life. The significant other provides this indispensable mirror of the emerging personality image. In this context, Fowler refers to the importance of the first experience of emotional intimacy outside the family, what psychiatrist Harry Stack Sullivan called the "chum" relationship. The chum is someone of either sex who provides a mirror to reflect the many new facets of the young person's inner life. The adolescent begins to develop the story of his or her life in relation to the chum. Erikson maintains that "puppy love" plays a similar role in helping to shape the story of the adolescent's self.

Fowler observes the difference between the role of story for the nine- or ten-year-old and for the adolescent. For the preadolescent, stories are the medium for describing relationships and roles, for giving unity and value to experience and for understanding life. Using the metaphor of life as a river, Fowler says the preadolescent tells stories that describe the flow from the midst of the stream. Meanings in the person's life are conserved and expressed in the stories, but also trapped in them because the preadolescent cannot yet draw general conclusions from the stories for the meaning of life generally. With adolescence, the development of formal operational thinking, with new possibilities for reflecting on one's thoughts and experience, permits stepping outside of the life stream and observing the stream as a whole.

In Fowler's (1981) view, this capacity represents a whole new level of story, what he calls the story of our stories. It allows the possibility of composing a story of the present self and a myth of the possible roles and relationships of the future self. Fowler believes that the new sense of a mysterious and ultimately inaccessible depth of personality that grows out of the chum or young-love experience sheds light on the frequent and powerful experience of adolescent conversion. The adolescent's spiritual hunger is for a God who knows and affirms the myth of personal identity and the values that are emerging at this time of life. We shall return to the major role of story in forming identity later in this chapter, but now we turn to the crucial place of identity in adolescent spirituality and religion.

IDENTITY AND RELIGION

Beit-Hallahmi (1989) sees religion as "an identity-maintenance system" (p. 104). He distinguishes three levels of identity: ego identity, social identity, and collective identity. The first level, ego identity, denotes the integration of the individual personality. This concept grows out of the psychoanalytic tradition, with its notions of internalization and identification as the foundations of the personality. Erikson has done the most to promote this idea of identity at the center of the ego, synthesizing the person's experience and providing a sense of continuity and self-sameness. Beit-Hallahmi considers religious beliefs and affiliations to be a source of stability and support for ego identity.

The second level of identity, social identity, refers to membership in an externally defined social group and the individual's integration into the group. The third level of identity is a strictly collective identity as defined by the group to distinguish itself from other groups. The theory of the second and third levels of identity grows out of the disciplines of sociology and social psychology. Beit-Hallahmi believes that, for most people, religion operates at the second level, i.e., as a social identity. In this regard, religion is similar to other group identities such as that of belonging to a political party. Religion, like other basic social identities, is a result of social learning that usually takes place within the family. For most people, religion is not primarily determined by choice, by believing certain ideas, but rather is a part of their identity as members of a certain religious tradition.

Beit-Hallahmi states that the social identity comes first, and that many people discover, sometimes to their surprise, that they have acquired a system of beliefs that is tied to their social identity. Considering religion globally, social identity determines how most people adopt their beliefs about the world and the meaning of human experience. According to Beit-Hallahmi, relatively few people actually adopt a religion or religious beliefs as a result of a spiritual quest or conscious choice. In sociological terms, religious identity is usually ascribed rather than achieved. In his view, the concern for a consciously chosen spirituality, discussed in chapter one, is a relatively recent and atypical phenomenon.

Beit-Hallahmi is particularly interested in the way ego identity relates to social and collective identity. For the majority of people, religion does not go deeper than a social-identity label denoting group membership. In his view, this means that religion has relatively little influence on ego identity when compared with its central role in creating social identity. Beit-Hallahmi speaks of the "religion of identity" to highlight this type of low-personal-involvement religion that is learned within the family of origin. However, he emphasizes that religious groups themselves aim for high levels of ego involvement among their members. For example, religious groups that require new members to change their ego identity by adopting a new name attempt to force high ego involvement on group members.

In those cases where there is high ego involvement with religion, the belief system becomes closely tied to identity and self-esteem. The goal of socialization is precisely to tie religious beliefs to personal identity. Beit-Hallahmi argues that religion as a belief system persists despite rational critiques and predictions of increased secularization because it is intimately tied to a sense of personal identity. People strongly resist any challenges to religious belief that are at the same time seen as threats to their sense of personal identity.

IDENTITY AND LIFE STORY

Thinking and talking about their life stories is for many adolescents the key to their spiritual and religious lives. Their stories help to create and clarify their identities which are central to spirituality and implicit religion. Anthony Giddens (1991) places biography or life story at the heart of self-identity. He maintains that a person's identity is not to be found in his or her behavior, nor even in the reactions of other people, but in the capacity to keep a particular narrative going. Such a narrative strives to integrate the person's behavior and people's reactions to it, as well as events that occur in the external world. All of this is arranged into an ongoing story about the self that includes who the person is now, who she or he was, and where she or he is going. Giddens points out that self-identity is fragile because the narrative that the person creates is only one among the host of potential stories that could be developed and told depending on personal and social circumstances. Gregg (1991) brings together the important roles of both ideology and narrative in identity formation by viewing narratives as ideological structures that help to situate the individual in the realities of social and political inequality. He states that people construct an identity narrative as an ideological tool to struggle for personal dignity as well as for power. The sad irony is that, in this view, the process of creating one's own identity typically leads to denying dignity, equality, and power to others as individuals and groups. Gregg sees the particular value of narrative psychology as its ability to highlight the social construction of the self and the role of ideology in shaping the social self.

In Fowler's explanation of the transition to the characteristic adolescent faith stage, he places in the foreground the central aspect of life story, noting how it changes as emerging cognitive capacities enable a new level of personal story. McAdams (1995) maintains that a number of factors, including physiological, cognitive, social, and cultural, predispose adolescents in contemporary Western societies to believe that they must construct a coherent self that incorporates their many different roles, values, and skills. He believes that the most effective form for constructing such a personal identity is the narrative, and he even defines identity as "an internalized and evolving life story, or personal myth" (p. 382). People author and revise their personal story over the years to make sense, for themselves and others, of their lives.

Michael Novak (1971) links the idea of life story directly to religion. He describes three levels of life story, each of which can be related to religion. At the first level, there is simply living out one's life without any awareness of its narrative character. For Novak, this is already a basic, though undeveloped, form of religion. This level corresponds to what we have been considering as implicit religion and spirituality. The second level is an awareness that one's life expresses a story. This level too reflects the person's implicit religion and spirituality, especially the key elements of a person's sense of self, identity, values, and worldview. At the third level, people give an explicit religious interpretation to their life story, interpreting it in relation to God's will, activity, or presence. At this level, the person might speak of being called by God, or converted to a particular religion, or experiencing the divine in some way. This represents the explicitly religious dimension of life story. Novak's levels two and three involve reflecting on, and creating, one's identity.

Like Novak, Robert Emmons (1986) emphasizes the role of religion and spirituality in shaping a person's life story. He holds that religious factors play a significant role in the narrative level of personality because, as people construct their life story, they often draw upon existing religious values, ideas, images, and metaphors. He notes that, in a number of collections of life stories, spirituality serves as a guiding, integrating, and empowering force, and religion functions as a potent source of identity. Conversion narratives help to consolidate and strengthen a new religious identity, and timeless religious metaphors such as death and rebirth give major life changes such as divorce and remarriage a deeper spiritual meaning. According to Emmons, religion and spirituality often provide a philosophy of life that serves to integrate the many disparate aspects of personality into a coherent life story. Such a philosophy of life also provides a framework within which people can locate their own narrative. He believes that, more than at any previous time in history, people at the end of the twentieth century appear to be concerned with determining their place within the context of an evolving universe. Embedding one's life within a larger, all-encompassing narrative seems to be a universal human need, and the inability to locate oneself in the context of the larger story leads to despair and self-destructive behavior (Emmons, 1999).

A growing body of research shows that much of the thinking of ordinary people does not follow the patterns favored by science, namely, inference, abstraction, and generalization. For most people, the narrative, rather than the generalization, is the prime medium for preserving and communicating information (Baumeister & Newman, 1994). Baumeister and Newman (1994) contrast the paradigmatic and the narrative modes of thought as two different ways to structure and process information. The former is the sphere of science, logic, and mathematics, involving context-free abstractions, while the latter captures the particularity of human actions and intentions, involving coherent stories about specific experiences. They see narratives as important alternatives to laboratory experiments, surveys, and questionnaires, the usual tools of research in personality and social psychology. In their view, even systematic surveys or carefully structured questionnaires may miss crucial information because the researcher sets the limits of response, whereas narratives may include a wealth of detail unanticipated by fixed-response instruments.

The role of narrative in structuring human experience has gained growing recognition in recent years. Hayden White (1978) places narrative at the heart of humanity itself and its search for meaning. In his view, narrative solves the general human problem of how to share reality, that is, how to translate something we know into something we can communicate to others. To be human is to tell stories that situate the individual and his or her world in a larger and more meaningful context. Creating narratives about the self allows people to confer on their identities the meaning and continuity they seek. Telling these stories may be a vital means of consolidating an identity at the same time as causing others to recognize it. People may desire a certain identity, but do not feel it confirmed until others accept and validate that identity as a social reality (Wicklund & Gollwitzer, 1982).

Although people often think about their experiences in terms of propositions and personality traits, more frequently they use stories and refer to particular incidents to formulate and communicate these to themselves and others. Narratives, it seems, manage to preserve the richness and ambiguity of experience whereas abstract propositions and conclusions narrow the interpretive field. Baumeister and Newman (1994) state that generalizing and drawing conclusions requires an extra step in cognitive processing, so telling a story is both easier and remains closer to the experience itself. They add that narrative thinking is more flexible and can accommodate inconsistencies better than paradigmatic thinking. Thus the narrative mode is more suited to reinterpreting inconsistent information and thinking about situations involving conflicts and contradictions.

Baumeister and Newman explain that stories are particularly suited to bring out the meaning in life events. They elaborate on how narratives help to find meaning in life by focusing on what they call the four "needs of meaning," namely, purposiveness, justification by values, efficacy, and self-worth. They maintain that people interpret their experiences in ways that satisfy one or more of these needs. Stories often satisfy the first need, for purpose, by interpreting events as causally linked to subsequent events. They may order a series of events that lead to some fulfillment or attainment of a goal. Stories meet the second need, to have a firm sense of right and wrong, by narrating events and interpreting them according to a set of values. Explaining reasons, motives, and intentions may help to justify certain events.

Narratives often serve the third need, efficacy, i.e., to make a difference and to control the environment, by recounting how a person reached some goal or by emphasizing a stable environment in which one can obtain positive outcomes. People frequently construct stories to affirm or even increase their sense of control over their lives. Narratives meet the fourth need for meaning by bolstering a person's sense of self-worth or defusing potential threats. Baumeister and Newman admit that there may be overlap in these needs for meaning, especially the needs for justification by values and self-worth. They attempt to distinguish justification from self-worth by arguing that the former usually concerns specific actions, while the latter often affects the whole person, yet they insist that both needs are served by generating stories that make the self look good.

So narratives provide meaning and direction for self-understanding. Some stories make us sick while other stories help us recover a coherent and healthy identity. Dan McAdams (1996) asserts that systematic research on life stories within personality theory is still in its infancy. He speaks of the turn toward narrative in the social sciences within the last two decades. In psychoanalysis, psychology, social psychology, personality theory, and the human sciences in general, the life story is increasingly seen as an important way human beings make sense of their experiences and organize them into a plot for a potential listener, including oneself. McAdams sees identity in terms of life story as the deepest of three levels of understanding the human personality. According to him, level one represents personal dispositions or traits (such as openness to experience or extraversion), and level two consists of strategies, plans, and concerns which enable people to complete life tasks and achieve crucial life goals. The third level seeks to describe and explain the personality through the narrative lens. McAdams (1995) characterizes the move from level one to levels two and three as moving from the psychology of the stranger to a more detailed and nuanced description of a real, flesh-and-blood person.

McAdams (1996) locates within the characteristic mind-set of modernity this effort to understand the personality through stories that create and maintain identity. In the modern world, individuals are expected to create, discover, and explore personalized selves that define who they are and how they are similar to, and different from, other individuals. According to McAdams, constructing a personal identity involves telling the story of oneself in a way that synthesizes diverse elements so that the self is seen as more or less unified, despite its many facets. Life narratives explain too how the self of yesterday becomes the self of today and will evolve into a future self of tomorrow. The creation of the life story depends on the way the individual weighs and arranges elements of the self into a sequence that includes the dramatic features of character, plot, and setting. McAdams emphasizes that a person may have more than one life story, or the overall narrative may be only loosely connected as a collection of stories about the self. However, he insists that most people seek opportunities to integrate their different stories into a narrative whole that exhibits unity and purpose. Identity, seen as a life story, allows psychologists to understand how and to what extent people in modern society are able to attain unity, purpose, and meaning in life.

The narrative of the self assumes a chronological framework that helps to give coherence to self-identity. The larger context of this trajectory of development is the lifespan and its various phases. Giddens (1991) notes that the core of self-identity in modern life is closely associated with the writing of autobiographies, a practice which developed only during the modern period. The analogy between creating and maintaining self-identity and writing an autobiography emphasizes that constructing personal identity through one's life narrative requires reflective effort and creativity. Giddens observes that the idea of a series of passages through the course of life helps to organize personal identity. He reminds us that each passage usually involves both losses and gains. Mourning such losses as the death of a parent or marital separation is part of the ongoing creation of identity. Undergoing major transitions in life, such as leaving home, getting or losing a job, forming a new relationship, or confronting illness, brings mixtures of risk and opportunity.

The construction of identity involves consciously assessing the risks of personal development in order to take advantage of the corresponding new possibilities. According to Giddens, personal integrity in the modern world comes from integrating these experiences of life transition within a self-development narrative. Giddens believes that people in modern society are at a disadvantage in facing these transitions because they lack the rites of passage found in traditional societies, especially regarding the key transitions of birth, adolescence, marriage, and death. Although modern people work through many of the psychological ramifications of these transitions in the process of reformulating their life narrative, they do not have the advantage of the clear cultural pattern and strong social support provided in more traditional societies. In modern society, each transitional phase tends to become an identity crisis, or at least the occasion for a major revision to the ongoing narrative of the self. The lifespan itself is viewed in terms of the expectation to meet and resolve such crises.

This discussion of life story and identity helps to show the relationship between religion, implicit religion, and spirituality from yet another perspective than that presented in chapter one. There, we viewed the three terms as having certain areas in common, illustrated as intersecting sections of circles. Here, it appears that the three are related as increasing degrees of awareness and interpretation of life experience. At the level of implicit religion (corresponding to Novak's first level of religion as simply living out a story), there may be little or no self-awareness about one's identity, values, and worldview. At the next level, that of spirituality (corresponding to Novak's second level of religion as being aware of the narrative one is living out), there is increased awareness of, and reflection on, one's identity, values, and worldview. This level of story as spirituality also reflects the view that spirituality consists in the narratives people construct about their spiritual journeys (Wuthnow, 1998). Finally, explicit religion adds to the first two levels an interpretation that links one's identity, values, and worldview to the divine or to one of the religious traditions that call attention to divine transcendence in the midst of human life.

EXAMPLES OF RELIGIOUS AND SPIRITUAL EXPERIENCES IN ADOLESCENCE

Douglas's Story

Douglas was the second youngest in a family of three boys and two girls. His mother was Jewish and his father an atheist. Douglas had a mild curiosity about his mother's Judaism, but otherwise thought very little about religion or spirituality. He loved cars and enjoyed working on automobile engines. In secondary school, he hung around with a group of like-minded young men who talked mostly about their jobs, earning money, and their desire to be independent. Douglas was sixteen when he met Joanne at a party one night. They seemed drawn to each other. She liked his down-to-earth attitude and friendliness and he found her sympathetic and easy to be with. They began to spend time with each other outside of school.

Joanne was a serious person, reflecting on who she was, her goals, and the meaning of her life. At first, Douglas was uncomfortable talking with her about himself, his values, and plans, but gradually he found himself thinking about their conversations and her way of seeing the world. She had a positive attitude and trusted people, giving them the benefit of the doubt. Even though Douglas felt she was naive at times, he admired her approach to life. When he learned that she meditated daily, he wanted to know what that was like and how it affected her. Joanne explained her meditation experience to him and he tried it himself.

Douglas found that meditating helped to calm him and center his mind. It also made him aware of a deeper dimension to his life. Although he did not want to share this development with his buddies, he felt that he was slowly changing, becoming more confident about who he was and what he valued. Both his relationship with Joanne and his meditation practice seemed to broaden and deepen his spirituality, though he did not use the word *spirituality* to characterize the changes taking place in his life. Although Douglas and Joanne parted ways after secondary school, he wanted to remain friends with her. He realized how much she contributed to his growth as a person. In Douglas's case, his development of identity, values, and worldview are probably best described as changes in his implicit religion.

Erika Sabo[1]

Erika was raised in the Apostolic Christian Church, a small denomination in Canada. When she was fourteen years old, she started sorting out her identity and worldview, trying to determine who she was and what she really believed. She thought about how much she was like her parents and how greatly they influenced her beliefs and values. She began to wonder if her ideas about God and the world were purely a result of her parents' viewpoint. She wanted to base her beliefs on her own experience and felt uncomfortable with not knowing exactly what she believed.

Erika was wrestling with these questions when she had a powerful religious experience. She was with her church youth group one evening at a campfire service. They were sitting around a large bonfire when she suddenly saw the profile of Jesus in the fire. She was shocked as she saw him walk in the fire and then turn to look at her. He looked compassionate and sad. He appeared to be of average height, with a robe and shoulder-length hair. He remained only a short while and then disappeared. After the service, a friend sitting on the opposite side of the fire from her came over to ask what happened to her as her appearance seemed to change, reflecting strong emotions. No one else around the fire said anything about having seen what Erika saw.

Erika now looks back on this visionary experience as a major turning point in her life. From that point on, she has been convinced that her religious worldview and her identity as a Christian are no longer based solely on her parents' or even her church's ideas, but on her own direct encounter with God. She has drawn on this identity and worldview to help her cope with life's difficulties, especially the death of her parents in an automobile accident. She believes that God is present even in her darkest moments.

---

1. Erika's story is taken from Wiebe (1997, pp. 64–65).

Mirjana Dragicevic[2]

Mirjana was one of a number of young people who experienced visions of Mary in Medjugorje, Bosnia, in 1981. She was sixteen years old when she and her fifteen-year-old friend saw a light hovering over a small mountain near where they lived. From a distance of about 300 yards, both girls saw a woman holding a baby, surrounded by rays of light. Frightened by this sight, they ran to a nearby relative's house to report this strange experience. The next evening, Mirjana and five other young people returned to the mountain and again saw the lady surrounded by light. A short distance from where they were standing, Mirjana fell to her knees in ecstacy. In that state she said she saw Jesus' mother, Mary, weeping in front of a shining cross and pleading for prayers for peace.

Yugoslavian authorities persecuted Mirjana and her family because they suspected the visions were part of a nationalist plot to undermine the ruling Communist government. Nevertheless, Mirjana and the other visionaries continued to experience and talk about the apparitions. She stated that, in her visions, Mary repeatedly requests prayers for peace and has given her disturbing information about future misfortunes and suffering in the world. These visionary experiences contributed greatly to Mirjana's identity and overall spirituality. She sees herself as an emissary for peace and a witness to the divine presence in the world.

Mirjana went on to study at the University of Sarajevo, where she met her future husband. She, her husband, and two daughters live in Medjugorje, though they were in exile during the Civil War of 1992. Mirjana has traveled widely and spoken about the urgency and meaning of her visionary experiences. She continues to pray and fast for peace, the central value that guides her life and work.

SUMMARY

In this chapter, we have seen that religion and spirituality can be central to the fundamental task of adolescence, namely, the formation of identity. We have observed that young people often doubt and criticize organized religion, but formal religion still means a great deal to many adolescents. Family and peers have a strong influence on young people's values and attitudes toward religion. Physical changes and social

---

2. Mirjana's story is found in Connell (1998, pp. 39–74).

demands also force young people to struggle with their own identity, values, and worldview, primary aspects of their spirituality. In adolescence, the ego strives to synthesize disparate family, social, and occupational roles into a coherent identity with meaning and purpose. Religion itself may contribute to identity as an "identity maintenance system." Young people may not reflect on, or be explicit about, the main features of implicit religion or spirituality in their lives, but their life stories express these features in a way that gives unity and meaning to their personalities. In this way, life stories may be a valuable measure of what is happening in the young person's spirituality and religion.

In relating these conclusions to our table of the overall movement of spirituality, we see in adolescence the level of conscious sorting involved in the formation of identity, values, and worldview, as young people gradually move to greater independence from the family. The efforts to achieve an identity and worldview represent the personal level of development which builds on the prior, largely emotional and unconscious prepersonal level. We should not imagine that the earlier unconscious foundation of identity is completely left behind. The conscious shaping of identity and worldview works with the givens of a person's life, which include a sense of one's body and the prepersonal sense of self that is based largely on experiences in early relationships.

Table 6: Implicit Religion and Spiritual Development in Adolescence

	Self-Stream	Values Stream	Worldview Stream
Transpersonal Level			
Personal Level	Shaping personal identity and story	Conscious sorting of values	Worldview expands beyond the family
Prepersonal Level			

In the table, we see that the prepersonal sense of self is gradually transformed into a more or less coherent personal identity that includes an outlook on life and values to live by. In the *sense-of-self stream of development*, personal identity is often expressed in the stories told about young people and in the emerging realization that their lives tell the story of who they are, their family background, nationality, race, religious or cultural tradition, and the unique relationships and experiences of their lives. In the *values stream of development*, the early attitudes and values internalized from parents and caretakers begin in adolescence to be questioned and sorted into values that fit into the emerging identity and life story. Peer pressure is often a significant factor in determining which values to live by.

Finally, in the *worldview stream of development*, attitudes and outlook on life developed in childhood begin to be examined at a relatively conscious level. Here adolescents often discover, to their surprise, that the world is actually quite different from what they learned to expect from their early experiences in the family. Meeting people from varied backgrounds in secondary school can cause the adolescent to compare and evaluate different assumptions about the nature of life, death, and even life after death. Young people's religious traditions may help to shape their outlook on reality and the meaning of life. In the table, adolescence represents only the beginning of the personal level of spirituality. The processes of the personal level of development continue to shape identity, values, and worldview throughout life, but they enter a crucial phase in early adulthood with its growing opportunities and responsibilities.

CHAPTER FOUR

THE TASKS AND TRIALS OF
YOUNG ADULTHOOD

———————— ❧ ————————

> For most of those in the twenties, a fantastic mystery story
> waits to be written over the next two decades. It races with
> excitement and jeopardy, fools us with false villains, diverts
> us from the real villains that are the divisions within our-
> selves, mugs us with surprise changes in our perspective,
> and leads us down secret passageways in search of our miss-
> ing personality parts.   — Gail Sheehy, *Passages*

Religion and spirituality are not always in evidence as young people
struggle to find their place in the adult world. Nevertheless, the main
elements of spirituality are involved as young adults begin to assume
responsibilities and make commitments based on the identity fashioned in adolescence. Empirical studies show few clear indicators of
the religious concerns of young adults. Life-cycle theorists offer a starting point as they describe the general context in which spiritual and
religious issues emerge, but ultimately it may be easier to see the role
of spirituality and religion at those points where people experience difficulties meeting the main challenges of adult life. In this regard, psychotherapy frequently offers the occasion for people to reassess their
present identity, values, and worldview in early adulthood.

To gain perspective on this life stage, we shall examine, in the first
part of this chapter, the portrait of early adulthood presented by prominent theorists of the life cycle. They provide a broad view of the chief
rhythms and concerns of early adulthood, emphasizing the degree to
which transitions play a major role in this period of life. Next, we

consider the empirical studies, which show complex patterns of religiousness in early adulthood. Studies indicate that young adults are moving toward the religious extremes: Some are drawn to conservative and fundamentalist religion, while many others adopt a growing liberalism in their religious ideas and practices. The major theories of young-adult religious development still focus on the cognitive aspects of religious and moral judgment and the overall organization of faith. These studies point to the importance of how people come to terms with the paradoxes of their experiences. Finally, a discussion of Gordon Allport's work on mature religion rounds out this section by highlighting how religion can help to integrate the adult personality.

The remainder of this chapter examines the context in which many young adults first become aware of important aspects of their religion and spirituality, namely, psychotherapy. As Erik Erikson (1995) observes, only when human beings are motivated to introspect can certain psychological and spiritual dynamics be observed, and ordinarily the best motivation for such introspection is when they need help. In recent decades, psychotherapy and clinical psychology have become more appreciative of the role religion and spirituality play in helping people to wrestle with their problems and redraw their maps of reality. When young adults struggle with inner conflicts and difficulties with sexuality, relationships, and work, they are often required to think about and reevaluate their identity, values, and worldview. Increasingly, they look to psychotherapists to help them sort out these religious and spiritual issues. Psychotherapy helps us to understand the developments of religion and spirituality throughout adulthood. Sigmund Freud's and Alfred Adler's contributions especially illuminate the primary concerns of young adulthood, stressing the importance of sexuality, relationships, and work for healthy psychological functioning. To oversimplify, Freud and Adler focus on the major dynamics of young adult development, while Carl Jung illuminates the events of midlife and beyond. These perspectives allow us to see the main features of religion and spirituality over the entire course of adulthood.

OVERVIEW: THE SEASONS OF ADULT LIFE

First, let us look at the big picture—how young adulthood fits into adulthood as a whole. Popular theorists of the life cycle provide an overview of the principal tasks and interests of early adulthood. Young adulthood is a time of significant transition. Two popular theorists of the life cycle highlight the major transitions of young adulthood. In this section, we focus primarily on Daniel Levinson's view of the chief tasks that face young adults and Gail Sheehy's vivid portrait of the key life passages of adulthood.

Social psychologist Daniel Levinson produced two major studies of the adult stages of the life cycle. The first, *The Seasons of a Man's Life*, studies forty men who were workers and executives from two companies. The main focus of this study is the period of early adulthood, with ages ranging from twenty to forty years. Levinson speaks of an early adult transition which covers the years from the late teens to about the age of twenty-two. In this transitional phase, we see how the concerns of adolescence are modified and extended to prepare the young person to enter the first period of adulthood. Levinson refers to the first phase of adulthood as a novice period in order to emphasize how gradual the entry into adult life can be in our society. A key aspect of Levinson's theory of the life cycle is that there are two distinctive eras in the main part of adulthood, divided by a more or less well-defined midlife transition. Levinson's follow-up study, *The Seasons of a Woman's Life* (1996), is an attempt to update and broaden his data by interviewing forty-five women from their late teens to their mid-forties. He concludes from this work that women go through roughly the same sequence of adult development, even though there are many differences from men in the concrete ways they traverse each era.

Levinson et al. (1978) describe four major tasks of early adulthood:

- forming a dream;
- establishing a mentor relationship;
- finding an occupation; and
- developing a love relationship and/or family.

By dream, he means the imagined possibilities of one's life that generate excitement. The life dream usually provides a general picture of how one's life may unfold in adulthood, although it sometimes includes particular images that anticipate or guide future developments. Levinson's choice of words for this task is instructive, because the life dream is akin to daydreams and night dreams. Daydreams frequently revolve around the kind of work one wants to do, the type of person one wants to become, or the kind of future life and partner one imagines. Sometimes night dreams anticipate and shape the life dream too.

Personally, I recall Emily, a young woman of twenty, whose dream showed her surrounded by sick animals that she was able to help. Deeply moved by this fulfilling dream, she sought out and pursued a career as a veterinarian. In another instance, I remember twenty-two-year-old Robert, who dreamed that an airplane wrote the first and last name of his future wife across the sky. He was shocked when a few years later he met and fell in love with a woman of this name. After some twenty years of marriage, they still marvel at the prescience of this amazing dream. For Levinson, it is important to entertain life dreams in a way that gives them a place in one's current life, thereby establishing a link between one's dream and present reality. He notes too that the life dream is malleable and may be modified to fit with changing circumstances in life. It may even be given up, for instance when people reach their forties and there is not enough in their current experience to sustain the early dream. Levinson found that the people who were able to shape their lives around their dream tended to be happier and more fulfilled than those who abandoned their dream or were unable to express it in their lives.

The second task involves finding a mentor, a person who is both a role model and a guide in the world of work. The mentor is familiar with a profession or a particular line of work, often through years of experience, and thereby is in a position to offer guidance on how to get started, what kind of skills and work habits to develop, and what to expect along the way. Even more than a source of information, the mentor provides a living example of what a particular occupation looks and feels like, and may offer emotional support or help through rough spots. The mentor relationship is generally connected to the third task, namely, finding an occupation. For instance, Linda, a first-year graduate student, gravitated toward her psychology professor, an accomplished researcher and writer and a woman she admired personally. She soon found herself in many of this professor's classes and later became her research assistant and doctoral student. Linda modeled herself after her mentor, even in her area of specialization and style of teaching and writing.

We have seen in Erikson's study of identity formation the crucial role that a job can play in helping people to gain a sense of themselves and their place in society. Richard Dayringer (2000) points out that this link between job and identity is reinforced because individuals are frequently called by job titles, such as mail carrier, nurse, or doctor, and in earlier times occupations often had their own unique hat or uniform so that a chef, chauffeur, or sailor would be easy to recognize. He adds that the Protestant work ethic and the focus on occupational success in modern Western countries have influenced people to merge their personalities with their jobs in order to solidify their identity. Settling on an occupation that fits with a person's talents and interests can contribute greatly to a stable identity during early adulthood.

The final task that is central to early adulthood involves developing a love relationship. This carries on and deepens the process of adolescent love wherein people continue to discover themselves and their values through ongoing encounters with others. Erikson characterizes this stage as intimacy, the ability to give oneself to another person, thereby sharing the personality that has been formed thus far. In Erikson's view, developing the capacity for intimacy and establishing a love relationship are the primary goals of young adulthood. Levinson recognizes that there is often considerable pressure from family and society to move such deepening relationships toward marriage and starting a family. He observes that people frequently experience one of the great paradoxes of development at this point in their lives: They have to make crucial choices before they have sufficient knowledge, judgment, and self-understanding; however, to put off these choices may have greater costs. This paradox has probably always been true, but in a modern society where vocation and marriage are seen as individual decisions, the difficulty seems to be heightened and experienced as a personal problem.

Psychiatrist Roger Gould (1978) identifies certain assumptions made by young adults that undergird the tasks of young adulthood. These assumptions are very simplified versions of our complicated reality and are unconscious attempts to make us feel more at home in the world. From late adolescence until about the age of twenty-two, the assumption develops that our parents will somehow ensure our safety and be there to help when we cannot do it on our own. In the earliest period of adulthood the conscious personality focuses on becoming more critical, analytical, experimental, goal-oriented, and persevering. Gould contends that the assumptions supporting these efforts are as follows:

- rewards come if I do as I am supposed to;
- rationality, commitment, and effort always prevail; and
- my loved ones can do for me what I cannot do for myself.

The first two ideas give us the confidence to put all our energy into the life projects that are emerging in adulthood. The idea that loved ones will carry us through when we cannot make it on our own continues the late-adolescent assumption that our parents will ensure our safety, though now a spouse or partner becomes the primary symbol of that safety net. In Gould's judgment, even though these assumptions are false, they have some value. They allow us to step out confidently into the world and strive for goals without too much uncertainty and hesitation; they protect us from being paralyzed by the real possibilities of failure or the threat of sickness and death, which are part of the human condition.

In his study of men, Levinson focuses on how a man seeks a special woman to support his dream, emotionally and sometimes financially. The woman, usually his wife, helps him to get started in adult life, sometimes by working while he finishes school or professional training. Bill and Amy represent one of many similar stories I have encountered. They met during their undergraduate years at the University of Toronto. After graduation, they married and Amy went to work at a bank to finance Bill's years of medical specialization. Amy thereby enabled Bill to achieve his dream of a medical career. In his study of women, Levinson does not highlight to the same degree how a woman seeks a man to support her life dream. Cultural patterns have led to differences in the way women experience the tasks of early adulthood, especially in regard to occupation and relationships. Levinson (1996) observes that we have only recently begun to overcome "gender splitting," which he defines as a rigid division between male and female, masculine and feminine in all areas of life. Gender splitting creates a division between the domestic sphere and the occupational sphere, which assumes the female is the homemaker and the male the provider within a "traditional marriage enterprise" (p. 414).

Although economic forces are making it less feasible for a woman to be a full-time homemaker, and new forms of marriage are developing where the lives of men and women are becoming more similar, Levinson finds that women suffer from an internal conflict between the "Traditional Homemaker Figure" and an "Anti-Traditional Figure." For the homemakers in this study, the Traditional Figure originated in childhood and became predominant in shaping their life structure during their twenties. For these women, their life dream revolved around home and family, and their relationship with a man allowed them to realize at least part of their original dream. However, Levinson found that most of the women who took this path found their life structure unsatisfactory as their lives developed. The career women attempted to modify the traditional pattern by working in the world and at the same time establishing a family life in which homemaking responsibilities were more equally divided. These women experienced both joy and suffering in their attempts to find a balance between work and family. Levinson underscores the hardships that face women in both groups as they seek to find their way in today's changing society.

Overall, Levinson believes that adulthood consists of alternating periods of structure-building and structure-changing. A current that runs through these changes is the ever-shifting balance between autonomy and connectedness. Levinson observes that separation from parents is not restricted to the individuation processes of infancy, childhood, and adolescence, but continues on into adulthood. The degree and kind of attachment to parents often plays a role in the transitions of adulthood, whether this be leaving home, returning home, establishing a family of one's own, or caring for sick or aging parents. Another prominent feature of early adulthood is the tendency to explore and, at the same time, create a stable structure. This dynamic can cause inner tension and pull a person in two different directions at once. The desire to explore may lead people to abandon a stable life structure in order to find new horizons of identity and worldview, whereas the desire to create a stable structure may inhibit such exploration and change.

Levinson maintains that *life structures,* defined as the patterns of a person's life at a given time, are in flux throughout adulthood. He argues that stable periods of structure-building and maintenance usually last about six to seven years, ten years at most, while transitional periods ordinarily last four or five years. This means that almost half of an adult's life is spent in developmental transitions. According to Levinson, these transitions are frequently experienced as times of crisis in which a person feels "in a state of suspended animation" (p. 51). The transitional periods end when the person's questioning and exploring lose their sense of urgency. *Marker events* often accompany, and sometimes precipitate, these transitions. Common examples of marker events would be marriage, divorce, illness, the birth or death of a loved one, war, experiences at work, or retirement. Such significant events may undermine the stability of a previous life structure, especially when people can no longer adapt to these events with the identity, values, or worldview of their current life structure.

An interesting feature of Levinson's view of early adulthood is what he calls the Age Thirty Transition, a period extending from twenty-eight to the age of thirty-three. He observes in both men and women that sometime after the main elements of the adult life structure have been put in place, a crisis arises. This is a time when both men and women appear to have second thoughts about the major commitments they have made to a job and relationships. Levinson (1996) states that 90 percent of the career women he studied had a moderate-to-severe crisis in life during this period. At this time, people often question how well their commitments fit who they are. After pouring their energy into creating a stable structure in their twenties, people may find that their life structure does not correspond to their early life dream. They may now view their earlier choice of job or marriage partner as more a product of social and family pressures than an expression of their own needs and interests.

LIFE PASSAGES

Gail Sheehy is a journalist who built on Levinson's research to produce the best-seller *Passages*. For that book she studied 115 middle-class Americans ranging from eighteen to fifty-five years old. Like Levinson, she emphasizes the frequency of changes within the adult period of life and she supports his view that no life structure seems to last more than seven or eight years. Sheehy (1978) finds that transformation periods differ from person to person in terms of the outer events, but are similar in regard to the inner turmoil experienced. She contends that, though the fundamental periods are the same for men and women, the tempo of development differs between them; rarely do men and women struggle with the same questions at the same age.

In her more recent study *New Passages*, based on some 500 interviews with people from the age of twenty to seventy, Sheehy modifies her previous understanding of the adult life cycle. She still finds a pattern in the way people move through adult life, but notes that some of their transitions occur at different ages than before. Sheehy speaks of a ten-year shift in the life cycle when comparing the 1990s to the 1950s. The two changes that bear directly on early adulthood are, first, the lengthened time of adolescence and, second, the increased tendency to delay marriage and family-building. In her view, adolescence begins earlier now and in some respects lasts through the twenties. Marriage and family-building, which in the 1950s began in the early twenties, may not start until thirty and extend to the mid-fifties.

Sheehy divides early adulthood into two periods, which she calls "provisional adulthood" (ages eighteen to thirty) and "first adulthood" (ages thirty to forty-five). Her term "provisional adulthood" highlights the tentative and exploratory character of early adulthood. The first stage of provisional adulthood involves "pulling up roots," distancing oneself from the family, often by going off to college, entering the military, traveling, or marrying early. At the same time, the young person strives to take hold in the adult world by finding a suitable job, a mentor, and a partner. All these steps are influenced by other people. Family expectations, cultural pressure, and peer models shape these important early choices. Sheehy's term, "the trying twenties," emphasizes not only the effort necessary to enter the adult world, but also the "trying" character of the pressures and obligations of this life stage. Religion, region, and class background are part of the "shoulds" of the twenties that create an atmosphere where key decisions about job and marriage may seem inevitable.

Sheehy labels her next stage the "catch thirties" to indicate that even when a person is outwardly successful in managing the tasks of early adulthood, there is an undercurrent of restlessness. Sheehy agrees with Levinson that alongside the desire to build a secure structure in early adulthood is the desire to explore and experiment. Sheehy speaks of the urge to bust out of the restrictions that go along with a job, marriage, and family. People may feel that while they have done all that they should do in establishing a job, relationship, and family, they are not sure it's what they themselves really want. This inner tension contributes to what Levinson calls the Age Thirty Transition. As life becomes increasingly attuned to the pace of career, home, and family, personal discontent often rises, frequently leading people to review their marriage and job.

Sam Keen (1978) describes this "catch-thirties" dilemma as a struggle between the "Adult" and the "Outlaw." For him, the Adult values cooperation and has the ability to perform various social roles such as husband or wife, worker, citizen, and consumer. Keen believes that the Adult has a certain measure of independence but mainly adapts to the demands of culture. Keen associates this stage with developing character and accumulating character armor. For him, the qualities of the Adult are summarized in the Boy Scout virtues: to be trustworthy, loyal, helpful, obedient, thrifty, brave, clean, and so on. The Outlaw, on the other hand, represents the undercurrents of restlessness and dissatisfaction that frequently disturb the established structure of the Adult.

According to Keen, the Outlaw commits the crime of "killing" the old authorities; it is the story of everyone "who decides to find out what life in the wild is all about" (p. 120). After years of conforming and coping, the Outlaw seeks to discover what lies beneath the duties and roles of adulthood. Keen sees this as a quest for autonomy. The Outlaw desires to explore the forces that have been held in check by the character armor built up in the process of socialization. During this time, the person questions all the old values and endures a period of experimentation, discovery, and disillusionment. Sheehy points out that marriage satisfaction often declines during the "catch-thirties" period, as couples socialize less and attend to children more. Their vision-supporting marriage of the twenties may now almost be forgotten with the practical demands of family and work life. This is the period of the life cycle when the incidence of divorce reaches its peak. Of course, to the degree that the life cycle is shifting as Sheehy describes in *New Passages* (1996), this period of discontent and reconsideration of the "catch thirties" may be pushed back to later in the thirties.

Sheehy (1978) sheds further light on the differences between women and men as they face the tasks of early adulthood. She describes six main patterns or lifestyles for women that are really various points on the spectrum between Levinson's Traditional Homemaker Figure and the Anti-Traditional Figure. The first pattern is that of caregiver, whose top priorities throughout adult life are her husband and her children. The second is the nurturer, who defers personal achievement. Although women in this group want to be caregivers, they hope to develop a career of their own after they have raised their children. Some of these women have already begun college or a job, but they take time out to care for their children and then return where they left off. Others in this group go back to school or begin their career after their children are in school or have left home. The third pattern is the achiever who defers nurturing. Women in this group devote themselves first to establishing a career, even though they intend to bear children later, often around thirty years old. The fourth lifestyle is the integrator, the woman who combines family with a career. This pattern is very hard on women unless they are married to men who also commit themselves to integrating family life and work. The fifth pattern is never-married women who represent about 10 percent of women, and the final pattern is the very small category of transient women who, according to Sheehy, do not appear to have much interest in nurturing or achieving.

The overview of young adulthood shows it to be a time of significant transition. Young people begin to find their way by tackling important tasks in life such as finding an occupation, developing a love relationship, and starting their own family. Levinson highlights the transitory nature of adult life and places in the foreground the constant challenge of adapting our identity, values, and worldview to changing circumstances. Stable periods may last five to ten years, but then give way to transitional periods lasting four or five years. This means that adulthood is not a plateau or a final place to arrive at, but rather a dynamic time, a continuous series of passages that require us to come to terms with our dreams in the context of family and social expectations and physical realities. Sheehy emphasizes the "shoulds" that greatly influence our decisions about occupation and relationships in our twenties. Part of the "Age Thirty Transition" involves a restlessness with the structures so eagerly sought, and sometimes hard won, in the twenties. This unease is often the occasion to reexamine the basic components of spirituality and implicit religion. Having established the broad contours of young adulthood, we now focus on the empirical studies that show patterns of religion and spirituality in young adulthood.

EMPIRICAL STUDIES

The pattern of religious involvement in early adulthood reflects and continues the developments we have seen in the religion of adolescence. Young adults are less religious than middle and older adults in North America and Europe (Hood et al., 1996). In Canada, Bibby (1993) found that 17 percent of eighteen- to twenty-nine-year-olds attended religious services weekly in 1990, as compared with 40 percent of those over forty-nine. He points out that this places Canada in roughly the same category of adult religious involvement as countries such as the United Kingdom, Germany, the Netherlands, Sweden, Norway, and Denmark.

Hood et al. (1996) find contradictory patterns in adult religiousness in the United States. On the one hand, there is a significant trend toward the growth of conservative churches and a marked increase in those who define themselves as "evangelical" or "born-again" Christians. On the other hand, there is a trend toward "loosening of traditional bonds" and a growing liberalism in religious ideas and attachments. They believe that these contradictory tendencies may indicate that people are moving toward the possible extremes within Western religion. At the same time, they conclude that socialization remains the most important factor in the religiousness of early adulthood. While parents exercise less influence on young adults than they do on adolescents, parents still represent the strongest single influence on patterns of religion for people in their early twenties. They add that the verdict is not unanimous on whether mothers or fathers play a greater role here, though available data suggest that mothers exert more influence.

Hood et al. (1996) recognize that the growing interest in spirituality, both within and outside mainline religion, is increasingly a characteristic of religion in early adulthood. For a large number of adults, the search for identity, values, and worldview becomes primary. If the search leads outside the bounds of mainline religion, people often seem willing to leave traditional religious communities and seek spiritual guidance and illumination wherever they can find them. Hood et al. conclude that the religion of early adulthood shows considerable variety, and people in this period often change their religious beliefs and practices as a result of their experience.

Raymond Paloutzian adds to the picture of religion in early adulthood by noting that women are consistently more religious than men in this period, and across the entire lifespan as well. He observes that there are sparse data available on the changes in people's religious views over a lifetime, but what there are seem to indicate little overall change in most religious attitudes. Paloutzian (1996) describes two significant empirical studies of religion during early adulthood. To begin, he describes a long-term study of 154 students from an all-white male college. In 1942, these students were given a questionnaire on their views about various religious topics such as God's existence, the soul, and life after death. In 1964 and again in 1984, these same people completed an identical questionnaire. The results show the relative stability of certain religious ideas held by individuals over a period of forty years. The second study Paloutzian describes is based on data gathered from over 5,000 adolescents and adults ranging from thirteen to those in their eighties. He surveyed 561 congregations from five major Protestant denominations. When the data were analyzed according to age, they showed a continuous increase in the importance given to religion, the frequency of private prayer and Bible reading, and the integration of faith.

Paloutzian (1996) emphasizes the difficulty in determining and describing exactly how religion and spirituality develop from adolescence into early adulthood. In his view, there is empirical support for those models that show a hierarchical sequence of stages into early adulthood, but there is no necessary chronological sequence beyond the earliest phase of adulthood. Paloutzian maintains that the two current models offering the most useful guidelines for understanding religious development from adolescence through early adulthood are Fowler's model of faith development and Oser and Gmuender's developmental theory of religious judgment. Both models see maturity as a capacity to deal with the major polarities and paradoxes of life. Here, we shall consider how they contribute to our understanding of religious and spiritual development in early adulthood.

Fowler's Stage Four—Individuative-Reflexive Faith

James Fowler's fourth stage of faith[1] development highlights the responsibility people have for their own identity, outlook, and commitments. Fowler emphasizes the degree of autonomy that characterizes Stage-Four faith, with the person's ability to stand alone or apart from others' perspectives. Young adults at this stage recognize that their views differ, often considerably, from those of others and therefore realize that the truth or adequacy of their outlook may require justification. While underlining the independence of this perspective, Fowler insists it is not necessarily an individualistic stage. People at this stage do not always separate from former interpersonal relationships or social and institutional ties, though they may.

Most of Fowler's subjects in early adulthood were in Stage Four. He found that, in subjects aged twenty-one to thirty years old, 40 percent were at this stage, while one third showed characteristics of both stages three and four. Fowler believes that a truly individuative-reflexive faith is rarely well developed before the early twenties. The emergence of a Stage-Four outlook occurs not infrequently in the thirties or forties, and then it is typically experienced as more disruptive to an existing identity and worldview. According to Fowler (1981), a genuine move to the Stage-Four outlook requires an interruption of reliance on external authorities. This interruption can be painful and often forces a person to reflect critically on his or her previous assumptions and values. Compared with the vague and sometimes amorphous quality of Stage-Three faith, the person at Stage Four makes his or her worldview and values part of an explicit system. The person at this stage is concerned with how various aspects of identity, values, and worldview are coherent and fit together. Fowler notes that the psychological need to preserve self-boundaries and to justify one's outlook occasionally results in representing others' views and values in the form of a caricature of their actual stance. This defensive tendency is mostly unconscious, and people at Stage Four do not usually recognize that they are creating such caricatures.

Persons who adopt the Stage-Four perspective have a rather limited appreciation of symbols, myths, and rituals. They find such symbols to be useful only if they can be "demythologized," i.e., translated into ideas and propositions that make sense to the rational intellect. People at this stage constantly want to know the meaning of these symbols presented

---

1. The earlier stages of Fowler's theory are discussed in chapter two.

in clear and unambiguous statements. In Paul Tillich's (1957) terms, the power of the symbol is thereby broken and can no longer communicate the deepest mysteries of human existence and the world. According to Fowler (1981), the symbolic power of myth and ritual is broken when the participant-questioner takes the initiative over against the symbol rather than allowing the symbol to exert its power on the participant.

Interestingly, Robert Fuller (2001) finds the people who describe themselves as "spiritual but not religious" have almost invariably entered the individuative-reflexive stage. He holds that the "spiritual but not religious" take responsibility for their own beliefs and usually have reflected on many of the critical issues raised by modern science, biblical scholarship, psychology, sociology, and philosophy. In Fuller's judgment, this reflection places them in a more mature stage of spirituality than those at the level of conventional faith, which is largely secondhand, based on loyalty and obedience, rather than firsthand experience and reflection.

Religious Judgment of Young Adults

The work of psychologists Fritz Oser and Paul Gmuender (1991) complements Fowler's research by suggesting ways in which the religious judgment of young adults differs from that of children and adolescents. Their studies are similar to the work of Piaget and Kohlberg in that they too describe an invariant and hierarchical sequence of stages based on answers to a cognitive task. People are asked to respond to questions about three dilemmas presented during the course of an interview. In one of these stories, a young physician is on an airplane which malfunctions. As the plane loses altitude, the physician's life flashes before him and he resolves to alter his future plans and devote his life to helping people in the Third World if he somehow survives the crash. Miraculously, he does survive and, when he returns home, he is faced with this dilemma: He is offered a much-sought-after position at a private clinic and must decide if he should accept this extraordinary opportunity or keep the promise he made as he faced what seemed to be certain death. After presenting the story, Oser and Gmuender pose questions: Should Paul keep his promise? Why or why not? Do people have duties to God? Should people choose their own personal freedom over against the claims of a religious community?

Oser (1991) believes that the dilemmas posed require people to deal with the tension between competing values, which he characterizes as seven bipolar dimensions that are essential aspects of religious

judgment: first, the feeling of freedom versus dependence on the Ultimate Being; second, thinking that God's activity is either transcendent
(God acts directly) or immanent (God acts through human and natural means); third, the experience of hope versus absurdity; fourth, the
transparency versus the opacity of God's will; fifth, the feeling of either
faith or fear; sixth, focusing on the holy versus the profane aspects of a
dilemma; and, seventh, seeing things as involving the eternal versus the
ephemeral. He uses these dimensions to evaluate the stage of a person's religious judgment. Oser and Gmuender conclude from their
research that the higher stages of religious judgment involve the ability
to think about both ends of each of the polarities at the same time
rather than considering only one element of the polar opposites. They
believe that the underlying structure of religious judgments can be
measured by how people are able to coordinate these polarities. Their
view that the capacity to consider both sides of polarities represents a
higher level of religious judgment supports Fowler's observations that a
higher order of faith recognizes the polar tensions in the self and that
the paradoxical nature of truth requires a person to take into account
both sides of the fundamental opposites human beings experience.
The developmental models of Fowler and Oser and Gmuender show
the religion of young adults as a matter of gradually recognizing the
tensions and complexities of life, and becoming increasingly able to
manage polar opposites without denying or ignoring one of the poles.

Allport's Characteristics of Mature Religion

This section concludes with Gordon Allport's classic formulation of
mature religion, which describes the characteristics of religion that often
begin to appear in young adulthood. His analysis of mature religion
emphasizes the power of reason to organize and integrate mental life,
the central element in the individuative-reflexive faith that characterizes young adults. Allport did not describe a developmental progression
such as we find in Fowler's stages of faith. He remarks that chronological age is a comparatively poor measure of any kind of maturity,
whether it be mental, emotional, or religious maturity. Thus his criteria
for mature religion can be seen as goals to strive for throughout adulthood, whether in the early, midlife, or late adult periods. Allport
observes that religious attitudes in particular are likely to lag behind
other areas of development because an individual's religion is usually
regarded as something private and thus not under the same environmental pressures that push people to mature in other areas of life.

Gordon Allport (1960) was one of the first major psychologists to define the characteristics of mature religion in adulthood. Like the other writers in this section, Allport argues against the view that all religion is infantile. His understanding of mature religion stands behind his influential categories of intrinsic religious orientation (devotion to religion as an end in itself) and extrinsic religious orientation (using religion as a means to self-serving ends). Originally, he developed these categories to investigate the relation between religion and racial prejudice, but, since the 1960s, his religious orientation scale has generated a flood of empirical research on many different aspects of religion.

Allport's criteria for mature religion grow out of his personality theory and ego psychology. In his view, the mature personality has three attributes: first, self-expansion, second, self-objectification, and, third, self-unification. By self-expansion, he means that a healthy person should develop a variety of interests that focus on ideals and values beyond immediate biological impulses. Self-objectification refers to the ability to be reflective and insightful about one's life. Mature people are able to see themselves as others see them and even occasionally in a cosmic perspective. Allport believes a sense of humor is an important aspect of this second attribute. Self-unification implies that a mature person has some unifying philosophy of life, even if it is not explicit or religious. This attribute provides life with direction and coherence.

According to Allport (1960), the religious sentiment often plays a major role in developing these important personality characteristics. By "sentiment," he means a personality component that joins both emotional and cognitive factors. Allport's notion of the religious sentiment includes crucial factors of spirituality, such as identity, values, and worldview. He believes that the religious sentiment synthesizes everything that a person regards as "permanent or central in the nature of things" (p. 64). Allport reminds us that this life task is always unfinished and more than any human being can actually accomplish. So while he speaks of the mature religious sentiment, he insists that mature does not mean perfect. Thus, the characteristics that Allport describes as essential to the mature religious sentiment should be seen as targets to aim for rather than as completely attainable goals. The religious sentiment can contribute to the human personality even when it is not absolutely consistent. Allport sees the mature religious sentiment as:

- well differentiated,
- dynamic,

- consistently directive,
- comprehensive,
- integral, and
- heuristic.

Well differentiated refers to the fact that the religious sentiment contains multiple interests that can be organized and woven into an intricate pattern. Initially, the child is unable to articulate the many components that make up the religious sentiment, but, with a growing capacity for critical reflection, older children and adolescents begin to sort out the various parts, reorganize them, and value some more than others. This capacity stands in sharp contrast to an immature religious sentiment based solely on imitation and blindly accepting every aspect of faith equally. According to Allport, this sorting process transforms the secondhand faith adopted from parents during childhood into a firsthand faith based on one's own experience and choices. To achieve a differentiated religious sentiment, the person reflects on such issues as the existence and nature of God, the soul and immortality, ordering values to guide life, questions about sin and freedom, and attitudes toward prayer and relations to others. Allport maintains that the particular issues will vary among different cultures and individuals, but the mature person will fit all relevant matters into a pattern that embraces an ever-widening reality.

Allport considers the dynamic aspect of the mature religious sentiment to be the most important one for distinguishing it from an immature religious sentiment. By dynamic he means that the motive energy behind the mature religious sentiment is autonomous, i.e., to a large extent independent of organic desires and childhood needs. Although Allport believes that the religious sentiment in childhood is originally rooted in the drives and desires of the body, something new emerges with the growth of personality. The religious sentiment becomes largely independent of the magical thinking, self-justification, and creature comfort that motivates immature religion.

The mature religious sentiment is consistently directive, i.e., it provides ethical standards that have a steady and persistent influence on the personality. Allport recognizes that there is no simple relationship between religion and morality; while religions do offer ethical guidelines and moral injunctions, many people believe that their morality is not dependent on religion. Increasingly, people are finding other sources of ethical guidance and moral behavior, as we have seen in some nontraditional spiritualities and in implicit religion. Allport wonders whether, in the long run, we can sustain high ethical standards without the idealism and "myth of Being" furnished by religion, but grants that nonreligious or secular spiritualities may perform the same function that he sees as essential to the mature religious sentiment.

The comprehensive character of the mature religious sentiment contributes directly to the healthy personality's need for a unifying philosophy of life to bring the disparate elements of experience into some kind of order. Allport recognizes that various secular philosophies such as humanism or communism can provide relatively powerful worldviews, bringing unity to the mind and significance to one's life. He concedes that for many people, wholehearted devotion to a secular cause may act like a religious sentiment. Commitment to such secular causes would correspond to Bailey's view of implicit religion as a commitment that expresses and embodies one's values. However, in Allport's view, even the most absorbing secular cause usually fails to include all of a person's horizons and falls short of dealing with matters central to all existence. For him, the religious worldview recognizes the wider spiritual reality in which our lives are set and thus has a greater capacity to bring together all dimensions of the human personality. Allport adds that a comprehensive outlook on reality should encourage tolerance as one comes to realize that different vantage points are necessary for fuller experience and the expression of infinite reality.

The comprehensive character of mature religion is closely connected to the fifth feature, its integral nature. The former characteristic ensures broad coverage, while the latter seeks a total design that is harmonious. The religious sentiment is able to hold everything together and find meaning in the totality. Allport sees two great challenges to the integrative task of mature religion. The first is the universal and omnipresent problem of evil. The suffering of innocent people is one of the most difficult facts of human existence to integrate into the mature religious sentiment. The Jewish Holocaust of the mid-twentieth century is often cited as such an obstacle to faith in God. Various religious traditions have struggled with the problem of evil and have come to different conclusions about its nature and meaning. Even if there are no final answers to such questions, Allport believes it is vital to wrestle with them if the religious sentiment is to become integral. The other major obstacle to integration is posed by modern science, in particular psychology. According to Allport, a mature religious sentiment must take into account the fact that much human conduct is determined by psychological and social factors beyond the individual's choice.

Finally, the mature religious sentiment is heuristic, i.e., it acts as a working hypothesis held tentatively until it is confirmed or disproved. People with a mature religious faith may have some doubt about elements of their religion, so their beliefs often have a provisional character. As Allport puts it, the mature religious sentiment is usually fashioned in the workshop of doubt. He maintains that the basic values and beliefs of religion always exceed the grasp of the inquiring mind, and so absolute certainty in these matters is not possible. Allport insists that it is better to act with optimism in the face of doubt than simply to lapse into an unproductive skepticism. He concludes that the mature religious person finds that the energy generated and the values conserved by religious faith prove that faith affirmation is superior to indecisiveness.

Allport's description of the mature religious sentiment goes beyond the institutional aspects of religion to include elements of spirituality and implicit religion, namely, identity and worldview. His criteria primarily address the cognitive aspects of religion, and he gives both reason and doubt a central place in forming the mature religious sentiment. Reason helps the mature person to clarify and differentiate the diverse elements of religion; it continually pushes the boundaries of personal experience and allows faith to become more comprehensive, and it aids personality integration by examining how various aspects of experience fit together. Allport sees doubt as a potentially valuable function of critical reason that helps the religious sentiment to mature. In this regard, he differs with those representatives of traditional religion who maintain that doubt is an obstacle that undermines religious faith, a sign of weakness or even a temptation of the Devil (Clark, 1958), and others who emphasize the pain and suffering of religious doubt, considering it a lack of integrated wholeness (Helfaer, 1972). Allport is certainly aware of the tensions and inner conflict caused by religious doubt, but he believes the overall gain far outweighs the distress experienced in religious doubt. His research emphasizes how the religious sentiment often plays a large role in helping young adults organize their mental life as they face the primary tasks of this period. Allport recognizes that the religious sentiment can help to shape a person's identity, values, and worldview in a way that integrates the richness of young-adult experiences.

Overall, the empirical studies give us an idea of general trends in the religion of young adulthood. They show that young adults are less religious than middle and older adults and that there seems to be an increasing polarization around conservative and liberal forms of religion.

These studies confirm that for a growing number of young adults, the spiritual search for identity, values, and the meaning of life lead beyond the bounds of traditional religion. Fowler emphasizes that the priority of young adults is to create and preserve their self-boundaries. This effort leads them to clarify their identity, values, and worldview in ways that distinguish them from others. Frequently, this means trying to demythologize complex religious symbols, reducing them to a set of discursive truths about human life and the nature of reality. The positive side of this tendency is that young adults may consciously sort out their beliefs and integrate them, thus transforming secondhand beliefs absorbed from parents and religious institutions into firsthand beliefs based on their own experience. The negative side of the individuative faith of young adults is that it tends to ignore the complexity of the human condition. Oser's studies describe development in religious judgment as a growth in the capacity to consider both sides of fundamental polarities such as freedom versus dependence and the holy versus the profane. Both Fowler and Oser recognize that this capacity for dealing with complexity and polarities is established in young adulthood, but usually does not fully develop until midlife. Allport underscores the unequaled power of the religious sentiment to integrate the diverse experiences of young adulthood, although some authors would say he seems to downplay, if not overlook, the role of the unconscious in personality integration.

RELIGION, SPIRITUALITY, AND PSYCHOTHERAPY

Frequently, young adults become aware of some of the most important aspects of their religion and spirituality when they encounter problems in their psychological lives, relationships, and work (Applebaum, 1985). From one perspective, every case of psychotherapy contains a crisis of spirituality, where the client's way of seeing and being in the world has somehow failed (Westbrooks, 2003). Psychotherapy is often the context in which people are forced to wrestle with their identity, values, and worldview—all key elements of spirituality, but these elements of religion and spirituality are not always apparent in the problems that cause young adults to seek psychotherapy. Part of the difficulty of observing spirituality in psychotherapy lies in the nature of the typical difficulties of young adults, namely, problems of love, work, and relationships. These issues may not always be viewed in light of their deeper spiritual implications. Another difficulty lies in the way psychotherapy has traditionally sought to distance itself from matters of values and religious beliefs.

Nonetheless, psychotherapy can help people make necessary changes in their spiritual outlook. First, it allows people to reflect on their identity and life story, thus furnishing insight as to the enduring positive features of their identity and the parts of their life story that need adjustment. By helping people to rewrite their personal story, psychotherapists work directly with the core of their spirituality and implicit religion. Second, psychotherapy helps people to revise their maps of reality to make them more accurate. It is often necessary to redraw these cognitive and moral maps as life circumstances change. Psychotherapy explores the degree to which people's worldviews reflect their actual personal and social situations rather than outmoded assumptions growing out of earlier, and sometimes traumatic, experiences. With an updated map, people are better able to find meaning in life and personal fulfillment.

The relevance of psychotherapy for understanding religion and spirituality applies to the entire adult lifespan, although its focus in young adulthood differs considerably from that of middle and late adulthood. For young adults, problems of work, relationships, and sexuality are primary. Sigmund Freud and Alfred Adler pioneered these areas of psychotherapy. Freud emphasized the importance of developing mature sexuality. When asked what constitutes good psychological health, Freud responded simply, "lieben und arbeiten," that is, the ability to love and work (Erikson, 1968). This statement concisely identifies the key challenges of young adults and where their problems are likely to develop. Adler (1964) also saw the significance of love and work for psychological health, though he focused largely on people's drive to achieve success and find satisfying human relationships. Carl Jung (1931) too found the Freudian and Adlerian perspectives fruitful in working with young adults, but his experience with patients entering midlife led him to the conclusion that another fundamental task emerges at that time, requiring a different kind of therapeutic intervention. Here, we shall consider how psychotherapy has gradually changed to accommodate patients' religious and spiritual concerns and then focus on how this change affects young adults. What we shall observe here about psychotherapy's growing awareness of important religious and spiritual issues also applies to the role of religion and spirituality in midlife and in late adulthood, which we shall consider in the next two chapters.

Changing Attitudes in Psychotherapy

In the early years of clinical psychology, psychotherapists considered themselves to be objective and value free, as psychology aspired to be scientific on the model of the natural sciences. The quest for value neutrality seemed to rule out a discussion of religion or spirituality, especially if it involved beliefs about ethics, spiritual forces, or life after death. Many therapists feared that considering patients' views regarding human nature and human destiny would go beyond the limits of a truly scientific psychology and psychotherapy. Other therapists ruled out religion in psychotherapy because they believed that religion inhibits personality growth (Ellis, 1980; Fallot, 1998b; Richards & Bergin, 2000). The clinical literature dating back to Freud and Leuba interprets mystical experience as ego regression, borderline psychosis, psychotic episodes, and temporal lobe dysfunction (Lukoff et al., 1992a). This pathologizing of spiritual experience generated therapeutic strategies designed to stop such "pathological" symptoms as quickly as possible. Hospitalization and anti-psychotic medication became the way to deal with spiritual crises even if such approaches might derail the potential growth that could derive from integrating such experiences. Hans Kung (1990) refers to this lengthy history as a repression of religion in psychiatry and psychotherapy. Thus, mental health professionals tended either to ignore or pathologize religious and spiritual aspects of life (Cortright, 1997; Lukoff et al., 1992b).

Carl Jung provided the first extensive examination of the role of religion in clinical practice (Bergin, 1980; Elkins, 1995). He recognized that the patient's religious attitudes and spirituality are at the heart of psychotherapy. Some years later, Karen Horney (1939) and Erich Fromm (1950) emphasized that psychotherapy is ultimately a vehicle for self-examination and self-realization. They saw psychotherapy as consistent with the ancient wisdom of Greek philosophy and the injunction of Apollo to "know thyself." From this perspective, techniques of modern psychotherapy such as supportive relationship, confession, suggestion, persuasion, and exhortation continue the age-old tradition of *cura animarum*, the care or cure of souls (McNeill, 1951).

Many writers have called attention to psychotherapy's growing awareness of the importance of spirituality and the spiritual dimensions of the personality (Fallot, 1998b; Lukoff, 1985; Thorne, 1998; Worthington et al., 1996). Within the last four decades, humanistic and transpersonal psychology have broadened clinical practice to include religious and spiritual issues (Lukoff et al., 1992b). William O'Donohue (1989) maintains that it is inevitable that religion and spirituality are involved in psychotherapy because psychologists are concerned with how their theories and practices fit into the larger scheme of things. He even calls psychologists "metaphysicians" because they help people clarify their identity, values, and attitude toward life. Many psychotherapists now believe that earlier aspirations toward pure objectivity and value neutrality are not compatible with the complex reality of the therapeutic situation. Increasingly, patients feel the need to articulate their values, worldview, and search for meaning, and they demand that psychotherapists assist them in sorting out these spiritual matters.

Stanton Jones (1994) argues that psychotherapy's previous negative and noninteractive stance toward religion was premised on an outmoded view of science and an overly narrow notion of professionalism. The philosophy of science at the beginning of the twentieth century maintained that either a religious explanation or a naturalistic explanation of an event or behavior (say, a vision of Jesus or speaking in tongues) could be valid, but not both (Paloutzian, 1996). This perspective assumed that an explanation or interpretation at one level contradicts the truth claim of an explanation at the other level. Many in the contemporary philosophy of science now challenge this earlier either/or perspective, dissolving the radical demarcation between natural science and other forms of human knowing such as religion (O'Donohue, 1989). Because the human being is so complex, multiple viewpoints are often necessary to capture the truth of an experience or situation. There may be useful naturalistic accounts of a vision or speaking in tongues, but these do not necessarily invalidate the meaning and value of religious interpretations of the same events. In current philosophy of science, religion and science are increasingly recognized as different but not mutually exclusive modes of knowing. So there is a growing movement within psychotherapy to include religious and spiritual concerns. Nevertheless, some studies show that a gap still exists between the religiousness of psychotherapists and their patients which may be an obstacle to dealing with religious issues.

Religiosity Gap, But No Spirituality Gap

A number of surveys and studies indicate that psychotherapy patients and the general public are considerably more religious than mental health professionals (Bergin & Jensen, 1990; Pargament, 1997). One study shows that about half of the psychiatrists surveyed describe themselves as atheists or agnostics, and almost 60 percent of psychologists do not believe in a transcendent divinity as compared with less than 5 percent of the general population who consider themselves atheists or agnostics (Lukoff et al., 1992a). Another study indicates only 18 percent of psychologists surveyed considered organized religion to be a significant dimension of their lives, in contrast to two thirds of the general population who report that religion is either very important or the most important aspect of their lives (Shafranske & Malony, 1990).

While there is considerable evidence of a religiosity gap, studies do not show a comparable spirituality gap between the general public and mental health professionals (Lukoff et al., 1993). In a survey of members of the California State Psychological Association, one third of the respondents stated that they were involved in an alternative spiritual path not connected with religious institutions (Shafranske & Gorsuch, 1984). The study concludes that most of the psychologists surveyed perceived spirituality to be important in their lives, even though they were less religious in terms of traditional religious affiliation and participation than the general public. Similarly, an American national survey of 425 psychotherapists indicates that they are involved in less conventional forms of religion (Bergin & Jensen, 1990).

The California Psychological Association study refers to this spiritual involvement as "unrecognized religiousness" and "unexpressed religiosity" and hypothesizes that psychotherapists' spiritual interests are currently unexpressed because they do not fit into the secular framework of professional psychiatry or psychotherapy. The terms "unrecognized religiousness" and "unexpressed religiosity" correspond to those areas of religion and spirituality we have designated as implicit religion, namely, patients' identity, values, and worldview. The study suggests that a willingness to be more open about this unvoiced spirituality, which they term "spiritual humanism," could bridge the "cultural gap" between a still largely secular psychotherapeutic profession and a more religious public (p. 3). It concludes that such a spiritual humanism would be welcome to a majority of the population that wants psychotherapy to be sensitive or even sympathetic to spiritual viewpoints (p. 6).

In another large survey, clinical psychologists characterized their beliefs and practices in personal rather than institutional terms, as an "alternative spiritual path which is not a part of an organized religion" (Shafranske & Malony, 1990, p. 74). In this study, "religiousness" means adherence to beliefs and practices of a religious institution and "spirituality" covers attitudes, values, worldview, and the more personal practices of a religious nature. Subjects generally considered spiritual beliefs and questioning to be valuable. Forty percent of respondents endorsed a personal, transcendent God orientation, and 45 percent were in the "quest religious orientation," which refers to a person's religiousness as a questioning attitude and open-ended dialogue with existential questions.

The psychologists surveyed in this latter study viewed spiritual and religious issues to be highly relevant in their clinical work. Sixty percent reported that their clients frequently expressed their personal experiences and outlooks in religious language. While most of the clinical psychologists thought it appropriate to know the religious background of their clients and even to use religious language and metaphors in psychotherapy, they believed it inappropriate for a psychologist to use religious texts or pray with a client while conducting psychotherapy. They recognized an important role for religion and spirituality in the clinical context so long as counseling interventions did not become too explicitly religious and participatory in nature (p. 75). Only about one third of the psychologists expressed a feeling of personal competence to assist clients with religious and spiritual issues. The psychologists' attitudes toward what are appropriate clinical interventions of a religious nature were influenced mainly by their personal religiousness and spirituality rather than any particular theoretical orientation in their psychological training.

These studies suggest an important change from earlier studies that showed most psychologists to be irreligious. Shafranske and Malony argue that because so many psychologists now recognize the relevance of religiousness and spirituality in psychotherapy, it is critical that clinical training be provided in these areas. In their view, clinical treatment of spiritual issues should be based on professional training rather than purely on the personal background and convictions of the therapist. Most of the psychologists surveyed reported that their education in psychology and religion was very limited, and 85 percent said that religious and spiritual topics were rarely or never discussed in their training. Even today, very little is being done to provide such training (Lukoff et al., 1992b). A survey of training directors for psychology internships revealed that none of them had received education or training in religious or spiritual issues, and little was being done at their internship centers to address these issues (Lannert, 1991).

Values and Psychotherapy

While there is currently little progress in training psychotherapists to work with religious and spiritual issues, a growing segment of the general public and the psychotherapeutic community consider these issues to be highly germane in psychotherapy. Many clinical psychologists today recognize the importance of discussing values and beliefs in psychotherapy (Bergin, 1980; Biggs et al., 1976; Vaughan, 1991). Regardless of therapists' own values and beliefs, they need to understand clients' religious situation as a crucial part of their life situation (Feifel, 1958). Even psychoanalysis, with its long history of critiquing religion's effect on mental health, acknowledges the significant influence of the analyst on the patient's values and worldview through analyzing the transference which is at the heart of psychoanalytic treatment. In the transference, the patient reexperiences major conflicts from the past that involve issues of identity, values, and worldview, factors central to spirituality and implicit religion (Meehl, 1959).

According to Brewster Smith (1961), values intrude into the therapeutic setting because the very definition of mental health involves values. He observes further that many people have turned to psychology for guidance on life values to fill the void left by the attrition of organized religion. The psychologist has as much right as anyone to posit values, states Smith, but those values should be recognized as a matter of personal choice and made explicit rather than disguised "under presumptive scientific auspices" (p. 306). In his view, the therapist and client should focus on the empirical consequences of particular values. Others emphasize that therapists communicate their values to patients in subtle and unintended ways, even when they try to avoid doing so (Rosenthal, 1955; Samler, 1960). Allen Bergin (1980) warns that when psychotherapists do not acknowledge their personal values, they tend to push them onto the client under the guise of professionalism and science.

Reviews of the literature on psychotherapy show that patients tend to adopt the personal beliefs of their therapist in the course of successful treatment (Bergin & Jensen, 1990; Beutler, 1981). David Rosenthal (1955) was one of the first to observe that patients who improve generally modify their moral values in the direction of their therapist's value system. At the same time, he noted that patients whose condition worsened or remained the same tended to move away from their therapist's values. Larry Beutler (1981) found that the convergence between patient and therapist in terms of beliefs and values is correlated with subsequent improvement in group and family therapy, and especially in individual therapy. This convergence of values may be seen as either good or bad, depending on what the therapist's values are.

Some believe that the values embedded in psychotherapy generally reflect the humanism, moral relativism, and hedonism of modern secular society (Rieff, 1966; Woolfolk, 1998). A national survey of mental health professionals in the United States found a high degree of consensus about a set of values that promote mental health (Bergin & Jensen, 1990). Many of these values are humanistic, including being genuine, sensitive, and nurturing; having self-control and taking appropriate responsibility; being committed in marriage, family, and other relationships; having orienting values and meaningful purposes; having self-awareness and motivation to grow; having effective strategies for dealing with stress and crises; finding fulfillment in work; and practicing good physical health habits. Although there was consensus on these important value themes, respondents differed considerably in their evaluation of how various religious and sexual lifestyles can influence mental health.

Bergin (1980) worries that therapists have become a kind of secular priesthood advocating values that may be at odds with those of their clients' religious or spiritual backgrounds. He delineates two classes of values that currently dominate the mental health professions: first, clinical pragmatism and, second, humanistic idealism. Clinical pragmatism aims to implement the values of the dominant social system and is particularly evident in psychiatry and behavior-modification psychology, where mental health is seen as the *absence of pathology*, with pathologies spelled out in manuals of clinical diagnosis such as the *Diagnostic and Statistical Manual* (*DSM-IV*). The other class of values, humanistic idealism, describes mental health in terms of positive characteristics such as flexibility, self-exploration, independence, self-actualization, honesty, interpersonal involvement, and a guiding philosophy of life.

Bergin believes it is necessary for both therapists and clients to be aware of the values directing psychotherapy as well as the values that are excluded. As useful as pragmatic and humanistic values are, he considers them to be part of the problem of our deteriorating society. In his view, religious and spiritual values are largely absent from assumptions about mental health. He maintains that alternative religious values such as theistic realism, held by a majority of the people in the United States, could be important in the therapeutic process. According to Bergin, relevant elements of theistic realism include a belief that God exists, humans are creatures of God, and unseen spiritual processes link God and humans. Some of these elements are on the border between implicit religion and explicit religion, where identity, values, and worldview may or may not be expressed in overtly religious language and metaphors. At the moment, there is no consensus about what clinicians should or should not do about aspects of spirituality and religion in therapy (Odell, 2003). In Bergin's view, psychotherapists should be willing to incorporate such theistic views whenever possible into the therapeutic process. While doing so may present practical problems for atheistic therapists, it would give an important option to many patients with religious and spiritual concerns. Bergin suggests that because values in therapy are so pervasive and often discrepant from clients' values, therapists should be explicit from the outset about their values in relation to their professional work. He even advocates that therapists publicize where they stand on the relevance of religion and spirituality in their practice.

In a similar vein, R. D. Fallot (1998b) argues for considering spiritual and religious values in psychotherapy because a great number of patients maintain that religion and spirituality are at the core of their self-understanding, providing them with deep sources of meaning, values, and identity. These patients insist that their spirituality refers to who they are, and this is more important than what they do. To overlook religious and spiritual matters seems to them to neglect an essential part of their personalities. Many patients believe that their commitment to religion and/or spirituality provides them with strength for coping, social support, a sense of coherence and the feeling of being a "whole person" (p. 9). Clinicians working with people from cultural and ethnic groups with strong religious beliefs should be aware of how such commitments function and what they mean to them. A further reason that psychotherapy should attend to religion and spirituality, Fallot adds, is that empirical studies show a positive relation between most measures of religion and most measures of mental health.

Religion and Mental Health

The relation between religion and mental health is an important issue, but the relationship is complex and the evidence contradictory. Harold Koenig's studies demonstrate that religious resources allow patients to cope more effectively with mental illness. He found that patients who relied on religious faith to cope with their illness were less depressed than those who did not. Rodney Stark's (1971) work shows that conventional forms of religious commitment are negatively related to psychopathology. On the other hand, James Dittes (1969) reports that religious people score higher than nonreligious people on anxiety measures and lower on self-esteem measures. Similarly, Milton Rokeach's study (1960) indicates that persons with stronger religious beliefs experience more tension in their lives and have more difficulty sleeping.

Gartner et al. (1991) shed further light on the inconsistencies found in studies of the relationship between religion and mental health. In a major review of over 200 studies on religion and mental health, they conclude that the results of these studies depend greatly on how mental health is defined and measured. They underscore a crucial difference between "hard measures" and "soft measures." The former are real-life events that can be directly observed and the latter are paper-and-pencil personality tests and questionnaires. They maintain that the studies based on "hard measures" of mental health show a positive relationship between religion and mental health, while studies based on "soft measures" indicate a negative relationship between religion and mental health. They argue that the studies based on real-life events and actual behavior, "hard measures," such as physical health, drug or alcohol use, sense of well-being, marital satisfaction, suicide, delinquency, and depression, have proven to be more valid and reliable than those based on paper-and-pencil tests.

In another review of the empirical literature on religion and mental health, Masters and Bergin (1992) point out that some of the ambiguity and contradictions in the findings are due to the factors chosen to measure religion. They insist that it is not enough to ask "Is the person religious?" Researchers must move on to the more telling question "How is the person religious?" They suggest using Allport's intrinsic and extrinsic forms of religious orientation as a useful way to get at how people are religious. Taking up this suggestion, Larry Ventis (1995) reviews data from sixty-one studies of the relation of religion to mental health. For each study, he determines the type of religious orientation being used to measure religion, utilizing Allport's categories of intrinsic (religion as an end in itself) and extrinsic religion (religion as a means to self-serving ends), and Daniel Batson's quest orientation (an open-ended search and a readiness to face existential questions in all their complexity). Ventis contends that each of the three religious orientations may differ in relation to mental health, depending on the measure of mental health considered. He differentiates seven common definitions of mental health that are used in the studies reviewed:

- the absence of mental illness;
- appropriate social behavior;

- freedom from worry and guilt;
- personal competence and control;
- self-acceptance and self-actualization;
- unification and organization of the personality; and
- open-mindedness and flexibility.

Ventis examines the data of these empirical studies as correlations between the three religious orientations (end, means, and quest) and the seven definitions of mental health. Extrinsic (religion as means) religiosity had no positive relationship with any of the mental health criteria. On the other hand, most of the studies showed a positive relationship between the intrinsic religious orientation and various mental health criteria. The relatively little data available on the quest religious orientation showed mixed results. It was positively correlated with mental health as open-mindedness and flexibility, and negatively correlated with absence of illness and freedom from worry and guilt. In Ventis's judgment, this review shows that the relationship between religion and mental health is complex and that certain orientations to religion have specific implications for mental health. So, although studies vary in their conclusions about exactly how religion affects mental health, it is increasingly evident that certain types of religion and spirituality have a positive effect on mental health, while other types have a detrimental effect.

Spirituality in Psychotherapy

A key development in clinical psychology's openness to dealing with religious and spiritual issues in psychotherapy was the appearance of a new diagnostic category in the *Diagnostic and Statistical Manual-IV* (*DSM-IV*), namely, the "religious or spiritual problem." The new category was proposed to offset the tendency of the mental health profession to ignore or pathologize religious and spiritual matters. A clinician's initial assessment of a powerful religious or spiritual experience can greatly influence how the experience will affect the person, whether it will be integrated as a stimulus for personal growth or repressed as a sign of mental illness. A psychiatrist's negative reaction to a mystical experience can intensify the person's sense of isolation and block efforts to understand and integrate the experience.

Paul Horton (1974) discusses a case that illuminates this point. A young woman of twenty had a powerful spiritual experience in which she felt filled with light and united with her surroundings. She tried but was unable to repeat this experience, and consequently felt outcast and sought professional help. When her psychiatrist disapproved of her spiritual experience of light and union, she feared for her sanity and jumped from a building, but survived with near-fatal injuries. Horton believes that a more accepting view of her spiritual experience by her psychiatrist would have allowed her to integrate the experience and avoid the suicide attempts that followed. The previous diagnostic manual, *DSM-III*, consistently portrayed religion in a negative light; all references to religion in the "Glossary of Technical Terms" illustrated psychopathology (Cortright, 1997; Lukoff et al., 1992b). The new *DSM-IV* attempts to be more sensitive to the increasing ethnic diversity of patients, some of whom are profoundly influenced by religion and spirituality.

Turner et al. (1995) lobbied for this change in the diagnostic manual because they believe that religious and spiritual dimensions of culture are among the most significant factors structuring human behavior, beliefs, values, and illness patterns. They note that mainstream religious institutions are declining at the same time as an increasing number of people report that they believe in God or a spiritual force, have mystical experiences, and pray or have some kind of spiritual practice. Because the trend toward secularization has created an "unchurched" but not irreligious culture, it is important for psychiatry and psychotherapy to assess and deal with spiritual problems that may not be connected with organized religion. This fact explains why there are two parts to the new category, one covering religious problems and the other dealing with spiritual problems. The new category emphasizes the nonpathological end of the spectrum of religious and spiritual difficulties. The Task Force on Changes to *DSM-III* struggled with the many factors involved in defining religious and spiritual problems and settled on the distinction that religion refers to the beliefs and practices of organized religion while spirituality indicates a transcendent relationship to a Higher Being, beyond any specific religious affiliation.

The new *DSM-IV* category is intended to deal with various types of religious and spiritual problems (Turner et al., 1995; Lukoff et al. 1992a, 1993). Some of the typical religious difficulties include marrying into a different faith; intensifying a religious practice or having a religious experience; struggling with doubt or the loss of faith; being ostracized from a religious community; wrestling with guilt due to breaking one's moral code; and suffering from emotional conflicts as a result of certain cult experiences. Carl Jung (1963) relates a vivid example of one such problem stemming from moral guilt. He cites the case of a young woman in a psychiatric hospital diagnosed as schizophrenic. In the course of analyzing her dreams, he discovered a tragic secret which she had carried with her for many years: In a depressed state, she had bathed her four-year-old daughter with contaminated water from the river near her home. While bathing the girl, she saw the child sucking on the sponge, but did not stop her. Soon after, the girl contracted typhoid fever and died. At a deep level, the mother felt that she killed her daughter. Jung helped her to confront this painful realization, and within two weeks she was discharged, never to be institutionalized again.

The range of spiritual difficulties that may enter into psychotherapy is equally wide and may include questioning a whole way of life, a purpose for living, and the meaning of life; integrating various phenomena such as a mystical experience, an NDE, kundalini awakening, a shamanistic initiatory crisis, or psychic experiences; dealing with meditation experiences that aggravate latent or preexisting problems; separating from a spiritual teacher; struggling with addictions; and coming to terms with a fatal illness. A number of these difficulties labeled as "spiritual" may be considered implicit religion in that they involve the person's identity, values, worldview, and attitude toward life. Catherine's story illustrates one example of a spiritual problem dealt with in psychotherapy. At twenty-four, she began to experience numerous instances of telepathy and precognition. Most of these experiences occurred in her dreams, though some took place as intuitions when she was awake. In one case, she dreamed the details of a child's murder that she read about two days later in the newspaper. As she followed the newspaper accounts of the murder investigation for weeks, she was horrified to learn how accurate her dream had been. On another occasion, she was startled by the dream of an explosion in a distant city where her sister lived. The next day, she learned that her sister had been injured in a natural gas explosion that leveled five houses. As these psychic experiences mounted up, she became increasingly disturbed and entered psychotherapy, fearing she was going insane. Because the mechanistic worldview of science denies the possibility of such experiences, she felt her experiences were symptoms of severe psychopathology.

This new diagnostic category signals to therapists and the general population that there are crucial experiences and struggles involving religious and spiritual issues that are not in themselves pathological, but which must be dealt with in order to avoid their degenerating into pathology. What makes this process a thorny matter in clinical practice is that religious or spiritual issues may overlap with mental disorders (Lukoff et al., 1992a, 1993). For instance, obsessive compulsive disorder may use religion as a metaphor to express compulsions; manic psychosis often contains mystical elements; manic-depressive disorder frequently expresses religious and spiritual concerns; and psychotic episodes display mystical features (Lukoff, 1985; Turner et al., 1995). Marguarite's difficulties illustrate the overlapping of religious and mental problems. She was a devout woman of twenty-five, raised in a very religious home. Her moods would swing wildly from elation at being one of the saints to despair at being a sinner. In the extreme phase of her struggle, she was diagnosed with manic-depressive disorder. Her treatment included medication, but at the same time she discussed and worked through the spiritual meaning of her highs and lows, allowing her to gain insight into her spirituality and psychological life. Clinicians must be alert to these border regions where, on one side, religious and spiritual issues are part of the profound experiences and challenges that occur within the course of normal life, but, on the other side, may slip into pathological misery.

Some of the spiritual issues involved in psychotherapy can be viewed as an intensification of experiences of the normal growth and decay of life structures. In many cases, spiritual experiences develop gradually as a person's awareness extends beyond normal consciousness. Sometimes, however, people have powerful mystical and transcendent experiences, whether or not these experiences are defined by themselves or others as traditionally religious (Applebaum, 1985). In such cases, they may lack the inner and outer resources to assimilate the experience and hence they become lost on the inward journey. Spiritual experiences such as sudden illuminations, experiences of bliss, feelings of expanding into love or unity, or the perception of inner worlds may disturb people if they occur very dramatically or very rapidly. At that point, the process of spiritual emergence becomes a *spiritual emergency*, which is defined as a difficult stage or crisis in a natural developmental process. This term suggests both a crisis and an opportunity to rise to a higher state of being (Grof, 1993). Such experiences may radically alter one's sense of self, values, and worldview, central aspects of spirituality, and implicit religion.

Brant Cortright (1997) describes the two major circumstances in which spiritual emergencies occur: first, people lack a conceptual framework to deal with what they are experiencing; and, second, people do not have the physical and emotional resilience to integrate their experiences, and consequently their self begins to fragment. He maintains that the former circumstance is less common but more easily dealt with; the therapeutic goal here is to provide a conceptual map to help orient the person and a supportive environment in which the person can fully experience the spiritual process. The latter circumstance, he states, is more common and more difficult to rectify because it may require deeper psychotherapy, experiential work, bodywork, or even medication and/or hospitalization for a time in order to slow down the disturbing process. Cortright delineates the three main patterns of response to spiritual emergencies: first, the person integrates the experience and moves forward in life; second, the person becomes overwhelmed for a period of time but then is able to integrate the experience; and, third, the person cannot integrate the experience and subsequently has difficulty adapting to everyday life.

Therapists and clients should recognize that a person's spirituality and implicit religion may not always deepen and expand the work of psychotherapy but may indeed interfere with certain aspects of psychological development (Cortright, 1997). Certain aspects of a person's identity, values, and worldview may conflict with therapeutic strategies for increasing self-knowledge and more adequate functioning. Cortright (1997) describes a phenomenon known as *spiritual bypassing* which occurs when a person uses spiritual words and concepts as a rationalization to avoid dealing with genuine psychological problems (p. 210). Cortright cites an example of spiritual bypassing in group therapy, where a young man avoids dealing with his anger by stating that he does not want to express anger because it might hurt others and that it is inconsistent with *ahimsa* (nonviolence) and "right speech." At the same time, his anger comes out indirectly and unconsciously through biting sarcasm, coldness, and aloofness. In another case of spiritual bypassing, a woman avoids facing childhood wounds under the pretext of not wanting to dig up the past because it prevents her from living in the here and now. Here, the laudable goal of being present-centered is used to avoid dealing with painful unfinished business that continues to sap her psychological energy (p. 211). Cortright notes that even the important notion of forgiveness can be used to bypass essential therapeutic work. He insists that true forgiveness cannot be brought about by sheer will; to try to force it, without first working through pain, anger, hurt, and grief, is like putting a bandage on an infected wound which continues to fester underneath.

Psychotherapy as Revising Our Personal Story

Beyond the treatment of the specific spiritual emergencies and problems just mentioned, spirituality and implicit religion are regularly involved in general psychotherapeutic work. In psychotherapy, people often rewrite their personal story which embodies their identity. In the previous chapter, we saw the important part narrative plays in adolescents' creation of identity. In psychotherapy, where people wrestle with, and sometimes alter, fundamental aspects of their identity, values, and worldview, story again plays a significant role. Roger Fallot (1998a) focuses particularly on the spiritual and religious aspects of such stories in helping people recover from mental illness. He observes that recovery narratives provide a general orienting system by placing suffering persons in relation to their immediate and larger contexts and by offering a comprehensive scheme for understanding, adapting to, and overcoming mental disorders.

Recovery stories often include crucial elements of spirituality or implicit religion. One such element is understanding oneself as a child of God or as an integral part of the larger world. This perspective can be an effective counterbalance to seeing oneself as mentally ill (Fallot, 1998a). Another spiritual element is the notion that recovery is often a long and effortful journey. This idea is found in religious traditions that see spiritual development as an arduous quest or pilgrimage. People who incorporate this view are braced for the lengthy struggle typically involved in recovering from severe mental problems. They are able to emphasize their own responsibility and activity rather than expect a quick or magical solution to the difficulties attending their illness. Hope and loving relationships are other important spiritual factors for recovery. Hope is essential for coping with severe mental disorders. For many, a belief in God's benevolence or the idea that there is a force in the world allied with good allows the mentally ill to maintain a hopeful attitude. For those who believe in a personal God, the experience of divine love can provide a significant loving relationship. Those who feel themselves strengthened by such a relationship with God are able to tolerate stress more readily and are more willing to take initiative. According to Fallot, many people include in their recovery stories the important role played by their faith communities and spiritual practices such as prayer and meditation.

The appreciation of narrative has also found its way into psychoanalytic treatment. Spence (1982) remarks how psychoanalysis has gradually moved from the search for historical truth (seen in Freud's early metaphor of psychoanalysis as the archeology of the psyche in search of biographical facts) to the recognition that it is the "narrative truth" of an interpretation which is effective for the patient's insight and self-understanding. The facts alone are insufficient; they require a story to set them in context. While Spence admits that there is the actual historical "kernel of truth" in every interpretive construction, this is less important than creating a coherent and consistent account of events. This represents a shift from the discovery of psychological artifacts to the creation of a healing story. Spence describes the process by which this narrative truth takes hold of the analysand. First, the analyst's interpretation creates an idea or psychological connection; once it is shared with the analysand, it becomes increasingly familiar and plausible; finally, it is accepted as completely true. So, in psychoanalysis, story involves the analyst's creative insights and interpretations taking hold of the analysand. This new story generates a perspective that can free the analysand from the previous story characterized by neurotic conflict, along with the identity, values, and worldview embedded in that story.

Schafer (1980) describes the psychoanalytic process in similar terms. For him, the patient tells his or her story and the analyst retells it, highlighting certain features and interrelationships within the story. The analyst's interpretive retelling organizes the elements of the original story in a new way, transforming the narrative from the story about the problems of an incohesive self to the story about the insights and understanding of a more integrated self. By controlling the way in which events in psychoanalysis are told, the analyst creates a cluster of more or less coordinated new narratives that establishes a healthy identity and a more effective way of dealing with personal and interpersonal difficulties. Thus, revising the personal story at the core of one's identity, spirituality, and implicit religion is often central to psychotherapeutic change.

Psychotherapy as Redrawing Our Map of Reality

Psychotherapy also attends to the patient's worldview, another central aspect of spirituality and implicit religion. Odell (2003) states that issues surrounding the patient's worldview are the deepest, most personal, and most significant in psychotherapeutic work. Human beings need a moral and cognitive map of the universe to orient themselves and counteract "ontological anxiety" (Frank, 1977). A person's worldview includes a set of beliefs about the nature of reality and the meaning of life. According to Scott Peck (1978), people's ideas about reality frequently cause them psychological difficulties. He uses the metaphor of drawing a map of reality to characterize how people come to see and deal with the world (p. 44). If our view of reality is accurate, it is like having a map with which to navigate the course of life. An accurate map allows us to know where we are and how to get to where we want to go. If our view of reality is inadequate or false, then our map is less reliable and we are likely to get lost along the way.

Peck explains why so many people encounter problems with their map of reality. First, human beings are not born with such maps. A great deal of effort is required to construct a moral and cognitive map of reality. The more we are able to perceive and appreciate reality, the more accurate our map will be. Peck maintains that many people are unwilling or unable to expend the time and energy to make necessary alterations to their reality maps as life continues to unfold. Because the world and our place in it are constantly in flux, we are required to revise our worldview continually. When we are children, dependent on our parents for safety, the world looks one way. During the adolescent quest for identity, the world looks quite different. When we are preoccupied with the tasks of early adulthood, the world looks different yet again, and so it goes throughout life. We are continually forced to increase our understanding of reality or be left with an outdated and inaccurate map. According to Peck, clinging to an outmoded view of reality is a source of psychological misery and much mental illness.

Psychoanalysts try to get at such obsolete and problematic worldviews by analyzing the transference. Peck redefines the transference as a set of ways of perceiving and responding to the world, derived from childhood, which may have been appropriate to the childhood environment, but which is inappropriately transferred into the adult world. He contends that when psychotherapists help people work through transference problems, they are helping them revise their map of reality. In his view, the attempt to revise an outmoded worldview map is essentially a search for the truth. Mental health requires dedication to reality and the courage to face painful truths. Both worldview analysis and the quest for truth are central aspects of implicit religion and spirituality involved in psychotherapy. Those who stop making the effort to revise and update their reality maps are left with misleading and narrow worldviews. Peck estimates that by the end of middle age, most people feel certain that their maps of the world are complete and lose interest in gaining new information and continuing to explore the mystery of reality.

According to Odell (2003), fundamental work with the client's worldview is necessary even when the therapist and client share the same labels such as "Christian" or "spiritual." He believes that psychotherapeutic worldview analysis requires the therapist to ask about the patient's specific worldview as well as to reflect on his or her own worldview. Worldview analysis should be explicit in psychotherapy in order to avoid the danger of manipulating the patient toward the therapist's worldview. Where there is worldview incompatibility between the psychotherapist and the client, the client is usually being asked implicitly to give up or significantly adjust his or her worldview. In Odell's view, the therapist often deliberately influences clients away from their worldview and values, while operating within his or her own worldview. He maintains that the therapist's job is not to shape clients' worldview and spiritual values, but to help them explore the ramifications of that worldview as broadly as possible. Frequently, the therapist and client are not overtly aware of this process, and Odell insists that both need to become aware of it to ensure that the worldview aspect of the client's spirituality or implicit religion is respected.

Young adults often explore and develop the fundamental aspects of their spirituality and religion while in psychotherapy. Psychotherapists are increasingly aware of the central role values play in the course of their work. While there are still therapists who believe that religion militates against mental health, many now recognize that only certain types of religious orientation interfere with psychological development and that patients often benefit from becoming more aware of how their spirituality affects their lives.

While there may be a religiosity gap between the general public and mental health professionals, no corresponding gap in spirituality and implicit religion appears to exist. Surveys show that many psychotherapists are themselves engaged in alternative spiritual paths, allowing them to appreciate and work effectively with the spirituality and implicit religion of their clients. Psychotherapists who consider themselves to be on a spiritual quest are in a good position to understand how identity, values, and worldview play a major part in people's mental health and illness.

EXAMPLES OF RELIGIOUS AND SPIRITUAL EXPERIENCES IN YOUNG ADULTHOOD

Richard's Story

Richard was engrossed in his work most of the time. His wife, Julie, and their two children saw him only on weekends, because he was on the road during the week driving a truck. While he found it frustrating not to have much time with his family, he wanted to provide them with what he considered a comfortable style of life. He felt he had no choice but to keep up the hectic pace, though there were times when he felt that he hardly knew his wife and children. A remarkable experience during a deer-hunting trip with friends signaled an important change in his life when he was twenty-seven years old.

Richard went out at dawn to take his hunting position near a meadow and woods. He was there watching for about half an hour. As the sun rose, he was struck by the beauty of the light on the trees and grass. Suddenly, he felt paralyzed and could only watch as three deer appeared at the edge of the woods. He just stared at them. Then he saw a large stag emerge from the shadows of the woods behind them. In a state of shock, he saw light radiate from this magnificent animal. He had no idea how long he was observing this scene, as time seemed to stop. Richard said later that he felt he was in a kind of trance and did not even recall seeing the deer disappear back into the woods. For the next couple of hours, he sat there alone, disoriented and trying to recover his bearings.

Richard felt subdued for the rest of the hunting trip. When he returned home, he told his wife about his strange experience and said he was worried that he might be losing his mind. Julie suggested that he see a psychotherapist to sort out this matter. In the course of therapy, he was able to see this experience as an invitation to appreciate a wider dimension of life. He used this opportunity to reevaluate his priorities and recognize a sacred aspect of his life that he had previously ignored. Richard decided to cut back on his working hours in order to spend more time with his family. As he looks back on this event, he sees it as one of the most important experiences in his life, causing a major change in his attitude and values.

Maureen Hason

Maureen was in an unhappy marriage.[2] When she was twenty-nine years old, she and her husband decided to attend a weekend retreat for marriage enrichment. The theme of the final day of the retreat dealt with unconditional love and how important that was to a successful marriage. Maureen puzzled over the meaning of unconditional love and how this might apply to her marriage. At the break, she wanted to be alone and think about this matter, so she returned to her room. As she sat in her room trying to understand the meaning of unconditional love, she was startled to see Jesus appear in front of her. He stood

2. Maureen's experience is recorded in Wiebe (1997, pp. 70–72).

before her in a white robe, extending his arms toward her. His hair and beard resembled traditional images of him. Although he did not say anything, she felt that he knew and loved her. She began to weep.

Maureen sees this event as the turning point in her life. She suddenly understood aspects of her faith that had previously eluded her. After this religious encounter, Maureen imagined that many believers have similar visions, but she was surprised to discover that they were relatively rare. She believes that she had this religious experience because she is a doubter by nature and needed something striking and unusual to strengthen her faith. This event heightened her sense of identity and strengthened her religious beliefs. It also clarified her worldview, convincing her that God governs every aspect of life.

Gianna Talone

Gianna Talone of Scottsdale, Arizona, was thirty years old when she had her first religious experience.[3] She had a vision of Jesus' mother in which seven people were kneeling at Mary's feet while two people were standing nearby. This event disturbed and disoriented her so much that she telephoned her parish priest, Father Jack Spaulding, to tell him about it. She feared she might be going crazy and was somewhat relieved to hear that she was not the only person to tell Father Spaulding about recent visions. Eight other people between the ages of nineteen and thirty-one had already contacted him about voices speaking to them. Father Spaulding agreed to meet with all of them in a prayer group to provide them with mutual support and guidance. This support and acceptance of her vision meant a great deal to Gianna, strengthening her religious identity and worldview.

She had a doctorate in pharmacology from the University of Southern California and had been a fashion model and appeared in different television series. These extraordinary experiences motivated her to dedicate her life to serving others. Gianna and her husband, a physician specializing in internal medicine, now involve themselves in a medical care center for the rural poor, going out daily in a van stocked with medical supplies to sick shut-ins and those with no other access to a doctor. Their goal is to bring medical care, compassion, and dignity to the poverty-stricken sick.

---

3. Gianna's story is found in Connell (1996, pp. 283–296).

SUMMARY

For many, young adulthood is a time when they solidify personality developments begun in adolescence. We can see this process particularly as they face the main life tasks of this period. Finding a suitable occupation, developing satisfying relationships, and establishing a family can go a long way toward creating the identity of the young adult. In the course of these activities, people come to realize which values matter most to them and what the world is really like. The identity, values, and worldview developed during this time provide the main elements of the young adult's spirituality and life structure. However, Levinson has helped us to appreciate the transitory nature of these life structures; adulthood is not a plateau we arrive at, but a constantly changing reality.

Table 7 of the movement of spiritual development shows that young adulthood usually is centered at the *personal level* of development.

Table 7: Implicit Religion and Spiritual Development in Young Adulthood

	Self-Stream	Values Stream	Worldview Stream
Transpersonal Level			
Personal Level	A. Identity focused on job and relationships	B. Values centered around establishing self and family in the world	C. The world seen as manageable through reason and effort
Prepersonal Level			

At this stage, all aspects of spirituality and implicit religion are influenced by the main tasks of young adulthood. Identity (A) is usually built around occupation, relationships, and establishing a family. Values (B) revolve around efforts to establish oneself in the adult world, with corresponding goals and responsibilities. Worldview (C) is increasingly influenced by science, which portrays the world as controllable. Life is seen as manageable through reason and effort.

Even as young adults are establishing their identity, occupation, and close relationships, they often feel undercurrents of restlessness. While solid structures offer stability, they also entail restrictions. Frequently, toward the end of the early adult period, young adults have second thoughts about the life structure created in their twenties. The crucial question arises: To what degree does the foundation of young adult personality reflect family, social, and cultural pressures, and to what extent does it express the deepest currents of one's unique nature?

Keen dramatizes this conflict between the desire for structure and the desire to explore and change by stating that the Adult stage is followed by the Outlaw stage.

Spiritual development in the period of young adulthood is often marked by creating and preserving personal boundaries of identity and worldview. Young adults tend to emphasize their control over the forces of life and the qualities that distinguish them from others. Thus they fashion a "unique" identity and a worldview that fits with their experience and supports their current life tasks. They often simplify the world in this process and translate complex religious symbols into rational statements about a more or less predictable reality. This oversimplification is one factor behind the relatively low religious participation shown in empirical studies of young adulthood as compared with middle and late adulthood. The world seems quite manageable by rational means and does not require recognizing transcendent experiences that reveal a more complex and mysterious world.

Young adults frequently downplay the fundamental polarities of life and hold at bay contradictory realities that threaten the personality structures they have created. According to Gould's view, a major part of spiritual development for the young adult is to become aware of, and come to terms with, the faulty assumptions that shore up the personality during this period. Often a painful clash with the unbending realities of life forces young adults to realize the limitations of their current spirituality and implicit religion. For many, this clash with reality leads them to reevaluate their identity, worldview, and life structure. At such times, young adults may turn to some form of counseling or psychotherapy to help them adjust to new and sometimes complicated realities. In this context they may reexamine their identity, life story, values, and worldview. Psychotherapists may help them adjust their identity and reframe their life story, putting emerging realities in a broader and more fertile context. Psychotherapy may also help them redraw their maps of reality to accommodate new experiences. Such a revision of their life story and worldview is often at the heart of young adults' spirituality and implicit religion.

CHAPTER FIVE

THE MIDLIFE PASSAGE AND TRANSFORMATION

——————— ❧ ———————

Midway this way of life we're bound upon,
I woke to find myself in a dark wood,
Where the right road was wholly lost and gone.
Ay me! How hard to speak of it — that rude
And rough and stubborn forest! The mere breath
Of memory stirs the old fear in the blood.
— Dante Alighieri, *The Divine Comedy*

I felt that something had broken within me on which my life had always rested, that I had nothing left to hold on to, and that morally my life had stopped. . . . All this took place at a time when so far as all my outer circumstances went, I ought to have been completely happy. . . . And yet I could give no reasonable meaning to any actions of my life. And I was surprised that I had not understood this from the very beginning.   — Leo Tolstoy, *My Confession*

The midlife transition has become generally recognized as a major event in the life cycle. Today, even in ordinary conversations, we hear about people having a midlife crisis. One of my middle-aged friends bought a motorcycle and began seeking dangerous adventures that greatly disturbed his wife and family. Another friend left her husband to start a new career and develop a whole different circle of friends after she turned forty. These outward and sometimes startling events may cause tremendous disruption for those in the middle years, as well as for their family and friends.

While such changes may dramatize the midlife passage, they are only part of an important transition, which may or may not involve a crisis.

This chapter focuses on the role of religion and spirituality in the midlife transition. Here, as in the previous chapter, insights from psychotherapy help to highlight the deepest developments of this period. The overall movement of spiritual development often reaches the transpersonal level of identity, values, and worldview during the midlife passage. Two examples illustrate how striking these religious and spiritual changes can be.

Next, we explore how the personal story constructed in adolescence and young adulthood is influenced by the timeless stories of mythology. The collective stories of myth provide a broad map of spiritual development and help situate the evolving personal story of the individual in a larger meaningful context. The many variations of the hero myth symbolize and guide the age-old quest for self-realization. Even when people no longer seem able to understand the symbolic language of myth, they continue to generate personal myths that shape their life story. Finally, we consider how myths and metaphors help us to picture the invisible processes of religious and spiritual development that are so important in the midlife passage.

BROAD CONTOURS OF MIDLIFE

Daniel Levinson sees the midlife transition as a dividing line between early and middle adulthood. In his view, this passage usually occurs sometime between the ages of forty and forty-five and represents a time when people review their lives and reappraise what they have done up to that point. This reassessment is more thorough and foundational than the one that may occur at the "Age Thirty Transition." In the earlier transition, people have second thoughts about the life structure created in their twenties and may have regrets about how they have met the main tasks of early adulthood, with all the limitations and restrictions that accompany their jobs, relationships, and family life. Levinson (1996) describes the tensions of the earlier transition as a clash between passions and ambitions from within and family and social demands from without. By contrast, he sees the midlife transition as rooted in a gradual decline in physical and psychological powers, which, for many, is experienced as a loss of vitality and a growing emptiness. He recognizes great individual differences in how people come to face midlife changes, but he maintains that there are crucial tasks that challenge most people at this time in life.

According to Levinson, three major tasks face people at midlife. The first is reviewing one's life to see how the present reality compares with the early dream that shaped the novice period of adulthood. This review leads to the second task, namely, modifying the existing life structure in order to bring it closer to one's current emotional and spiritual needs. This change includes trying out different behaviors and testing new choices. The third task is coming to terms with the major polarities that can cause inner tension and even division in one's life. In Levinson's view, the major polarity people struggle with at midlife is young/old, but the polar opposites of destruction/creation, masculine/feminine, and attachment/separateness may also contribute to the malaise of midlife.

Gail Sheehy places a great deal of emphasis on the midlife passage, even though she believes it is now frequently experienced about ten years later in the life cycle than it was in the 1950s. The range of ages marking the midlife passage (thirty-five to fifty-five years old) show that the term "midlife" is not very precise, referring roughly to the middle period of adult life. Sheehy describes some of the main factors that shape this passage to "second adulthood." In her view, the most fundamental shift occurs as we begin to experience our own perishability. Often the death of a parent occurs during this period, bringing our own mortality into focus as we realize that we are "next in line" in the cycle of generations. She adds that the death of the remaining parent is one of the most consistent crisis points in a person's evolving sense of self. According to Sheehy, a vague awareness emerges that the forces of decay are not entirely outside us, and even our own death dwells within. There is a growing sense that time is starting to squeeze and may not allow us to realize the dreams and possibilities of early adulthood. There is often grieving to be done as we see parts of our old self dying.

Sheehy (1996) refers to the midlife passage as "middlescence" (p. 82) to call attention to the similarities between this period and adolescence. In middlescence, people often lose their bearings and react to their disorientation in ways that resemble teenagers' sometimes frantic attempts to cope with rapid changes in their bodies and environment. People often describe the feelings accompanying the midlife passage as a sense of fainting, vertigo, losing one's balance, and being in a state of suspended animation. Sheehy maintains that the midlife passage is frequently the time when people become aware of underdeveloped aspects of their personalities. Men often begin to get in touch with a previously neglected receptive and nurturing side of their personalities, while women may become more aggressive and more interested in tasks and accomplishments. This development is part of what Sheehy refers to as the "sexual diamond," an image of the changing relationship between males and females throughout the life cycle.

Diagram 6: The Sexual Diamond

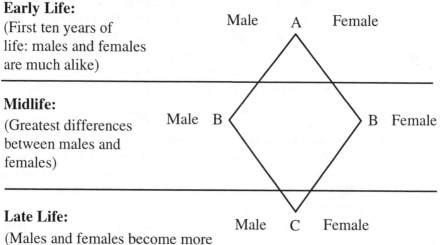

Early Life:
(First ten years of life: males and females are much alike)

Male   A   Female

Midlife:
(Greatest differences between males and females)

Male   B   B   Female

Late Life:
(Males and females become more like each other again)

Male   C   Female

The top of the diamond (A) indicates the years before puberty when males and females are much alike. The breadth of the diamond (B) shows that male and female personalities become most different from each other in the late thirties. The bottom of the diamond (C) signals an increasing convergence, when males and females again become more like each other.

Sheehy (1996) emphasizes the physiological basis for this male and female convergence at midlife. She notes that, as women enter midlife, the ratio of the "female" sex hormone, estrogen, to the "male" sex hormone, testosterone, decreases significantly. The ratio of testosterone to estrogen in postmenopausal women may be up to twenty times higher than in premenopausal women. She believes this midlife period of testosterone dominance contributes to a resurgence of adventurousness and assertiveness in women. For middle-aged men, there is a corresponding shift in the opposite direction: the ratio of testosterone to estrogen becomes much lower than in young men. These hormonal changes represent the physiological substructure of the psychological and spiritual changes observed in women and men during the midlife passage.

Erik Erikson (1995) emphasizes that the ethical dimension generally reaches maturity at midlife. He places the midlife passage in the context of the struggle between generativity and stagnation. Erikson extends the notion of generativity beyond its biological meaning, as procreating children, to include caring for following generations. He describes the main virtue to be cultivated throughout adulthood as care, beginning with care of one's family and gradually extending to an ecological care for the world. In this regard, he considers the teaching instinct to be as fundamental as the sexual instinct because it ensures that one's offspring have the values and skills required for life.

In Erikson's view, care builds on love (the capacity to commit oneself to others) and fidelity (the ability to stick by commitments). With the full development of the virtue of care, human beings are able to transcend a too-narrow allegiance to their own family or group. Erikson (1995) coins the term *pseudospeciation* to indicate the human tendency to split humanity into imaginary separate species, encouraging people to reject others as subhuman. This defensive tendency creates a kind of tribal consciousness and racist identity that threatens to undermine the harmony, and even the survival, of humankind. According to Erikson, only a universal ethic based on the principle of *reciprocity* can overcome the fatal flaw of pseudospeciation. Reciprocity, he holds, is common to all the world religions and enshrined in ethical principles such as the Golden Rule and compassion. In terms of spirituality and implict religion, Erikson shows the midlife development as a broadening of identity, values, and worldview to include the entire species and the interconnectedness of all things. Some see Erikson's emphasis on generativity and care as a "pragmatic spirituality" that joins rather than divides people (Rubinstein, 1994).

Carl Jung was the first psychologist to give a modern formulation of the midlife transition (Elkins, 1998; Levinson et al., 1978). He saw this period as a major turning point that divides the preoccupations of early adulthood from the primary work of the second half of life. Jung distinguishes between the morning of life, which in his view ends at around thirty-five to forty years of age, and the afternoon of life. The main tasks of life's morning enable the conscious personality to extend life's horizons beyond the world of the family and to manage the demands of the external world. The adolescent quest for identity and the tasks of early adulthood form a major part of the preoccupations of life's morning. Education and socialization contribute greatly to personality formation during this period of life.

The afternoon of life is a very different matter, in Jung's view. If life's morning is directed primarily toward adapting to the external world, the afternoon is about becoming more aware of, and coming to terms with, the inner world. According to Jung, a "diminution of personality" occurs as people focus their psychological energy on the demands of family and work in the first half of life. This diminishment of personality is a consequence of neglecting the inner life, leading to a one-sided personality (Jung, 1930). Jung believes that early personality development is mainly about strengthening ego consciousness and creating the *persona*, a Greek word that means "mask," referring to the masks that actors wear as they play a role. The *persona* embodies the various roles people play in life, such as wife, mother, daughter, or career person. In Jung's view, people become increasingly identified with these roles and subsequently ignore important aspects of their inner lives.

During the midlife passage, neglected and repressed personality elements may become split off from the conscious personality and develop a life of their own as unconscious processes. They may interfere with normal functioning by producing a host of symptoms such as boredom, a sense of meaninglessness, self-destructive thoughts and acts, depression, anxiety, and compulsive behavior. Jung analyzes these symptoms as the psyche's way of signaling the conscious personality that something is wrong and needs attention. The message is that "business as usual" is not working. Changes have to be made. Jung's prescription for the malaise of a midlife crisis is to reconnect with one's neglected inner reality. He recommends cultivating an attitude of attention to the inner world of emotions, intuition, and dreams. In the section on transpersonal perspectives, we will discuss Jung's view of the midlife transformation in more detail.

EMPIRICAL STUDIES

When it comes to empirical research, there is relatively little said specifically about midlife religion and spirituality (Hood et al., 1996). Peter Benson's (1992) study of 561 Protestant congregations provides some information about midlife religion inside these churches. He asked questions about the importance of religion, the frequency of private prayer, Bible reading, and church attendance. According to this study, those in midlife (ages from thirty to fifty years old) show a gradual increase in each of the areas surveyed, as compared with those in adolescence or early adulthood.

Wade Roof's (1993, 1999) research on the "baby boom" generation in the United States suggests three main patterns of midlife spirituality, which he labels "loyalist," "returnee," and "dropout." Loyalists remained within their original religious traditions through midlife.

Returnees left their original religious tradition to experiment with various forms of religion and spirituality before returning to traditional mainstream religion at midlife. Dropouts included those who left traditional forms of religion or were never associated with the mainline religions. The returnees and dropouts represented a substantial number, more than 60 percent of those from religious backgrounds.

Roof (1993) observes that attendance at religious services has become increasingly a matter of personal choice for these baby boomers as they reach midlife. Those Roof refers to as "intense seekers" think of themselves as spiritual rather than religious. Exposure to the 1960s, with its questioning of established authority and experimentation with altered states of consciousness, may have helped to shape the attitudes toward religion and spirituality of those currently in midlife.

Fowler's Stage Five: Paradoxical-Consolidative Faith

James Fowler's research sheds further light on midlife spirituality. While he does not link the stages of faith development to age, his fifth and sixth stages aptly characterize the major spiritual and religious changes of midlife. Fowler (1981) admits experiencing great difficulty when he attempts to describe Stage Five, which he calls paradoxical-consolidative or conjunctive faith. At this stage, the person goes beyond the self-certainty and "either/or logic" of the previous stage to recognize that human beings and reality are much more complex than articulated in the earlier individuative-reflexive stage. This recognition rarely happens before age thirty, according to Fowler, and most often occurs at midlife, if at all. In this stage, one begins to realize that the clear boundaries of identity and worldview constructed in Stage Four overlook much of life's complexity in an effort to adapt successfully to reality.

People at Stage Five take a deeper and broader look at their past, coming to terms with the personal and social unconscious, including myths, values, and prejudices built into the self-system already achieved. They become aware of the accidents of their upbringing, such as their family's ideals and values, ethnic identity, sex, race, religious tradition, social class, and geographical region, and how these influence their outlook. At this stage, people are ready for an identity beyond the boundaries of tribe, race, class, or ideology. To put it in psychological terms, people begin to realize that the conscious ego is not the master in its own house and does not rule the personality.

Truth is now understood as more paradoxical than it previously appeared to be. People at this stage are able to live with apparent contradictions because they appreciate that truth can be apprehended from various standpoints. They are able to see many sides of issues and situations simultaneously, embrace polar opposites, and risk altering their own perspectives, values, and material conditions. Fowler (1981) describes the style of knowing at this stage as dialogical, by which he means that the known is allowed to speak and the knower is listening. People at this stage seek to accommodate their "knowing" to the "known" rather than to impose expectations and categories on what is known. This attitude attends to things as they are, rather than trying to control them or shape them for one's own purposes.

This style of knowing influences the person's attitude toward symbols. Where people at Stage Four question symbols and translate them into concepts, those at Stage Five are aware of the limits of this strategy. At the conjunctive stage, people acknowledge that the depth and reality of symbols escape all efforts to reduce them to clear statements. Paul Ricoeur (1978) refers to this appreciation of the nonreducible value of symbols as "second naivete," where one accepts again the power and initiative of symbols to convey truths and realities that cannot be captured by critical reason alone.

Fowler maintains that the outlook of Stage Five is not something that can be taught, but arises from the reflective interaction with other people and the circumstances of one's life. He asserts that this perspective presupposes a wide range of life experiences, including suffering and loss, responsibility and failure, as well as the grief that accompanies irrevocable commitments of life and energy. People at this stage experience the pain, struggles, and divisions of the human race, and recognize the possibilities of a more inclusive and harmonious situation. They are able to live with ambiguity, apparent irrationalities, and the mysteries of human existence. The paradox of this stage, according to Fowler, is that while people recognize the importance of justice, they focus on the need to preserve their own well-being. There is a tension between these conflicting loyalties. The impulse to self-preservation and the survival needs of their family and group temper their desire to sacrifice themselves for the requirements of justice.

Stage Six: Universalizing Faith

At Stage Six, people overcome the paradoxical conflict between concern for themselves and the needs of the larger world. They become heedless of personal consequences to respond to the demands of absolute love and justice. According to Fowler, such people commit themselves entirely to transforming the present state of the world into its transcendent possibilities. Their zeal for universal moral and religious values and their inattention to self-preservation may challenge our usual ideas of normalcy and psychological balance. Such people seem to defy the typical human preoccupation with survival and security. Fowler states that their ultimate respect for life and nonviolent strategies constitutes an affront to practical realism and self-interest, frequently creating conditions where they become martyrs at the hands of those they seek to change.

This willingness of Stage-Six persons to sacrifice their lives for the sake of justice or love indicates *an alteration in their sense of self.* Fowler speaks of a "significant epistemological shift" to characterize their feeling of oneness or unity with the world and the deepest aspirations of humanity. Their extension of the usual self-boundaries to include humanity and the world relativizes the status and significance of the individual ego. The person at Stage Six experiences a larger identity than the ego identity which is so carefully nurtured throughout the early stages of life. Now, the person identifies with all humans and even with Being itself. Fowler admits that this stage is exceedingly rare and that his description of it pales before the reality of actual universalized people, a reality that goes beyond the common categories of personality analysis.

Ultimately, Fowler (1981) believes that the only way to grasp this stage is by studying the lives of those who incarnate this universalized faith, such as Mohandas Gandhi, Martin Luther King Jr., and Mother Teresa. He adds that to embody the qualities of this stage does not mean to be a perfect human being, nor even a "self-actualized person" or "fully functioning human being" in terms of psychological health. The extraordinary commitment and vision of such people often coexist with psychological and moral blind spots and limitations in leadership ability, according to Fowler. He grants that a radical monotheistic faith influences his description of Stage Six, and a Jewish-Christian image of faith in the Kingdom of God informs his view of the end point of faith development. To those who see this view as a kind of religious and cultural imperialism, Fowler responds that drawing from a particular religious tradition to express the goal of faith development does not necessarily deny its possible truth. He also believes that this image of the highest level of his theory is consistent with the central thrust of all of the great religious traditions.

The empirical studies provide useful background for our attempts to understand midlife religion and spirituality. Benson's study indicates that there is a gradual increase in religious activity in midlife as compared with adolescence and young adulthood. Roof emphasizes the diversity of midlife religion and a growing trend toward an eclectic spirituality that is largely independent of a single religious tradition. Fowler rounds out the empirical view by showing that the faith developing at midlife increasingly recognizes the great complexity of human beings and reality. Coming to terms with this more complex reality can mean a new appreciation of symbols and their power to apprehend both conscious and unconscious dimensions of our paradoxical and mysterious world.

TRANSPERSONAL PERSPECTIVES

Ken Wilber: The Spectrum of Consciousness

Two basic paradigms lie behind transpersonal research and theory as it has developed over the last thirty years: the structural-hierarchical model hypothesized by Ken Wilber and the dynamic-dialectical framework formulated by Carl Jung (Washburn, 1988). Wilber has been the most prominent contemporary theorist in transpersonal studies and virtually defined the field of transpersonal psychology in the 1980s (Rothberg, 1998b). Hailed as the Einstein of consciousness research, Wilber (1977, 1981, 1982) brings together a remarkably broad range of sources from contemporary psychology and comparative religion within a transpersonal framework. His integrative approach views various psychological and philosophical theories as points on a full spectrum of consciousness and experience. The central idea behind all of Wilber's work is that there is a fundamental drive that propels matter and life toward Spirit. This is the impetus behind physical, biological, and cultural evolution. Wilber (1993b) understands this core idea to be in the tradition of the "perennial philosophy," which holds that there is a common view of the nature of reality, knowledge, ethics, and spirituality underlying all of the world's religions and spiritual traditions, despite their surface differences.

Wilber (1981) traces human evolution from infancy to self-realization at the individual level, and from the earliest hominids to contemporary societies at the collective level. He sets the development of the individual in a larger, evolutionary context, describing five broad stages in the development of human consciousness. In the first stage, the sense of self is determined by the physical being and the elementary forces of nature. During the second stage, consciousness gradually becomes differentiated from the body's physiological base. He characterizes the consciousness of this period as a kind of magical and dreamlike thinking. The third stage of consciousness, the mythical stage, emerged with the development of more complex forms of language about 12,000 years ago, according to Wilber. Cultural myths grew up during this stage to structure the human sense of self and reality. The fourth period of consciousness, the rational stage, is a relatively recent development which, in Wilber's judgment, evolved within the last 4,000 years. It is characterized by the differentiation of an individual ego or personal consciousness.

The rise of ego consciousness and self-reflection permits the individual to move beyond strictly instinctual and socially determined behavior, but it also alienates the mind from the body. Wilber sees the inability of the ego to integrate its physiological and social foundations as our culture's primary dilemma. As rationality has become valued over instinct and individualism over community, a widening dualism threatens the unity of embodied human consciousness. The fifth stage of consciousness, which Wilber sees rising in our own time, presses toward a higher level of integration that can reunite the individual ego with its physiological and social foundations. Wilber labels the emerging stage of human consciousness "centauric." The name "centaur" refers to the being in Greek mythology which was part human and part horse; in art, the centaur has been portrayed as a human being from head to waist, attached to the body of a horse. According to Wilber, the centaur symbolizes a "perfect state of at-one-ment" of mind and body, the integrated and total self.

In Wilber's view, cultural evolution is the nourishing backdrop of individual development. Culture largely establishes the models and limits of personal development, though Wilber recognizes that there are always persons in any given society whose individual developmental stage goes beyond the collective stage of consciousness of that society as a whole. Wilber (1995) sees these cultural forms of consciousness as parallel to the stages of individual cognitive development described by Piaget. The first cultural stage corresponds to the sensory-motor stage of child development; the magical consciousness of humanity's second stage is like Piaget's preoperational stage; the mythical consciousness of the third stage corresponds to the concrete operational stage, and the rational consciousness of stage four parallels Piaget's formal operational stage of cognitive development. At the centaur stage, there is no parallel level of cognitive development as described by Piaget, so Wilber creates the term *vision-logic* for the individual cognitive level that corresponds to this cultural stage of consciousness. Vision logic is a higher-order capacity to synthesize a whole network of ideas and to unify opposites in a dialectical, nonlinear fashion, enabling greater integration of mind with body and emotions (Wilber, 1990).

According to Wilber (1993a), the human psyche and reality have an essentially hierarchical structure: the "higher" levels of reality and human development are considered "superior" to the "lower" levels. Thus, the thrust of evolution is a slow but persistent movement toward newly emerging, higher forms of psychological, spiritual, and social development. Wilber sees individual development as an ascending path that originates in the prepersonal experiences of infancy and childhood, passes through the personal developments of consolidating ego consciousness, and potentially leads to transpersonal experiences that may allow us to recognize our connections to the divine. Wilber draws on the works of mystics and thinkers through the ages from both the West and the East to describe four basic transpersonal or spiritual stages of development.

Table 8: Table of Transpersonal Stages

	4. Absolute Level
	3. Causal Level
	2. Subtle Level
Transpersonal Level	1. Psychic Level
Personal Level	
Prepersonal Level	

At the *psychic level*, the first transpersonal stage, the experience of a "soul" emerges, a broader sense of self than the ego. This state may include overcoming the subject-object split that is such a characteristic feature of normal ego consciousness. According to Wilber, *nature mysticism* epitomizes this first transpersonal level. He considers philosopher Ralph Waldo Emerson a prime representative of this stage of consciousness, where a person may experience identity with human beings or aspects of nature that were considered "other" at the personal levels of consciousness. For Emerson (1941), the basis for this unitary consciousness is an awareness of nature's unity: "Everything in Nature contains all the powers of Nature. Everything is made of one hidden stuff" (p. 153).

At the second transpersonal stage, the *subtle level*, a person becomes aware of "archetypal" images and forms that are not available to the normal senses. These forms may include the experience of shamanic power animals, sacred beings, deities, inner light, and primal sound.

Wilber sees this level embodied in *personal mysticism,* especially as exemplified in the life and works of St. Teresa of Avila, who described with intimate bridal imagery the soul's progress toward God as a growing but difficult love relationship.

At the *causal level,* particular images and forms of earlier levels drop away and only pure consciousness remains. For Wilber, this level represents *formless mysticism* and encompasses the Buddhist nirvana, the Gnostic abyss, and Meister Eckhart's notion of the Godhead that is beyond the personal mysticism often found in Christianity. For Eckhart, the Godhead is beyond God, beyond all images of God, and is the incomprehensible origin of all things.

The highest stage, the *absolute level,* is represented by a *nondual mysticism,* where phenomena are experienced and observed, but are spontaneously recognized as manifestations of consciousness. Wilber sees this stage epitomized in certain forms of Hinduism and Mahayana Buddhism. He considers the Indian holy man Ramana Maharshi as an example of this ultimate stage. According to Maharshi, the individual soul is identical with the world soul, and phenomenal reality, including death and evil, are illusory.

In Wilber's view, the transpersonal stages are based on not merely metaphysical speculation, but on direct phenomenological descriptions given by people who have navigated these realms of experience. He believes validity claims for these transpersonal experiences and stages follow the same basic principles as scientific verification and valid knowledge accumulation in other realms. He describes these principles as injunction, observation, and confirmation. Injunction tells us what to do in order to observe a phenomenon, whether this be constructing a telescope, building a microscope, or cultivating a form of meditation. Then, we observe the phenomenon and, finally, we test those observations against the observations of others who are trained to study such phenomena.

Wilber (1993a) distinguishes sharply between prepersonal states (psychologically "lower," primitive, or infantile) and transpersonal states (psychologically "higher" or spiritual). Because prepersonal and transpersonal appear to be similar from the vantage point of ego consciousness (i.e., both are *not personal*), they may easily be mistaken for each other. A prime example of this confusion is Freud's (1930) interpretation of mystical experience as a pathological regression to the earliest psychological state of the infant. In the history of psychoanalysis, psychiatry, and psychotherapy, such judgments have had unfortunate consequences, as many people with genuine spiritual experiences have been labeled "mentally ill." In Wilber's view, this tendency to equate prepersonal and transpersonal states is regrettable because they actually reflect very different psychological structures, even though they bear a superficial and misleading similarity. In effect, such an equation of the prepersonal and transpersonal removes any higher goal of psychological development that might point beyond the ego consciousness that governs the everyday world.

Wilber maintains that healthy psychological development presses toward transpersonal psychological structures and levels of experience, ascending beyond the prepersonal and personal levels. He highlights a number of crucial differences between prepersonal and transpersonal structures. For instance, the oceanic fusion of infancy (prepersonal) contrasts with spiritual wholeness or mystical union (transpersonal); the illusory, magical thinking of early childhood (prepersonal) is distinguished from genuine psychic ability (transpersonal); and prerational mythic thinking (prepersonal) differs from the suprarational archetypes that influence human thought, feeling, and behavior (transpersonal). Wilber concludes from examining these contrasting structures of consciousness that two types of confusion have occurred throughout history: first, higher transpersonal structures such as mystical union have been interpreted as lower prepersonal ones, reducing the former to the latter; and, second, lower structures, such as magic (prepersonal), have been considered the same as higher transpersonal ones, elevating the former to the latter. Where Freud represents the reductionist error, Jung represents the elevationist error, according to Wilber (1981). He sees both of these misinterpretations as examples of the "pre/trans fallacy," which results from an inability to distinguish prepersonal states from transpersonal states.

Prior to his analysis of the pre/trans fallacy, Wilber was in substantial agreement with the Jungian view that prepersonal and transpersonal states have a common basis in the psychological resources available in childhood. However, with his formulation of the pre/trans fallacy, he rejected the view that certain similarities between prepersonal and transpersonal states mean that they are rooted in the same or similar psychic structures. While Michael Washburn (1998) values the pre/trans distinction as a way to avoid confusing prepersonal with transpersonal states, he believes that Wilber's linear, hierarchical-structural model overlooks the possibility that many nonegoic structures have both pre- and transdevelopmental expressions. However, even with the limitations of an excessively linear model, Wilber's work has been important for its effort to set transpersonal psychology on a scientific foundation and relate its findings to mainstream disciplines. Now we turn to Jung, who provides an alternative transpersonal model that emphasizes the nonlinear aspects of spiritual development.

Jung's View of Midlife Transformation

Carl Jung, more than any other psychologist, highlights the religious and spiritual implications of midlife. He sees midlife as a time when people begin to turn their attention to aspects of the inner world that have been neglected or ignored. In Jung's view, the transformation of midlife is at the heart of "individuation," his term for the overall process of psychological development. He defines individuation as "the process by which individual beings are formed and differentiated," a process that might be described as a dialogue between the conscious and unconscious (Jung, 1921, p. 448). The conscious-unconscious dialogue involves individuals attending to their dreams, intuitions, and emotional states. Though the conscious and unconscious are equal partners in this "dialogue of individuation," their perspectives differ greatly: The conscious mind focuses directly on adapting to the here and now, while the unconscious draws from the past, present, and future. Jung believes that the interaction between these different perspectives developed as an evolutionary survival mechanism that takes into account both the short-term and long-term needs of the human being.

This dialogue between the conscious and unconscious involves all areas of human functioning. The unconscious expresses the state of the physical and social environment, as well as the body, mind, and spirit of the individual person. According to Jung, the unconscious comprises material from the individual's personal history (the personal unconscious) and material from the cumulative experience of the human race (the collective unconscious). Individuation entails becoming aware of, and assimilating, the neglected and repressed aspects of the personal unconscious, as well as the largely unknown images and symbols emerging from the collective unconscious. Jung looks to dreams, intuitions, and other products of the unconscious for information about all levels of his life and work. He contends that both the conscious and unconscious are changed as a result of this encounter and dialogue. The conscious personality becomes more attentive to the inner world and the unconscious increasingly cooperates in guiding personality development through dreams and intuitions. This psychological and spiritual transformation is at work in life generally, but is often intensified in the course of psychotherapy.

Jung describes this personality transformation from two different angles, namely, the conscious and the unconscious perspectives. In regard to changes in the conscious personality, Jung speaks of acquiring an attitude of attention to the numinous, a term he borrows from Rudolf Otto (1958) to signify the divine will as it manifests itself in life. Further, he maintains that a sense of "I-ness" fades as the ego ceases to be the primary director of a person's life. While the ego does lose some of its former prominence in this personality transformation, the ego (I-ness) does not disappear entirely. In fact, Jung emphasizes the need to retain a healthy ego throughout personality transformation. A more marginalized, reconstructed ego continues to play an important role in focusing attention on the numinous and orienting the person to both the outer and the inner world. A primary task of the conscious ego becomes assimilating unconscious contents as they are presented in emotional states, intuitions, and dreams. So, while the ego is removed from its former preeminent position, it remains a crucial partner in the dialogue between the ego and the unconscious.

In regard to the changes in the unconscious, Jung speaks of the emergence of the self-archetype and the reconciliation of opposites. The self-archetype, or simply *the self*, represents the center that moves the totality of the psyche toward wholeness. The word *archetype* refers to symbols and images that occur across cultures and in various times in human history. For Jung, the archetypes are universal symbols that express the collective heritage of the human race; they are the images and forms of what he referred to as the "collective unconscious." The self is a union of opposites that holds together and reconciles divergent and conflicting psychological tendencies such as good/evil, female/male, and spirit/matter.

Jung highlights the self's capacity to reconcile psychological opposites when he describes the self as the transcendent function. By "transcendent" he means a point of view that *transcends* both the conscious and unconscious perspectives on life. According to Jung, this transcendent vantage point takes into account conscious reflection and judgment as well as intuitions and dreams from the unconscious. The confrontation of the conscious and unconscious creates a tension of opposites charged with energy, and their sustained interaction brings about this third viewpoint that is something unique, something more than just the sum of the conscious and unconscious perspectives. Diagram 7 may help to picture this psychological development.

Jung observes two key polarities of life that are involved in the material presented by both the personal and collective unconscious,

**Diagram 7: The Essence of Midlife Transformation—
Establishing the Transcendent Function**

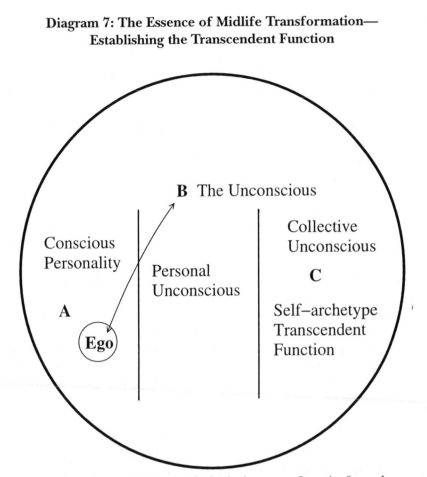

This diagram shows the shift in psychological center of gravity from the ego to a larger personality center Jung calls the self or the self-archetype. This shift represents the essence of midlife transformation, which involves the conscious ego (A) confronting the unconscious material (B) presented in emotional states, dreams, and intuitions. From the interaction of these two perspectives, a third position emerges (C), the self-archetype or transcendent function, which is a unique perspective taking into account both the conscious and unconscious vantage points on life. While the circle representing the self or transcendent function has its center in the unconscious (indicating that it is never fully grasped by or in control of the conscious ego), its circumference includes the conscious personality to show that the new personality center organizes the whole personality, in both its conscious and unconscious dimensions. This shift from A to C can be thought of as a move from *ego identity* to a broader and more universal *self-identity*.

namely, good/evil and feminine/masculine. The first polarity, good/evil, Jung speaks of in terms of the "shadow." The personal shadow is not necessarily bad, but it involves the inferior and underdeveloped aspects of the personality. The personal shadow is discovered primarily in psychological projections and in dreams. Psychological projection means that we see in the external world those qualities that we reject or are unaware of in ourselves. For instance, when we are not aware of our own anger, we tend to see others around us as being angry. In dreams, shadow figures often appear dark and menacing. Jung believes that shadow figures in dreams are usually the same sex as the dreamer. He also recognizes a collective shadow that may be expressed in traditional religious symbols of evil, such as a devil figure.

The second major polarity that people come to terms with in the course of psychological transformation is feminine/masculine. In Jung's view, the conscious personality usually reflects cultural expectations and a person's physical body. Thus, men cultivate male characteristics and females develop female characteristics as defined by a particular society. For most people, this means they ignore the qualities their society attributes to the other sex, and their own countersexual characteristics atrophy or never develop. Especially during midlife, the unconscious presents emotional states, dreams, and intuitions of these neglected and underdeveloped potentials that can confound the conscious personality.

EXAMPLES OF MIDLIFE TRANSFORMATION

It may be difficult to imagine what spiritual and religious transformation at midlife might be like. The stories of two people may help us understand what is involved in such developments. Admittedly, the following examples of spiritual transformation at midlife are more dramatic than most instances, but, as William James noted, extreme cases allow us to identify and understand a phenomenon more readily.

The Transformation of Richard Alpert into Baba Ram Dass

The remarkable story of social psychologist Richard Alpert is told in the autobiographical *Remember Be Here Now* (1971). It records three distinct stages in Alpert's spiritual journey. The first stage is that of the upwardly mobile Harvard psychologist, who describes his academic achievements and measures of worldly success, including his Mercedes-Benz sedan, MG sports car, Triumph motorcycle, Cessna airplane, and sailboat. Although everything appeared to be going well in his academic life, he was beginning to have doubts about his career path. He was doing all the right things—writing books, getting research contracts, and teaching interesting courses on human motivation and Freud, but he started to feel something was wrong with his life, that he was caught in a meaningless game, even though he was good at the game. He became a heavy drinker to offset his depression and anxiety. He then spent five years in psychoanalysis in an effort to resolve his problems and discontent.

This dissatisfaction, coupled with the fact that Timothy Leary took an office just down the hall from him at Harvard, led Alpert to the next stage in his life. Alpert became friends with Leary and they started to teach courses together. One summer in Cuernavaca, a Mexican anthropologist introduced Leary to the local "magic mushrooms." When Leary returned, he obtained a test batch of psilocybin, a synthetic version of the magic mushrooms, and shared it with Alpert. Alpert recounts his first extraordinary experience as follows. Hours after ingesting a small amount of psilocybin, he was in a room by himself when he saw a man standing about eight feet away from him. To his surprise, the man he saw was himself, as a professor in cap and gown. He felt as though that part of himself had separated from him and was not an essential part of himself. Then the figure changed to himself as the social cosmopolite. He slowly realized this too was not the real him. The figure changed again and again, into all the different aspects of himself. He felt he was being asked to let go of each nonessential aspect of his life. Just as he was resigning himself to doing without all his personal and social roles, he was struck with horror as his body seemed to disappear and he could now see only the couch on which he sat. As the panic mounted, he heard a quiet voice say, "Who's minding the store?" As he focused on this question, he realized that without all his roles, and even without a body, there was an aware "I" that was watching the whole drama with calmness and compassion.

Suddenly his panic left and he felt profound joy that he was experiencing an identity that existed independent of any social and physical identity. Alpert now realized that he participated in a larger identity and more interconnected world than he had imagined. The problem for him now became the transitory nature of this realization. No matter how many times he would reach this state of consciousness through chemical means, it would gradually fade and he would return to his previous identity and social roles. Always coming down again to the everyday perspective on life frustrated and depressed him. Nevertheless, he grants that these experiences at least showed him new horizons of identity, values, and worldview.

A turning point occurred when Alpert was introduced to the *Tibetan Book of the Dead*, which contained descriptions of experiences strikingly similar to his own experience with psilocybin. This ancient text, over 2,500 years old, was used to prepare Tibetan Lamas for death and reincarnation. While studying this text, he came to believe that the Tibetan preparation for physical death and rebirth was parallel to the psychological and spiritual death and rebirth he had experienced with psilocybin. In an effort to learn more about Eastern spiritual wisdom, Alpert set off for India with a friend. After roaming around India for some time, he was introduced to an elderly holy man who was able to reveal things about Alpert's mother and how she died. Alpert's mind raced as he tried to understand how this man was able to know his thoughts and secrets from his past. At this point, he felt that he had finally arrived, and he became a follower of this guru.

Alpert describes his transformation as experiencing himself and the world from a different perspective. He observes that when you crack the ego, you do not lose your personality, but you no longer identify with it. Alpert now experiences his ultimate identity as consciousness, energy, and love. Following an ancient religious custom, he took on a new name, Baba Ram Dass, in order to symbolize this radical transformation of his identity, values, and worldview. "Baba" is a term of endearment and respect, meaning "father," and Ram Dass means "servant of Ram" (one of the incarnations of the God Vishnu). This example highlights the explicitly religious character that midlife transformation can assume.

Jean Shinoda Bolen's Transformation as a Grail Pilgrimage

Jean Bolen's *Crossing to Avalon: A Woman's Midlife Pilgrimage* (1994) represents a second example of midlife transformation. Her story begins with an invitation to a pilgrimage to Glastonbury, England, the site of the ruins of a famous Christian abbey and also the legendary place where people were said to cross to Avalon, the realm of the Goddess. Bolen, a well-known psychiatrist and Jungian analyst, was forty-nine years old at that time and struggling through pain and disillusionment after the end of a nineteen-year marriage. While she and her husband had been good at being parents and supporting each other's work, their communication broke down and they became unable to express their needs, anger, disappointments, and vulnerabilities. Feeling lost, she accepted this pilgrimage invitation as an opportunity to reflect on her unfolding midlife path. Bolen emphasizes that a pilgrimage is a fitting metaphor for the spiritual journey, especially when it is directed to the site where the Holy Grail was once supposedly hidden.

The Grail, usually thought to be the sacred chalice used by Jesus at the Last Supper, has been a powerful symbol in Western Christianity for a thousand years. In another version, the Grail is the chalice that caught some of the blood flowing from Jesus' wounded side when he hung on the cross. The Grail legend contains many different stories and versions, the most famous of which tells of a wounded Fisher King, whose kingdom has become a wasteland and will remain so until his wound is healed by the Holy Grail. In one story, Joseph of Arimathea brought the chalice from the Holy Land to Glastonbury, the location of Britain's first church, and then it was lost. The stories of Camelot take up this theme as the Knights of the Round Table seek the lost Grail. One legend has it that King Arthur, wounded after his last battle, was taken to Glastonbury to die.

Bolen comes to see the Grail symbolism on two levels in her midlife journey of transformation. At the psychological level, the Grail is a symbol of Christ or the self-archetype, a spiritual center of the personality that reconciles opposites and provides meaning. The wounded Fisher King represents the ego that is cut off from the self-archetype and subsequently suffers from chronic anxiety and depression. At the sociological level, the Fisher King's wound symbolizes our competitive, materialistic society's cynicism toward spiritual values, where science largely ignores the realm of the spirit, resulting in a spiritual wasteland of despair, fear, meaninglessness, emptiness, and addictions. This barren spiritual climate manifests itself in the external world as deforestation, famine, armed conflicts, and potential nuclear and ecological disasters that threaten to turn the whole planet into a physical wasteland. For Bolen, the Grail and the Goddess represent the promise of life and meaning that can heal the individual's injured spirit and the wounded earth.

On her pilgrimage, Bolen reflects on her midlife situation. She thinks back upon a mystical experience she had when she was forty years old. At the time, she was preoccupied by the recent death of a patient who was the mother of a young son. A week later, toward the end of an analytical hour, a woman patient sensed that something was wrong and asked Bolen about it. When tears appeared in Bolen's eyes, the woman came over and held her. Bolen says she felt that they were both in the arms of an invisible divine presence. A deep ache in the center of her chest seemed to open and expand her heart. She believed this experience manifested the Goddess, mediated through another woman's compassion. This powerful experience of a maternal divine presence had a lasting effect on Bolen. From that time on, whenever she was moved by compassion for someone, she would feel an upsurge of love and that same ache in her heart.

Now, contemplating her pilgrimage to Glastonbury, she understands her profound religious feelings about the Goddess in that analytical hour as a Grail experience. She has come increasingly to feel the presence of the Goddess as a maternal, feminine, and deeply comforting energy. Her experience has led her to rethink the Grail stories from a feminine perspective. Bolen hearkens back to the Celtic and Druidic myths of the Grail as a sacred vessel, the Cauldron of the Goddess, which brings rebirth and inspiration. Those stories of the Goddess stand behind the Christian Grail legends and no doubt influenced them. Reflecting on her own experience and that of many other women, she now views the Goddess as a nurturer and comforter whose presence can be evoked through human touch. Her spiritual experience convinces her that the Grail is found in the realm of the Goddess and women's mysteries: The Goddess manifests herself through the Grail that is a woman's body. Bolen sees the emergence of goddess consciousness as a return of the Grail into the world to bring necessary healing to both individuals and the planet.

Bolen recalls a dream from her earlier years about Glastonbury and discovering a secret room with a wall that pivots open, revealing a different world. This dream came back to her as she approached Glastonbury, and she felt as though she was reentering the dream landscape, where the veil between ordinary reality and a transcendent world is thinner. She felt herself to be in a mythical time and place, where her personal story merged with the Goddess who was so closely tied to this magical place. To cross to Avalon is to enter the unknown world of the Goddess, where time and eternity intersect. In this place, dreams and synchronistic events (meaningful coincidences) became the compass to guide her through unfamiliar terrain. Bolen describes her transformation as dying to her old way of life and no longer being the person she had been.

Now, having struggled to find her way through the midlife forest, she sees herself as circling the self-archetype, which for her is signified by God, the Goddess, Dao, or Spirit. She feels that the meaning in her life is a result of circling around this divine, ineffable source that warms and illuminates like the sun. She likens this circular movement around the self to her experience of circumambulating (walking around) the sacred sites at Glastonbury, while her thoughts moved in a circular pattern around the Grail and the Goddess. Bolen sees her pilgrimage as an outward expression of an inner process of circumambulating the self, the nourishing contact with the divine center that transforms the personality.

Other Examples of Spiritual Experiences in Midlife

The following cases cited by Alister Hardy (1979) show that midlife transformation is not restricted to intellectuals. A forty-six-year-old woman who was in good health had an out-of-body experience that greatly expanded her sense of identity and worldview. As she was lying on a sofa during the day, she began to feel very light and suddenly was surprised to be looking down at her body from just below the ceiling. She said she felt liberated as she realized that she was not identical with her body which was lying on the sofa, but was more closely identified with the consciousness that was observing her body. She stated that she knew she had to return to her body but did so reluctantly. After this experience, she had a keen sense of her spiritual nature and had no fear of physical death.

In another case, a forty-seven-year-old man experienced a three-week period of quiet ecstacy which transformed his identity and worldview. He describes this time as a constant sense of being loved and life being good. His personal identity seemed to merge with the external world. Even though he and all the things around him seemed to enter into each other, he still did not lose a distinct sense of himself. During this period, he felt he was in communication with all things, but not through words or images. This remarkable experience left him feeling very much a part of the world around him and aware of the interconnectedness of all things.

A forty-one-year-old man had a powerful spiritual experience which impressed on him the unity of all things. He began to feel all of his mental barriers falling away as his sense of self and happiness expanded. At first, his identity enlarged to include those near him, but this expansion continued until he felt connected to everyone and everything. As the ecstacy intensified, he was filled with a great desire and strength to help others. His worldview became focused on the goodness in everything. His unitive experience led him to believe that all religions and sciences are paths to the ultimate reality that underlies everything.

MYTHIC DIMENSIONS OF TRANSFORMATION

At this point, we will consider myths, because they guide our movement through the life cycle, especially the midlife passage (Campbell, 1973). Myths provide valuable maps to orient people during the sometimes radical religious and spiritual changes of midlife. The example of Jean Bolen, which we have just described, brings to light exactly how myths can guide a person through a midlife transformation. We saw that she drew on the mythical theme of the Grail to symbolize the religious significance of her transformation. The Grail myth, with both its pre-Christian and Christian connotations, deepened her transformative experience and connected her to ancient human longings for union with God and the Goddess. Myths and mythic themes represent the deeper levels of the unconscious material that contribute to the conscious-unconscious dialogue Jung described as the essence of midlife transformation. In Jung's (1934) view, myths reveal the nature of the soul, and mythical themes of the collective unconscious are often a major stimulus and guide to midlife transformation. Myths crystalize the wisdom of innumerable generations that have experienced the stages of the life cycle, from birth through death. In this light, myths can assist us in understanding, at a deep, spiritual level, what we are going through and how to deal with it. Important aspects of a person's story transcend biographical facts of family origins, occupation, relationships, and social or geographical location.

The individual's personal story interacts, or at times even coincides, with humanity's universal aspirations as they are preserved in myth (Jung, 1963). We have already seen in chapter three how people's stories function to create and maintain their identity, and symbolize their values and worldview. Here, we consider a further dimension of the personal story as it is influenced by the universal themes of mythology. The word "myth" means different things to different people. Dictionaries often define "myth" as a traditional story focusing on the deeds of gods or heroes. In common parlance, "myth" is frequently used to denote a belief that is based on false premises or fallacious reasoning. The "flat earth" myth is an example of such a view that is now considered wrong, being incompatible with a scientific understanding of the world. However, according to Rollo May (1991, p. 23), the definition of myth as "falsehood" proves how impoverished our contemporary culture is.

The connotation of myth as a false belief no doubt derives in part from the fact that some myths were thought to explain the origins of the world and its countless phenomena. For example, when we read creation myths today, we may view them as a kind of primitive science which early people used to understand and manage a mysterious and dangerous world. If taken literally, these stories seem to be talking about the actual physical origin and nature of things. But myths, like dreams, are multilayered stories that go deeper than their literal meaning. If we penetrate the surface stories, we realize that myths are fundamentally concerned with the *meaning* of the world, its phenomena, and our existence. At this deeper level, mythology is a record of how human beings have understood their encounter with their world and the major events of life.

Myths provide information about the psychological and spiritual life of entire cultures or even humanity as a whole, in the same way that dreams illuminate the inner world of an individual human being. Both myths and dreams are symbolic stories that reveal the inner dimensions and depths of human experience. Psychoanalysts have long noted the intimate relationship between myths and dreams. Sometimes myths and mythical themes appear in the dreams of contemporary people. For instance, Bolen (1994) had a number of dreams about the Grail myth, symbolizing her own spiritual quest. Freud (1933) maintains that mythical themes are often found in the dreams of his patients. In his view, such themes shed valuable light on the psychological condition of the dreamer, showing how that person's situation in life resembles, in some respect, the mythical themes that appear in the dream. These myths provide a larger context for understanding the patient's dream and psychological condition. At the same time, contemporary dreams reciprocate by throwing light on the original interests that first inspired a particular myth at the dawn of history (Freud, 1916). For example, Freud understood modern Oedipal dreams to show that the timeless rivalry between a boy and his father was at work in the unconscious origins of the Oedipus myth itself. Thus Freud used myths and dreams to illuminate each other. Confident that both myths and dreams arise from the same unconscious ground and share a common symbolic language, he applied many of his insights about dream interpretation to understand mythology.

Carl Jung (1912), too, explored the close relationship between myth and dream. He believed that in humanity's earliest times, the originators of mythology thought, while awake, in patterns similar to the way we think in dreams; when we dream, we return to an earlier stage of humanity, and from our dream experience we can better understand the inner life of our earliest ancestors (p. 23). Jung valued myths greatly, considering them to be treasures of humanity's youth. In psychological terms, he came to view myths as projections arising from the collective unconscious. Jung observed that mythical themes emerge in contemporary dreams because they are part of human beings' psychological and spiritual heritage. However, not all dreams touch these archaic depths, only those "big dreams" which people consider particularly important, and especially those referring to a larger community beyond the dreamer. Jung points out that in ancient Rome, such "big dreams" were sometimes announced to the Senate, and, among many Native peoples, they would be told to the tribal assembly. These dreams were recognized to convey important information to the larger community or to express a vital collective human truth, and thus were not considered to belong exclusively to the dreamer (Jung, 1935a).

Mythology deals with timeless human concerns about the kind of world we live in and the meaning of our lives. Joseph Campbell, who has written extensively on the various roles mythology plays in human affairs, describes four general functions of myth, namely, the sociological, cosmological, psychological, and mystical functions. In their sociological role, myths work to harmonize individuals with their society; they are stories that express life's wisdom in relation to a specific time and culture. The cosmological function helps put people's minds and bodies in accord with nature. These stories present the physical world in a way that highlights the meaning and mystery of the universe. The psychological function shows life's stages and how people have understood and dealt with life's passages; these stories show how to live a fully human life, even in the most difficult circumstances. The mystical function opens people up to the transcendent in their lives and allows them to experience the divine presence in the world.

In Campbell's (1973) view, myths guide human beings through all the fundamental problems of life. Myths, like dreams, offer guidance through the stages of life. Campbell believes that our contemporary world no longer has living myths of passage to guide individuals and societies, so dreams increasingly assume this function: "In the absence of an effective general mythology, each of us has his private, unrecognized, rudimentary, yet secretly potent pantheon of dreams" (p. 4). Following the insights of Freud and Jung, he sees dreams as personalized myths, and myths as collective dreams of an entire people or society. Campbell argues that dreams can carry out the guiding role of myths because both spring from the unconscious and the same symbolic universe. The main difference he sees between them is that dreams reflect the peculiar difficulties of the dreamer, whereas myths portray problems and solutions for whole societies and even all humankind.

However, many, perhaps most, people in the modern world are at a disadvantage when it comes to tapping the wisdom of mythology. For Campbell (1988), the modern inability to appreciate myth is due to the effects of science. As science has undermined the literal interpretation of mythology, many have concluded that these stories linking them to transcendent depths and meaning are simply false, and that nothing remains to believe in except science itself, with its focus on empirical facts and the physical universe. Science and reason appear to have become the new mythology, promising to solve the riddles of life and the universe. Mary Midgley (1994) captures this idea very well in the title of her cogent book *Science as Salvation: A Modern Myth and Its Meaning*. The attitude of science resembles Fowler's Stage-Four faith, where the world seems to be adequately comprehended by reason, and religious myths can be translated into discursive statements about life. David Elkins (1998) criticizes the current scientific model as being excessively one-sided, ignoring other epistemological approaches such as the metaphorical way of myths and dreams. He identifies myth as one of the primary alternative spiritual paths to the sacred. Like Campbell, he views myths as metaphors that bridge the gap between our visible world and the transcendent. Myths are openings where the sacred can enter our world and nurture our souls. Elkins speaks of mythology as a spark that ignites the fires in the caverns of the soul, providing light to explore this primordial domain and deepen our spiritual lives.

The Hero Myth and the Spiritual Journey

Now that we have considered how myths in general guide people through the religious and spiritual changes of midlife, we turn to the hero myth, which some see as the prime metaphor for the spiritual journey of both males and females at midlife. Campbell (1973), for example, maintains that the hero's quest is the constant story or "mono-myth" of human transformation that appears in countless variations throughout human history. He provides evidence from a wide range of sources to show that the hero myth has oriented spiritual seekers in virtually all cultures and at all times in history. Jung too views the core of the hero myth as a symbolic portrait of midlife transformation. He sees the hero as a central archetype that expresses and guides the overall process of human development, which he calls *individuation*.

Overall, Jung sees individuation as the process by which people are increasingly differentiated from their mothers, families, and the physical and social environment. This differentiation enables conscious personality to emerge and develop. However, for Jung, individuation entails more than differentiating and developing the conscious personality, because that represents only the first half of life. In the second half of life, the conscious personality encounters the inner world of the unconscious. In the hero myth, this encounter is often symbolized as crossing a threshold or being devoured by a monster. This stage is seen in the story of Jonah entering the belly of the whale. The Eros and Psyche myth represents the potentially lethal aspect of the transformation process, as when Psyche is commanded to marry a terrifying serpent (Gollnick, 1992). These are mythical descriptions of the hero's (ego's) confrontation with the unconscious.

Jung (1912) refers to this transforming experience as the "night sea journey," a term he takes from Frobenius, who studied this theme in countless myths. During the night sea journey, the hero is locked in the symbolic mother's womb for a time and often faces all kinds of trials and dangers. The details of this transforming night sea journey differ from myth to myth. However, one of the standard features of these stories is that the hero lights a fire in the belly of the monster, symbolizing how psychological and spiritual transformation occurs. The fire represents the light of consciousness which provides orientation in the overwhelming darkness of the unconscious. For Jung (1912, p. 211), fire-making is "a pre-eminently conscious act" that ends the state of undifferentiated union with the unconscious.

The heart of psychological or spiritual transformation is represented in the hero myth as an apotheosis or divinization of the hero. In stark terms, the human being is transformed into a god. For Jung, this transformation symbolizes the emergence of the self-archetype, which becomes the larger personality center that now organizes the entire psyche, including the "heroic" ego. As Jung describes it, the self-archetype is most frequently expressed in dreams and myths as the circular pattern of the mandala. Thus we find that the mythic images of transformation include a combination of linear and circular metaphors: The hero's quest suggests a linear movement of development, while the transformation itself is described as dwelling in the monster's belly and contemplating the unconscious depths. This aspect of the hero myth emphasizes a circular movement around the center, the self. The hero's journey moves from the everyday world of ego consciousness across an initiatory threshold through a series of tasks or trials and back again to the everyday world. The hero who returns to the everyday world is a transformed version of the person who began the quest. Two examples will illustrate how the hero myth epitomizes the religious and spiritual journey of midlife.

TWO EXAMPLES OF THE HERO MYTH

A prime example of the hero myth is the Eros and Psyche story, one of the central myths of Western civilization, which has greatly influenced literature and art over the centuries. During the twentieth century, this story received more attention from depth psychologists than any other myth, save that of Oedipus. We should hardly be surprised that psychoanalysts and psychologists have been drawn to such a universal tale about the human psyche and its transformations. This extraordinary mythic portrait of spiritual transformation particularly captured the imagination of Jung and his followers. Jung was intrigued by the myth itself as well as by the literary setting in which the myth first appears, *The Metamorphoses*, because both stories deal with psychological and spiritual transformation. Apuleius, a second-century-CE author, born in a Roman colony in North Africa, is responsible for the literary form we have of both stories, which he shaped from preexisting sources.

In this myth, the oracle of Apollo commands Psyche, a girl renowned for her beauty, to dress for a funeral and wait on a mountaintop for a terrifying serpent. While waiting on the mountain, the wind carries her to a magnificent royal palace, where a ghostly voice tells Psyche to enjoy all the treasures there and wait for her bridegroom. Her husband visits her only in the dark of night and leaves before sunrise, so she does not know his identity. When her sisters discover that Psyche, now pregnant, has never seen this mysterious husband, they become jealous, imagining that he is a god and that Psyche's child might also be divine. They tell her that the unseen husband must be the deadly serpent spoken of in Apollo's oracle, so she should light a lamp when he is sleeping and cut off his head. At night, when Psyche lights a lamp to see Eros, she is overwhelmed by the sight of his beauty, but, as she embraces him, oil from the lamp burns him and he flies away. When Aphrodite discovers what has happened, she denounces Psyche and imposes upon her four seemingly impossible tasks. With unexpected help from forces of nature, Psyche manages to complete the first three tasks. In the final and ultimate task, she must descend into the realm of Hades, where she is overcome by a deadly sleep. At that point, Eros rescues her and Psyche is taken to heaven where she becomes divine and marries Eros. In time, they have a child, whose name is Voluptas.

Most Jungian interpreters have focused on how the Eros and Psyche myth illustrates key aspects of human development: Psyche's heroic journey symbolizes the way human beings are transformed and come to full self-realization. Some interpreters believe the myth portrays the essence of spiritual development, namely, the coming together of the human and the divine (Gollnick, 1992; Von Franz, 1970). The human psyche is ultimately divinized by its encounter with love (Eros) and other spiritual forces symbolized by the gods, goddesses, and nature. In this view, Eros symbolizes the divine which draws human beings forward and eventually leads to their divinization. As a representation of the self-archetype, Eros symbolizes the psyche's self-transcendence and potential for transformation (Johnson, 1976). Other Jungians consider the birth of the divine child, Voluptas (from the Latin for joy or pleasure), as a fitting symbol of the self-archetype because it is the fruit of the union of the psyche and the unconscious (Eros) and emerges from that interaction (Ulanov, 1971). Psychological commentators have interpreted the four tasks given to Psyche as symbolic representations of psychological development (Houston, 1987; Neumann, 1956).

So the Eros and Psyche tale is a prime example of the hero myth that shows the hero's ultimate victory over life's seemingly insurmountable obstacles. Psyche struggles throughout life and finally appears to be overcome in death, as symbolized by the deadly sleep that overtakes her in Hades. Only the divine power of Eros can rescue Psyche from death in the end. This tale shows that love brings human beings into relationship with the divine and furnishes the hope that sustains spiritual transformation at midlife.

The *Metamorphoses* and Spiritual Transformation

The *Metamorphoses*, the original literary context of the Eros and Psyche myth, is itself an important symbolic portrait of religious and spiritual transformation. Jung was particularly intrigued by this strange and remarkable story. Over the centuries, many have attempted to penetrate the meaning of Apuleius' mysterious novel that combines descriptions of serious religious experience with bawdy tales (Gollnick, 1999). This work, one of the oldest extant Latin novels, remains to this day a primary source for our understanding of the mystery religions in the ancient world. Jung focused on the powerful symbolism in the description of religious initiation at the heart of this novel because it portrays the essence of religious and spiritual transformation. At several points in his collected works, Jung highlights this famous account of ancient religious initiation. Before considering the symbolic meaning of the religious core of this story, a brief summary of the story provides necessary background.

The *Metamorphoses* (Greek for transformations) is the tale of a young man, Lucius, in search of the secrets of witchcraft, who through magic is inadvertently changed into a donkey's body. The novel recounts the vicissitudes of Lucius' asinine life as he passes from owner to owner, enduring one humiliation after another. Finally, to escape his miserable existence, he breaks away and gallops off to a secluded seacoast. There, in the night, he is overwhelmed by the beauty of the moon, which he believes to be an image of the goddess, Isis. In desperation, he prays to her to release him from his misery and then falls asleep. In a dream, he sees the goddess in the form of a glorious woman who promises to deliver him. On the next day, a priest of Isis in a procession of worshipers gives Lucius a garland of roses, exactly as pictured in his dream. Lucius eats the roses and is changed back into a human body. He then dedicates his life to Isis in return for her merciful intervention. She continues to guide Lucius in dreams and visions, eventually leading to his ritual initiation into the cult of Isis.

At the heart of the Isis initiation ceremony, Lucius enacts a symbolic death and then is crowned as the sun. Jung interprets this culmination of the Isis mysteries as a prime example from the ancient world of ritual transformation, in which the initiate identifies with the god. He regards such an identification with the divine as the essence of the "religious relationship" (Jung, 1912, pp. 86–87). The symbolism of this initiation ceremony expresses a timeless truth about human transformation, namely, that human beings are related to, and participate in, divinity. Jung is especially interested in the ancient mystery religions because they acknowledge the potential divinity of the human psyche (Jung, 1935b). He values this classical portrait of religious transformation because it emphasizes the importance of experiencing the divine directly.

Jung does not see this transformation as being restricted to a particular religious cult or doctrine, but rather considers it as a general psychological and spiritual process. In this regard, the spiritual quest can be viewed either in terms of a particular religious tradition or in terms of implicit religion. Thus, Jung speaks of the divine aspect in human transformation as the emergence of the self-archetype, which may be expressed in a variety of symbols, some traditionally religious, as God, the Goddess, or the gods and goddesses, and some natural, such as a circle, flower, stone, or star. Both the religious and the implicit religious descriptions of spiritual transformation can effectively orient people in the course of their changing lives. Jung frequently refers to the self-archetype as the God-image in order to underline the ultimately religious or spiritual nature of the self and the transformation of the psyche. For some, Jung's description of transformation is problematic because he juxtaposes traditional religious language with psychological terminology. This ambiguity leads some psychological critics to accuse him of deifying the psyche. At the same time, religious critics insist that he psychologizes the divine. The question remains as follows: How does Jung understand the relationship between the self-archetype, as God-image, and the transcendent divinity of Judaism, Christianity, and Islam?

From a psychological point of view, Jung defines the God-image as a complex of archetypal ideas and a concentration of energy in the psyche. These definitions suggest that the God-image is strictly a psychological phenomenon, but such descriptions represent only part of the picture, as it is presented from the human angle. The transcendent side is shrouded in darkness. Jung (1952) states that we cannot distinguish whether our experience of the God-image emanates from a transcendent divinity as symbolized in theistic religions, or from the unconscious. In other words, he cannot say whether God is different from, or coincides with, the unconscious. Psychologists, as empirical scientists, cannot identify the experience of the self-archetype or God-image with the transcendent divinity of theistic religions. But, as clinicians, they can substantiate the importance of the God-image in the psychological functioning of their patients, whether or not it reflects realities in an external transcendent sphere. In Jung's view, psychology cannot determine, in any final sense, whether our religious ideas and symbols actually correspond to the realities they describe or evoke. Jung considered such questions matters of metaphysics, which are not verifiable by empirical science. While he refuses to assert uncategorically that the psychological God-image reflects a transcendent divinity, he grants that human beings *may be* in direct contact with the divine through the medium of unconscious processes.

Mythical themes, such as the hero's quest for self-realization and the psyche's divinization, highlight the possibly divine level of the unconscious and enable people to become aware of the mythic depths of their personalities. At this deep level, the personal story created in adolescence and early adulthood is influenced by the collective stories of mythology. Jung describes his own midlife transformation as discovering the myth or myths that were seeking expression in his life. He speaks of his encounter with these mythical depths as universalization, a state in which he no longer lives primarily for himself but rather for a purpose in the larger scheme of things. Jung attempts to do justice to both the personal story and the mythical story. Transformation involves coming to terms with the myths that are influencing the individual, but without surrendering uncritically to them. This means the mythical dimension of one's story must be integrated with the conscious personality. The individual person is not simply the stage on which mythic themes play themselves out, but a conscious and willing subject who helps adapt and personalize a myth in terms of a particular culture and historical period.

PERSONAL MYTH

Because cultural myths no longer guide many people through predictable life stages, "personal myths" increasingly organize their identity and reality. Feinstein et al. (1988) define "personal myth" as a constellation of ideas, images, and emotions that serves as an inner model. Ernst Kris (1956) introduced the term "personal myth" to denote crucial aspects of personality functioning that must be taken into account for effective psychotherapy. Feinstein (1979) employs the concept of personal myth to bridge the gap between the rational and the imaginative aspects of human functioning. His research on personal myth is closely connected to the development of "narrative psychology" which, as we saw in chapter three, deals with the creation and maintenance of identity.

Throughout the life cycle, personal myths order our lives. Some of these myths are rooted in early family life. Various myths may grow up around family members, reflecting their experience and location among siblings, such as "the responsible one," "the rebel," the peacemaker," "the martyr," "the talented one," or "the slow one." As children struggle to find their identity in the family, they begin to shape their personal myths. Alfred Adler (1964) in particular explored this dimension of personal myth under the rubric "life style," by which he meant a pattern of ideas and attitudes about other people, oneself, and one's movement through life. In Adler's view, sibling birth order and the family constellation of siblings and parents greatly determines a child's "life style" or personal myth as he or she strives to find a place in the dynamic set of family relationships.

Other personal myths may be strongly influenced by the culture, such as "the working-class hero," "the risk taker," "the upwardly mobile success," "the failure," "the survivor," "the self-made person," or "the underdog." Sometimes these personal myths are embodied in cultural expressions, such as "hard work always pays off," "you get what you pay for," or "everything will work out in the end." A cognitive approach to psychotherapy often examines and challenges certain dysfunctional personal myths when they interfere with psychological functioning and rational decision making. "I am indispensable," "I always fail," "I must always be first," or "I cannot rely on anyone" are examples of personal myths that often lead to problems. We have already noted Gould's discussion of myths that govern early adulthood and his conclusion that maturity involves becoming aware of, and overcoming, such faulty personal myths.

Guiding myths that order our experience are frequently called into question by new experiences and new information from various sources. We experience such changes in our personal myths especially during life-cycle transitions. When our experiences do not correspond to our existing myths, we are forced to distort our experience or alter our myths. Alternative or countermyths continually emerge and may compete with our prevailing myth or myths. This situation can create inner tension and anxiety. Feinstein et al. (1988) urge that we recognize both sides of the inner conflict represented by these opposing myths. Some people try to suppress the emerging myth because it is too painful to imagine life without the familiarity and comfort of an old prevailing myth. Others rush to embrace an emerging myth and totally reject the old myth when it becomes dysfunctional. Feinstein et al. recommend that we face squarely the inconsistencies and contradictions of the clash between the old myth and the new countermyth. They maintain that, if we do not run away from the tension of these opposing myths, further mythic images will emerge that transcend the old myth and the countermyth and preserve the most beneficial aspects of each.

An illustration may help to clarify the relationship between personal myth, countermyth, and reconciling myth. Feinstein et al. (1988) describe the case of a man who was experiencing a midlife crisis. Marco was the fourth son in an immigrant family of six children. Although he loved plants and wanted to become a gardener, his parents pushed him into a business career that would guarantee financial security. By the age of fifty-three, he had risen to an executive position and had a wife and three grown children. His life was predictable and dull. He felt dead. Then Marco fell in love with a new office secretary at his workplace. She reawakened his emotional life. Within a few months they moved into a beach house together. His employer strongly objected to this behavior and his outraged wife filed for divorce. Eventually, the secretary left Marco for another man. With his life in shambles, he fell into a deep depression.

Through psychotherapy, Marco came to realize that the personal myth governing most of his life revolved around security and upward mobility. This myth eventually isolated him from his own feelings, his family, and other interests. He called this the myth of the "Working-class Hero." During the course of therapy, a countermyth emerged from a dream in which he was tiny and climbing onto a beautiful but carnivorous Venus flytrap. Though he remained petrified on the edge of the deadly flower for a long time, he finally managed to escape its fatal embrace by climbing down a strong vine. Marco labeled this countermyth the "Playboy of the Western World," a dangerous personal myth, but one that put him in touch with an exciting, sensual, and youthful side of his personality. In the therapeutic setting, he brought these opposing aspects of himself into dialogue and began to recognize that both the myth and the countermyth represented important values for him. He called the reconciling myth that emerged from this dialogue "Zorba the Thoughtful," which incorporated his seriousness and industriousness along with his feelings and vitality. Working with these personal myths allowed Marco to gain insight into his identity and to recover from his depression.

Feinstein et al. (1988) maintain that personal myths inspire and direct our action, orient us, and help to interpret our experience, even though they typically operate outside our awareness. Personal myths reflect a culture's mythology, though they may be relatively independent of it. Feinstein et al. note that personal myths perform the same functions for the individual that mythology traditionally performs for entire societies. Personal myths explain the world, guide personal development, provide social direction, and express spiritual longings. Personal myths concisely express the key elements of our identity, namely, where we came from, who we are, where we are going, and why we are going there. In this regard, they can be seen as another, deeper dimension of personal story, which is a prime embodiment of identity and spirituality.

Drawing upon depth psychology and current clinical theory, Feinstein et al. employ personal myths to facilitate personal growth in clinical, educational, and community settings. They use personal reflection, dreams, conversations, journal writing, and psychotherapy to make people more aware of their personal myths, opposing countermyths, and the reconciling myths that are taking shape. According to Feinstein, myth-making is the primary psychological mechanism human beings use to find their way in life, and there is an urgent need in contemporary cultures for people to become conscious of the mythologies they are living out. As people begin to understand their underlying myths, they beome less bound by their cultural and childhood mythologies and more able to influence life patterns that previously seemed predetermined and inevitable.

THE SELF AND ITS DEVELOPMENT IN MYTHS AND METAPHORS

Cultural and personal myths symbolize and portray various models of the human personality. In Jung's view, the self that is forged in the first part of the hero's journey is increasingly individualized, i.e., differentiated from an unconscious immersion in, or fusion with, the mother and the environment. However, once individual consciousness is established and developed, the hero is able to encounter the unconscious without being swept away and losing the light of consciousness altogether. For Jung, the psyche's structure is essentially dialogical. The conscious personality constantly interacts with, and attempts to assimilate, contents of both the personal and collective unconscious. The psyche's fundamental dialogical structure can be characterized as the ego-self axis, as illustrated in Diagram 6 earlier in this chapter.

The self represents the multiple elements and influences of the unconscious that affect the personality at any given time. In this sense, Jung recognizes that the human self is multiple, though in a healthy psyche this multiplicity is organized as a coherent and cohesive whole. Views of the self that are embodied in the mythic maps of transformation emphasize the dialogical and relational aspects of the self. The self is by nature connected to others in the family, community, and larger environment. These other people shape the self, as do the timeless motifs of the deep psyche and mythology. The self that emerges from mythical maps is connected to an underlying invisible reality that supports and gives meaning to the everyday aspects of the self's waking world.

Some have dramatized this Jungian view of the multiple self by saying the human psyche is "polytheistic" and calling these various "selves" deities (Hillman, 1975). The entire pantheon of gods and goddesses represents various archetypal patterns in the collective unconscious which influence, and sometimes take over, the personality. James Hillman believes in giving these deities their due by recognizing their autonomy and contemplating their activity and meaning. He treats these deities as ends in themselves and downplays the ego's attempts to integrate these archetypal contents in order to produce a more cohesive self. In dreams, these deities appear as characters alongside figures from our personal experience. Hillman (1979) advises sinking into these deities when they appear in our dreams to absorb their meaning, rather than asking how they can benefit the conscious personality.

Kathryn Rabuzzi (1988) argues that the unitary self symbolized in the hero's journey emphasizes the male's goal of a single, unitary, and separate self. Rabuzzi contrasts this androcentric view of the "heroself" with women's experience, especially women who are mothers. The "motherself," as she labels this alternative perspective, involves two "separate selves," mother and child, coexisting in such a way that they are almost one. Rabuzzi speaks of this motherself as a "binary-unity," a two-in-one kind of selfhood, though she recognizes the inadequacy of language to capture this type of selfhood. For the motherself, the interrelationship between the mother and child is fundamental. In her view, the Jungian multiple-self model is a useful jumping-off point for exploring and understanding the motherself aspect of women's experience.

Rabuzzi offers the following example of how a woman might apply the Jungian perspective to make sense of her various and sometimes conflicting roles in the course of a day. Her decisive action in the business world can be thought of as incarnating the goddess of Crafts, Athena; later, her harsh criticism of male colleagues at a women's consciousness-raising group can be seen as the influence of Artemis, the goddess of the Hunt; still later, her love-making may appear to incarnate Aphrodite, the goddess of Love. However, Rabuzzi rejects the androcentric presuppositions that she believes underlie this use of goddess archetypes to illuminate female experience. In particular, she questions the idea that archetypal patterns built into the human psyche are unchanging, because this seems to lock people into predetermined, biologically unalterable thought and behavior. With other feminists, she considers these patterns to be socially constructed and therefore changeable. Even with an expanded and more adequate set of female models, Rabuzzi finds that a woman's experience of herself eludes even the best framework for understanding her multiple self. For her, the motherself cannot ultimately be grasped by a notion of selfhood that involves serial selves, in which the person is governed first by one personality or archetypal goddess, then by another. The paradox of the motherself is that the mother and child relationship is experienced as two personality foci *simultaneously* rather than serially. She adds that the motherself is confusing because it constantly changes, due to the ever-changing relationship between mother and child.

Just as the developmental models of Piaget, Freud, and Erikson have been criticized for being based on male experience, Rabuzzi (1988) believes that the developmental map provided by myths has also been distorted by the male perspective of the originators and interpreters of myth. Even where the Jungian perspective offers women a variety of roles, or goddesses, to identify with, it draws on the gods and goddesses of the Greco-Roman pantheon for models of experience (Bolen, 1984; Hillman, 1975). Rabuzzi criticizes these models as being shaped by waves of patriarchal invaders who altered the earlier matrifocal qualities of the goddesses. She believes that deities from other cultures, especially those less contaminated by patriarchal perspectives, might offer more fitting patterns of thought, feeling, and behavior for women to understand their complex experience.

Rabuzzi finds Campbell's view that the hero myth is the central myth of development in Western civilization persuasive as it applies to men, but she argues that the hero's quest for selfhood does not adequately reflect female experience and goals. Though Campbell maintains that the hero may be either male or female, Rabuzzi believes that the hero is a thoroughly androcentric construction. When a woman tries to take on the hero role, she has to modify the traditional tale or see herself in a male role. While Rabuzzi grants that the hero myth may be found at all times in history and in all cultures, she denies that it has been universally applied to women. She points out that for every one story about a heroine in myths, fairy tales, and novels from various cultures, there are ten stories about male heroes.

Rabuzzi argues that, for most women, the female "story" is the way of the mother. She contends that the way of the mother does not always involve a woman literally becoming a mother, but that it offers an essentially different perspective on the hero myth. In the typical hero myth, the protagonist is the force for good who struggles against evil forces that try to prevent him from obtaining his goal. In classical versions of this myth, one of the evil forces is a monster who symbolizes the "bad mother" (Neumann, 1954). Rabuzzi insists the same story looks very different from the perspective of the mother. From this altered vantage point, the mother becomes the protagonist and the person with whom we identify: She is not a monster preventing the fulfillment of the hero's quest for selfhood, but rather the symbol of a different kind of selfhood, what Rabuzzi calls the motherself, which values connection and relationship. This different perspective turns the typical hero myth upside down: What the male hero views positively, namely, separation from the unconscious, may now appear as negative; what the hero sees as negative may now be regarded as positive, namely, connection to the unconscious and the depths of life.

Rabuzzi points out that many women find themselves living out both patterns in their lives. Often, in the public sphere, they take on the hero's quest as a male norm of the development of selfhood in our society, even when it frequently seems incongruous to their own inner experience. At other times, they sense that the way of the mother is a better fit for their experience. Rabuzzi argues that as long as women are clear about which pattern they are following, they can function adequately. The problem arises when they find themselves following the wrong pattern at the wrong time.

Rabuzzi characterizes a woman's efforts to come to terms with the new sense of selfhood connected with motherhood as a life-and-death struggle. A woman must relinquish her previous sense of self to make room for her emerging motherself. If she is unable to accomplish this, her baby may die or fail to thrive; but if she does, she may feel as if she, or at least part of her old self, is dying. Rabuzzi likens this dilemma to a kind of Siamese twin who cannot simultaneously satisfy the demands of both heads. At its extreme, this situation is experienced as a state of perpetual ambivalence that differs so greatly from the single-minded decision making of a unitary sense of self that it may appear pathological. Rabuzzi questions the typical Western view that women are deficient in self because they are too dependent for truly independent selfhood. She reminds us that women's sense of self and spirituality may differ considerably from the pattern of midlife transformation described by Jung, with which many men readily identify. The motherself involves finding a balance between the needs of the woman's "own" self and those of her child. According to Rabuzzi, an appropriate balance is suggested by the phrase "I am a mother," as opposed to "I am mother," which indicates that "mother" is not her sole identity and that the woman considers herself to be other things as well.

Myths and Metaphors

The myths we have considered offer metaphors to guide our self-understanding and movement through the midlife passage. When we try to describe the religious and spiritual changes at midlife, we are forced to rely on metaphors. These developments are inner processes which cannot be directly described in precise scientific terminology. Even psychology's most valiant efforts to analyze spirituality pale before the reality of the human quest for meaning and value. Models of spiritual development are, at best, efforts to understand invisible processes that we trace through their effects on human behavior, thinking, and feeling. Transpersonal psychology has employed both linear and non-linear metaphors to characterize the spiritual transformation that may occur at virtually any point along life's journey, but especially at midlife.

Ken Wilber favors linear metaphors in his descriptions of spiritual development. Essentially, he views the spiritual journey as a one-way trip from prepersonal to transpersonal levels of consciousness. Wilber interprets any movement by the ego in the direction of prepersonal states as a regressive descent into the primitive and infantile, a move away from transpersonal states and structures. For him, there is only one constructive direction for human development and that is ascent. Wilber (1982) employs metaphors of using an elevator moving to higher floors or climbing a ladder rung by rung to describe spiritual development. A key question is whether these ascending, hierarchical models adequately take into account the ebb and flow of psychological and spiritual life.

If Wilber favors linear metaphors of ascent, such as an elevator or ladder, Jung prefers circular and spiral metaphors to describe spiritual development. Jung recognized that psychological development requires maintaining contact with unconscious depths that contain both the highest and lowest human potentials, an idea Wilber rejects because he interprets any return of the ego to its origins in the depths of the collective psyche as a movement away from transcendence and transpersonal structures. Jung saw the importance of contemplating and circumambulating (walking around) the central images produced by the self-archetype. For him, the most important circular images are seen in mandalas. The mandalas produced spontaneously by the psyche and those painted in religious art testify to the importance of the circle as a metaphor for spirituality. The Sanskrit word *mandala* means "circle," and in India it refers to circles used in religious ceremonies to render the whole cosmos present for the ritual (Gaeffke, 1987; Jung, 1950; Saunders, 1987). Here, I want to consider Jung's (1963) mandala dream which helped him to understand the goal of psychological development in midlife.

The dream setting is a dark and rainy winter night in Liverpool, England. In the dream, Jung and a small group of Swiss walk from the harbor to a square, dimly lit by streetlights at the center of the city. There is a round pool containing a small island at the center of the square. Although everything around is covered in fog and rain, the island itself is somehow bright with sunlight. A magnolia tree with magnificent red blossoms stands in the blazing sunlight; the tree seems to stand in the light and at the same time be the source of the brilliant light. Jung is overwhelmed by the extraordinary beauty of this illuminated tree, while his companions do not even notice it and wonder why anyone would want to live in a city with such abominable weather. He states that when he awoke from this dream, he felt certain that it expressed the goal of psychological development. Later, inspired by this dream, Jung drew a picture of a mandala with a symbol of the awe-inspiring tree at its center. In his interpretation, the luminous tree represents the self-archetype, the goal of development, which provides human life with orientation and meaning.

Jung's interest in mandalas initially grew out of his therapeutic work on himself during the long period of psychological disorientation he suffered after parting ways with Sigmund Freud. He felt the need to express his emotional state by sketching circular drawings in a notebook. For a time, Jung (1963) drew these circles every day and found that they helped him monitor his own psychological transformation. Gradually, by contemplating these mandalas that arose in his dreams and emotional states, he acquired a conception of the structure and dynamics of the psyche. As he began to recognize the importance of mandalas in his own efforts to regain psychological stability, he noticed mandalas in the dreams of his patients, especially when they were suffering from severe neurotic conflicts, psychic dissociation, and psychological disorientation. He came to believe that the order represented by mandalas compensated an inner state of confusion and that their spontaneous emergence represented nature's instinctive attempt at self-healing. These therapeutic mandalas created a protected space where the center of the personality could not be disturbed by scattered and conflicting elements of the psyche (Jung, 1950). Mandalas help introduce some harmony into states of psychological disorder by relating to a central point the various conflicting psychological elements, even those split off in neurosis or psychosis. The mandala thus reflects the self-archetype as the central structure that coordinates the entire psyche.

Some time after he discovered the therapeutic importance of his own mandalas, he was struck by their resemblance to the classical mandalas found in Eastern religions. At the center of the classical religious mandalas stands a sacred realm, occupied by an image or symbol of the divine. Jung observes that the religious mandala promotes concentration and centers the personality, parallel to the therapeutic effect of spontaneous mandalas. However, he notes that the symbols shown at the center of spontaneous mandalas observed in psychotherapy are not explicitly religious, but may be various natural symbols such as a flower, stone, sun, star, serpent, or human being. Jung believes that the central symbol still represents the highest value, but with the cultural shift toward humanism, that value is no longer symbolized by God, but rather by symbols of nature and human wholeness. We might consider these modern spontaneous mandalas as an expression of the nonreligious spirituality described in chapter one. Nevertheless, even the modern mandalas whose centers no longer depict the deity express a religious attitude, according to Jung. He uses the term *religious* here in the broader meaning of *spiritual* rather than in a traditional doctrinal and institutional sense. The modern mandalas are spiritual in that they express a centered worldview and an attitude of attention to the human totality or self.

So, in Jung's view, mandalas are particularly important symbols of spiritual development. They symbolize the concentration or attention of the conscious personality; they also express what is happening in the unconscious, namely, the emergence of the self-archetype. Jung (1936b) interprets the growing number and increasing clarity of mandalas in a long series of dreams as an indication of the development of the self-archetype. The circular mandala, representing the concentration of the conscious mind and the harmonious order of the self-archetype, is closely related to the circlelike figure of the spiral. Jung (1944, pp. 177, 217) links the circle with the spiral when he describes the movement of unconscious processes leading to spiritual development as a "spiral-wise movement round a center," gradually getting close to the center. Jung (1944, p. 180) speaks of the "spiral of inner development" where one appears to come around to an earlier point, though now at a higher level. This spiral movement emphasizes the gradual character of human transformation, which can be so discouraging for spiritual seekers, especially if they are unprepared for occasional periods of apparent regression.

It is at the midlife point that these circular symbols of wholeness become most prominent in guiding spiritual transformation. According to Michael Washburn, midlife is precisely the period when people are most likely to reach a transpersonal level of development, where creative and contemplative capacities emerge and the major dualisms of life are transcended. Like Jung, Washburn (1998) prefers nonlinear metaphors to describe spiritual processes at the transpersonal level. He argues that spiritual development is far too complex to see it primarily as an ascent and to view a descent into the deep psyche as a counterproductive and regrettable regression. He maintains that a return to the prepersonal potentials of the deep psyche is not simply a regressive U-turn to an earlier infantile and primitive state.

For Washburn, like Jung, the ego's encounter with the unconscious leads to a higher integration of the whole psyche. Extending the notion of "regression in the service of the ego," Washburn speaks of "regression in the service of transcendence" in order to put the seemingly regressive movement toward the unconscious in a larger and more positive context. He characterizes the ego's encounter with unconscious processes as the "downward loop of a developmental spiral that reconnects the ego with its nonegoic sources on the way to a higher integration with those sources" (p. 71). This statement nicely summarizes Washburn's view of the spirallike movement of spirituality toward transcendence. This viewpoint is consistent with the long clinical experience of Jung, Grof (1975), and analytical psychology. It also finds support among spiritual teachers such as Joseph Goldstein and Jack Kornfield.

Goldstein (1998), a longtime student of Buddhist contemplative traditions, believes even the best models provide only a glimpse of the vastness of the spiritual life and its movement. All developmental models, whether linear, spiral, or circular, are, at best, means to help liberate the mind from attachment. In his view, these models do not describe things as they "really are," but may provide useful orientation for particular people in a given culture at certain times in their lives. Goldstein emphasizes that spiritual development is a very individual journey that defies all attempts to capture it in a single model. Different models and metaphors are appropriate for different people. That having been said, Goldstein notes that, in his experience, the spiritual path spirals around, dealing with many of the same psychological and spiritual issues again and again.

Kornfield (1998), another well-known spiritual teacher of Buddhism, stresses the importance of the downward movement that is part of the spiritual journey. He emphasizes that his own path required a "descent" into the emotions and the body after years of transpersonal realizations as a monk in Southeast Asia. Kornfield maintains that Westerners tend toward the "linear mistake" when they draw upon Eastern spiritual models and maps, believing that if you have spiritual experiences of *satori* or *nirvana*, the rest of your physical, emotional, and psychological life will automatically take care of itself. However, he insists that you cannot do a spiritual "end run" around the basic need to come to terms with your body and emotions. He finds that the metaphors of the spiral and the mandala are particularly helpful in his experience because they allow for the great variations and vicissitudes of transpersonal or spiritual experiences and states.

SUMMARY

The midlife transition is increasingly recognized as a time of significant religious and spiritual changes, when people review their lives, modify their existing life structures, and come to terms with the major polarities of human existence, such as young/old, feminine/masculine, and life/death. During these changes people often become disoriented and lose their bearings. A host of psychological and spiritual symptoms may accompany this period of "middlescence," including depression, anxiety, boredom, a sense of meaninglessness, and compulsive behavior. This malaise often pushes people to explore their inner world in order to discover hitherto-unknown dimensions of their identity, values, and worldview.

Table 9 of the movement of spiritual development indicates that identity, values, and worldview often begin to reach the transpersonal levels during the midlife passage.

Table 9: Spiritual Development and Implicit Religion in Midlife

	Self-Stream	Values Stream	Worldview Stream
Transpersonal Level	A. Identity begins to extend to recognize possible participation in the divine	B. Values focus on universal principles: justice, compassion, life, love, peace	C. Worldview recognizes the interconnectedness of all things
Personal Level			
Prepersonal Level			

The midlife transformation involves all aspects of spirituality and implicit religion. Identity (A) begins to extend beyond the boundary of the personal level forged during adolescence and young adulthood. People may come to view their identity as participation in a divine drama, or experience an ultimate identity as part of God or the Goddess. Values (B) reach beyond self-preservation and the survival needs of family and nation, toward universal principles such as life, justice, peace, compassion, and love. Worldview (C) enlarges to recognize the interconnectedness of all things.

The transpersonal perspective provides a useful framework for understanding spiritual experiences and midlife transformation. It broadens science's traditionally mechanistic worldview to study spiritual and religious experiences and states of consciousness. This broadened viewpoint recognizes that human beings are more than biological machines;

they are also extensive fields of consciousness that transcend the physical body's space-time limitations. The spiritual experiences that frequently surround midlife transformation, such as mysticism, precognition, telepathy, and spiritual healing, testify to human beings' transcendent dimension.

Ken Wilber attempts to chart the various transpersonal levels of experience as a progression from nature mysticism to a nondual mysticism, where all phenomena are recognized as manifestations of consciousness. While the midlife transformation may entail some or all of these levels of consciousness, it may not involve such dramatic developments as we noted in the stories of Baba Ram Dass and Jean Shinoda Bolen. Jung describes the spiritual transformation of midlife as establishing the transcendent function, which takes into account both conscious and unconscious perspectives of life, and transcends them. This third point of view incorporates conscious judgment as well as dreams and intuitions of the unconscious, and shifts the psychological center of gravity from the ego to a larger personality center, the self, which reconciles divergent and conflicting psychological tendencies such as good/evil, female/male, and spirit/matter.

At midlife, people may encounter the mythical level of religious and spiritual experience as they confront the deeper levels of the unconscious, what Jung calls the collective unconscious. Here, the timeless images and symbols of the unconscious provide energy, support, and guidance for spiritual transformation. The hero myth expresses the ancient human quest for self-realization. The Eros and Psyche tale represents one of the most famous variations of the hero myth in Western civilization. Psyche's story portrays the essence of spiritual development, namely, the coming together of the human and the divine: It indicates that the human psyche attains the final heroic victory against seemingly overwhelming odds. The psyche is ultimately divinized by its encounter with love (Eros) and other spiritual forces (the goddesses, gods, and nature) in the story.

Timeless myths such as Eros and Psyche still provide guidance as people experience the depths of their spiritual development, though as many in the modern world are increasingly unable to appreciate traditional myths, they develop "personal myths" to orient them on their life journey. Personal myths are influenced by family and contemporary culture, and they evolve as people interpret and reinterpret their ever-changing experience. These personal myths are accessible to conscious reflection and journal-keeping, but they usually operate outside awareness and typically appear in dreams.

Myths and personal myths generally embody a view of the self that is relational. Human development takes place in relation to family, peers, and society in the external world, and in relation to figures of the inner world, including the goddesses and gods of mythology. Although the first part of the hero's journey is frequently about becoming an individual, separating from mother, family, and the environment, spiritual transformation involves a profound experience of the unconscious and relationship with figures of the personal and collective unconscious. Kathryn Rabuzzi emphasizes that the relational character of the self is even more apparent for women who experience the "motherself," wherein two selves, mother and child, coexist in a "two-in-one" kind of selfhood.

Myths and metaphors help us to imagine and understand invisible inner processes of religious and spiritual development, especially in the midlife passage. The spiritual life is so vast that it cannot adequately be grasped by a single metaphor. Linear metaphors emphasize a positive direction in the course of religious and spiritual development. Wilber's view of ascending stages of transpersonal experience and levels of consciousness provides a sense of progress as we consider the life of the individual and the evolution of the human species. This metaphor has served us in our table to indicate the general movement of spiritual development in the life cycle, and particularly the entry into a transpersonal level of consciousness at midlife. Nonlinear metaphors add depth to our understanding of spiritual development and transformation. The spiral metaphor highlights the gradual and irregular character of human transformation, which often seems like ten steps forward and nine steps back. The spiral metaphor of inner development helps to explain discouraging setbacks and apparent regressions on the spiritual path.

CHAPTER SIX

THE SPIRITUAL JOURNEY OF LATE ADULTHOOD

——————— ?❧ ———————

> The real challenge of old age is to risk all habitual frames
> of reference and to open the mind to another field of possi-
> bility that lies beyond the physical. Having gained a foothold
> in the inner world, we then can encounter death with calm
> anticipation rather than horrifying fear.
>
> — Joseph Pearce, *Evolution's End*

Late adulthood in our society appears to be the most problematic stage
of life because of our emphasis on youth and growth and the avoidance
of aging. The many negative images of aging with its physical, psychological, and social limitations make it difficult to appreciate the positive
potential of old age. Nevertheless, here I wish to underline the opportunities for spiritual and religious growth in late adulthood. Throughout
this book, we have viewed the human life cycle as a progressive unfolding of implicit religion and spirituality in the direction of transpersonal
identity, values, and worldview. The transpersonal developments that
frequently begin during the midlife passage often reach their culmination toward the end of the life cycle.

This chapter focuses on commentators who highlight the spiritual
potential of late adulthood. Eugene Bianchi's notion of aging as a spiritual journey, Zalmon Schachter-Shalomi's concept of sage-ing, and Lars
Tornstam's theory of gerotranscendence help us to see the growing
edges of spirituality and implicit religion in old age. One of the peculiar-
ities of old age is the discrepancy between the elderly's sense of themselves and the objective changes brought on by age. For many elderly

people, a deep sense of self seems to be ageless despite changes in physical and social circumstances. Finally, we explore the inevitable question of death and what may lie beyond it. We shall see that ideas about death and a hereafter can greatly influence the elderly's spirituality, especially their sense of identity and attitude toward their remaining years.

Overview: Challenges of Old Age

In this section, we examine some of the main features that characterize old age generally, especially the rhythm of activity and withdrawal, and the frequent negative views of aging which challenge the spiritual and religious life of the elderly. Our understanding of late adulthood has undergone significant changes in recent decades due to increased longevity, frequent early retirements, and improved health. Just as childhood became a discernible period of life with unique characteristics in the seventeenth and eighteenth centuries, and adolescence is largely an invention of the twentieth century, so too conceptions of late adulthood have become more differentiated. Today gerontologists generally distinguish separate age groups among the elderly because considering all old people together obscures important differences between subgroups. The common age categories used are: the young-old (c. sixty-five to seventy-five years old), the old (seventy-five to eighty-five years old), and the old-old (eighty-five years old and beyond). However, there is no universal agreement on these categories. For example, gerontologist Bernice Neugarten (1996a) observes that retirement, which is itself variable, is often used as the marker that signifies the beginning of the young-old period. Thus, she extends the young-old category to include those who retire at fifty-five years old, with the consequence that there is overlap between middle age and the young-old; at the same time, she notes that some people call themselves middle-aged until their seventies.

Irving Rosow (1974) calls attention to the problems of adjustment facing the elderly due to a lack of social support. He states that old age develops gradually and informally in our society, though it may be punctuated by retirement, widowhood, or institutionalization. He finds it regrettable that our society lacks rites of passage to old age, making it more difficult for people to adapt in late life. The elderly in our society have little preparation for the role changes occurring in late adulthood, and they must learn to adapt for themselves, without cultural help in their transition to old age. The married elderly adjust better to life changes than do the single elderly.

Activity versus Disengagement in Late Adulthood

Even though we lack rites of passage to guide people in late adulthood, our society's theories of aging reveal cultural expectations for successful adaptation to old age. Two important theories of how people respond to old age, namely, activity theory and disengagement theory,[1] indicate the primary tendencies and goals of late adulthood in our society.

Activity Theory

Activity theory maintains that healthy aging means staying active and involved with others. According to this theory, people must remain active, even if this means discovering substitute activities when they suffer physical, financial, and social setbacks. Advocates of activity theory insist that the healthy old do not voluntarily seek disengagement from society, but are forced to the sidelines; they view disengagement theory as a rationalization to cover up society's rejection of the elderly. Robert Havighurst and Ruth Albrecht (1980), proponents of activity theory, insist that personal adjustment in old age is directly related to activity; the more active older people are, the better mentally, physically, and socially adjusted they are. "Keep active" is their basic recipe for happiness in old age. They argue that personal and social tasks give the elderly meaning and sense of purpose, which are so vital for human beings at every age. However, they recognize that physical helplessness, loss of spouse, family, and friends, and feelings of rejection can undermine the ability and desire to remain active.

Barrow (1992) states that research in gerontology during the last fifty years has generally found a positive correlation between being active and aging successfully, but recent studies recognize that elders need not maintain the same high degree of activity they had in their middle age in order to be satisfied with their lives in old age. Laura Carstensen (1992) observes two weaknesses in the activity theory of aging, stating that activity theory cannot account for the empirical findings that, first, social-activity levels do not necessarily predict physical or psychological well-being and, second, the vast majority of older people do not take advantage of available social opportunities such as senior centers. Eugene Bianchi (1993) notes another potential drawback of activity theory. He fears it might be interpreted to mean that the elderly will be considered successful in aging only to the degree that they sustain the

---

1. Activity theory preceded disengagement theory, but was not recognized as a distinct theory until after disengagement theory arose (Barrow, 1992).

activities of middle age. Activity theory in this guise, he charges, is really a subtle way to glorify youth at the expense of old age, especially when the prescribed activities are dictated by social convention.

Disengagement Theory

As people approach old age, they often withdraw from the activities and roles they engaged in during the early and middle adult years. This observation is the basis for disengagement theory, which holds that both the elderly and the wider community favor the disengagement of older people. The theory argues that older people develop different values than the young, leading them to become less emotionally involved in the activities and social relationships that occupied them in middle age. In this view, older people naturally disengage from their social roles as their place in society and their health diminish, leading them to become more preoccupied with themselves. Society reinforces this withdrawal through its lack of interest in, and opportunities for, the elderly, but essentially disengagement is seen as a natural rather than an imposed process.

Though they admit that no single theory fully accounts for the aging personality, Cumming and Henry (1961) describe their disengagement theory as a commonsense theory which highlights important aspects of aging. In their view, activity theory is mainly a product of the "outgoingness" of middle-aged Americans who believe in an ever-expanding life. They grant that disengagement occurs earlier for some people than for others, and that the number of bonds broken, and the number remaining, also differ from person to person. Further, they observe differences between the disengagement patterns of men and women, noting that men tend to make an abrupt transition from the engaged to the disengaged state, while women often have a smoother but longer transition period. They attribute this difference to men losing their lifelong instrumental roles, whereas women retain their same basic socioemotional roles, even though they are forced to redirect their previously developed skills.

Studies have found that disengagement occurs at differing rates and in differing aspects of behavior. Frances Carp (1968) identifies a number of areas in which disengagement may occur, including ties to persons, material possessions, and to worldly activities and ideas. To the extent that disengagement is part of preparing for death, it must be accomplished in each of these areas. Carp further notes that there are important differences between disengagement with family and with friends. Increased peer engagement is associated with increased satisfaction with both friends and family, while disengagement from peers may encourage the elderly to return to a controlling parental role, which can interfere with the parent-child relationship and cause maladjustment. Disengagement from a directive parental role, on the other hand, is associated with a more positive self-image for the elderly.

Critics of disengagement theory charge that this theory makes a virtue out of an unfortunate necessity. Robert Atchley (1971) agrees with proponents of disengagement theory that, as people age, they become more preoccupied with their own inner states, but disagrees with the conclusion that this automatically distances the elderly from their external environment. Others suggest that if disengagement is primarily an intrinsic process in old age, as Cumming and Henry argue, then it might begin in the eighties or nineties, when people feel nearer to death. Ultimately, there are varying degrees of disengagement as people move into old age and disengagement is not a unitary phenomenon.

Further, Atchley's (1971) research indicates that disengagement is not always functional for many individuals, and even for society. In his study of aging professors, he found that their desire to remain engaged triumphed over disengagement and that older professors are equally or even more committed to their work than younger and middle-aged professors. This research causes him to distinguish between physical disengagement and psychological disengagement. He believes that certain interesting and attractive roles in society may interfere with, or even prevent, psychological disengagement, even when age and health lead to physical disengagement. Such cases undercut disengagement theory's claim to universality and inevitability. Atchley argues that disengagement theory does not sufficiently allow for the personality and social-role differences he observed in his study of aging professors.

Activity and Disengagement as Complementary

The research of Bernice Neugarten and Robert Havighurst is designed to test the adequacy of both disengagement and activity theories of aging. Their work confirms selective aspects of each theory. On the one hand, they find that older people generally tend to disengage socially and psychologically as they move from middle age to old age, thus supporting one tenet of disengagement theory. On the other hand, their research shows that life satisfaction is directly related to social interaction, a main contention of activity theory.

Havighurst et al. (1996) draw on repeated interviews with 159 men and women between the ages of fifty and ninety years old, excluding people living in institutions and those too ill to participate. Their study attempts to measure both social and psychological engagement. They define social engagement as interactions with other people in everyday living, which they measure on the basis of reports of the person's daily round of activities and performance in life roles, such as worker, spouse, parent, grandparent, friend, and so on. These measures show a decrease of social engagement with increasing age. In addition, they find psychological engagement, defined as the extent to which a person is emotionally invested in persons and events in the external world, decreases with increasing age. These findings support disengagement as a process of aging.

At the same time, measures of life satisfaction based on positive self-concept, positive mood, and goals achieved indicate that satisfaction is positively related to engagement. In general, those persons with higher amounts of activity displayed greater psychological well-being than those with lower activity. This finding supports the activity theory of aging. Overall, the research of Havighurst and colleagues highlights diversity in patterns of aging. They maintain that the rate and patterns of disengagement vary considerably from group to group. In their view, this diversity is due to complex interactions between biological, psychological, and sociological factors, and to differences in personality type. They conclude that, while their research partially supports both activity and disengagement theories, it also reveals that neither theory deals sufficiently with the issue of individual differences.

We can view these competing theories as opposite poles on a spectrum of experience in late adulthood. Both are based on important observations of what is happening toward the end of the human life cycle. Disengagement theory focuses on the very real inclination of many elderly people to explore their inner lives and penetrate beneath the everyday world they have known all their lives. The curiosity and desire to know more about the profound mysteries encountered in the course of life can be particularly compelling when older people realize they are approaching the final chapters of their own life story. The powerful human drive for meaning often moves the elderly to consider how their personal story fits into the larger stories of society, history, and the cosmos. Of course, this curiosity and desire for meaning may be more or less prominent in older people, just as in other stages of life.

At the same time, proponents of activity theory correctly observe that people of all ages, including the elderly, feel better about themselves and life when they are engaged in meaningful relationships and activities. This fact leads activity theorists to view the elderly's disengagement as an unfortunate course brought on by negative images of old age rampant in our youth-oriented culture and by the exclusion of old people from active participation in society. Of course, there are great individual differences in the degree to which the elderly rely on other people and activities to attain the optimal balance between activity and withdrawal for their mental and physical health. The ideal balance may depend greatly on individual temperament.

When we recognize the experiential basis of disengagement and activity theories, we can view both as important ways of thinking about late adulthood. They call attention to different phases in the contact-withdrawal rhythm that many schools of psychotherapy see as fundamental to psychological health at any stage of life. Activity theory focuses on the importance of alert contact with others and the environment for healthy adaptation to the constant changes of life. The elderly need ways to interact with society for their self-esteem and sense of purpose. They need to contribute the wisdom gleaned from many years of experience to the community. Disengagement theory focuses on the need to withdraw, from time to time, in order to process and digest ongoing experience. The elderly should have time to reflect on their long experience and attend to their inner lives after years of pressure to conform to occupational and social roles. An accurate picture of late adulthood requires the insights derived from both theories.

Continuity of Self in Late Adulthood

Gerontological research shows considerable continuity in the personality from adulthood into old age, suggesting that major aspects of spirituality and implicit religion remain largely the same as in midlife. Most old people continue earlier patterns of thought, emotion, and behavior, although physical and mental disabilities may precipitate substantial personality changes. Some consider continuity theory a major alternative to both disengagement theory and activity theory for understanding late adulthood. Continuity theory holds that the personality continues basically unchanged throughout the life cycle, and people's adaptation to early adulthood and midlife predicts their adaptation to old age. While a powerful religious experience can cause dramatic shifts in a person's spirituality and religion at almost any point in life, the norm is continuity with past attitudes and values. This continuity leads some to emphasize the need to focus on developing spiritual interests in earlier adulthood if people are to realize their full potential in old age. Nouwen and Gaffney (1974) maintain that if people contact their inner self and learn not to depend on success as measured by external standards in early and middle adulthood, they are more likely to maximize the unique conditions of their old age and direct their attention toward the ultimate dimensions of human existence.

Robert Atchley (1991), emphasizing the continuity of the self through time, notes that continuity is an important strategy helping most old people to adapt to internal and external changes taking place in their lives. Continuity of self-image means that the elderly are sufficiently able to incorporate life changes so that they and others can still recognize them as the same unique persons they were. Continuity of relationships reinforces a continuous self-image in old people and minimizes the effects of aging. Atchley finds that most older people have a highly positive self-image which resists disconfirmation. In his view, the elderly tend to recall the past as a drama in which they are the leading players. This reconstruction of personal history shapes the elderly's spirituality and sense of self, giving them a feeling of having more control and influence than other actors in their life drama. They also typically take credit for positive developments in their life story and blame outside forces for negative events. Surprisingly, Atchley observes that older people can accept negative stereotypes about aging and the aged, but, at the same time, think that these stereotypes do not apply to them.

Anthropologist Sharon Kaufman (1986) observes from her fieldwork with the elderly that they express a sense of self that is ageless. They feel their identity, a major component of spirituality and implicit religion, is continuous despite the physical and social changes they have experienced, as can be seen in the following examples from Kaufman's study. Martha, a woman of seventy, states that she feels thirty years old, and when she sees recent pictures of herself she is taken aback, thinking that cannot be her. Even when she looks in the mirror, she does not see herself as old. Ida, a lady of ninety-two, says that she thinks of herself as much younger, as she was in the distant past. When she sees herself reflected in a store window, she is shocked at how old she looks because she never thinks of herself in that way. Percy, a man of ninety-two, believes he has the same attitude toward life that he had many years ago, and when he is unable to keep up when walking with younger people, he feels deep down that that slower person is not really himself. Ethel, a woman of eighty-four, says she generally feels like she did at thirty years old, except for the few times when she has been very sick. Kaufman holds that, contrary to popular conceptions of the elderly, they themselves emphasize the continuity of an ageless self that endures the changes of a lifetime.

Kaufman's case studies illustrate ways of how people organize, interpret, and connect life experiences to create themes of their identity. She argues that old people's ageless self maintains continuity by means of a creative process, whereby the self formulates and reformulates personal and cultural symbols of their past to create a meaningful and coherent sense of self in the present. Her method of analyzing the life stories of old people highlights their feelings about their experience and identity. She believes that her study of the ageless self shows that the aging process is about more than losses and deprivation. In her view, focusing on the integrative aspect of aging, namely, creating ongoing meaning and identity, broadens and deepens our knowledge of the aging process and dispels the negative stereotypes of aging as mainly decline and loss.

Sense of Limited Time in Old Age

Many believe that older people live primarily in the past because most of their years are behind them. Jon Hendricks (2001) disagrees. He maintains that it is misleading to think older people have a constrained sense of the future merely because their view may be more abstracted and less grounded in narrow personal concerns. Because their life expectancy is limited, they are aware that the future is about more than their personal presence. They conceive of a future that is about the people and issues they care about, namely, children, grandchildren, and younger generations. Hendricks labels this perspective a "generative futurity," one that looks beyond the individual's own life.

In Victor Frankl's (1986) view, anticipating the end of one's life allows people to attain maximal meaning. It often moves people to focus on what has already been accomplished. They can reflect with pride and joy on the life already lived, work done, love loved, and suffering suffered. Frankl advises those near the end of life to review their lives so as to derive the fullest possible meaning. Harry Moody (1988) stresses the importance of storytelling as part of this life review. Narratives of forgotten times help the elderly to recover meaning in their lives. Structuring the life story as a spiritual journey often helps individuals to appreciate the religious and spiritual aspects of their lives (Quinnan, 1994). Storytelling has always been at the heart of traditional cultures, where life stories contribute to respect and dignity for old age. Moody believes that in our society cultural policy must assist older people to recover their identity as culture bearers and culture creators. Crafts, writing, and creative drama in senior centers can allow the elderly to go beyond previous roles and explore new values that express deeper aspects of the self, thus broadening their spirituality and implicit religion.

Carstensen (1992) hypothesizes that the heightened significance of emotions for older adults is due to the realization that future time is limited. Awareness of the ephemeral quality of life and inevitable endings increases older adults' appreciation of what is important and precious in life. According to Carstensen's "socioemotional selectivity theory," the same basic goals operate throughout life, such as intimacy and knowledge about oneself and the world, but the importance of specific goals depends on whether time is perceived as expansive or constrained. In her view, knowledge-related goals are especially important during the early years of life and young adulthood, and gradually decrease in importance as knowledge accumulates and the future seems less expansive; emotion-related goals are especially salient during infancy and early childhood, and again in later adulthood. This increased emphasis on the emotional life contributes to the elderly's values and relationship to the world, key aspects of their spirituality and implicit religion.

Negative Views of Aging

The negative images of old age are many: a decline in health and physical strength, the death of family members and friends, and the loss of social status as productive workers. Researchers and the media have tended to focus on negative aspects of old age, such as disease, physical deterioration, impoverishment, widowhood, and a sense of meaninglessness—the many things that can go wrong at this stage in life. All of these losses can undermine self-esteem and a positive sense of identity. Death itself seems not that far off and presents a real threat for the aged. The potential suffering and indignities surrounding the dying process may be more frightening than death itself. Simone de Beauvoir (1972) presents a bleak image of old age in general, which she sees as a "calamity." She also criticizes industrial societies for adding to the misery of the elderly by treating them as discarded pieces of scrap no longer of use to the economic system.

Negative stereotypes encourage society to see all old people as stuck in their ways or unable to manage their lives. Kaufman (1986) sums up the negative stereotypes of old age that are shared by both scholars and society in general as "decline, loss, and disease." Robert Atchley (1991) lists a wide range of physical and emotional stereotypes of old people, mostly based on appearance, behavior, and capabilities.

On the negative side, people view the elderly as physically disabled, nearly deaf, senile, dependent on family, old-fashioned, forgetful, lonely, sad, and bored. On the positive side, people see the elderly as wise, understanding, happy, supportive, and loving. According to Havighurst and Albrecht (1980), most people in our society regard aging and old age as a burden they abhor, and this general attitude may lead them to reject the elderly or discriminate against them. Such discrimination based on age has been termed "ageism" (Nuessel, 1982).

An early study of old-age stereotypes shows that people perceive the elderly as unproductive, a burden on their children, stubborn, grouchy, and lonely (Tuckman & Lorge, 1953). More recently, Erdman Palmore (1990) lists the main negative stereotypes associated with old age as illness, impotence, ugliness, mental decline, uselessness, isolation, mental illness, poverty, and depression, although he maintains that current old-age stereotypes are not as negative today as they were in the 1950s. A more subtle form of stereotyping portrays old people as economically, socially, or psychologically disadvantaged. Even this kind of compassionate stereotyping perpetuates dependency and low self-esteem, lowering the expectations of what the elderly can achieve (Barrow, 1992).

Advertising contributes to a negative image of the elderly by promoting the values of the youth culture, emphasizing the need to cover up physical signs of aging. Advertisers help instill a fear of aging in order to sell products that promise to delay or remove negative signs of age. Making people dissatisfied with their present appearance, age, and circumstances is good for sales. By calling attention to or creating a need, advertisers can sell a whole variety of products to make us look and feel like we are not old. Becoming old is portrayed in advertisements as something to avoid at all costs, leaving us feeling like getting old is some kind of shameful failure.

According to Ram Dass (2000), aging remains one of our culture's last taboos. He charges that television presents a very small number of images of older people, and those few depict the elderly as silly, stubborn, vindictive, or cute. In his view, this limited portrayal of the elderly reflects our market-driven culture's antipathy toward the elderly. The overall message that comes through the media is that aging is a necessary evil, a great social ill, and an affront to esthetics. Ram Dass believes that women suffer more than men from the current obsession with staying young and physically attractive. He characterizes this fight to stay young as "a losing battle against time" that is "inhumane toward ourselves and the cycle of life" (p. 14).

In Ram Dass's view, the philosophical materialism that dominates Western culture contributes to our negative attitudes about aging and the elderly. The worldview that nothing exists beyond what we experience through our senses profoundly influences how we regard the cycle of our lives. Death appears to be the end of the road if nothing exists after our physical bodies die. Ram Dass believes that when we realize that the ego is only a fragment of who we are and that we are more than our bodies and minds, we can begin to reimagine getting older as a healing path rather than a decline into oblivion. Recognizing our larger self can allow us to regard aging as an important spiritual opportunity.

Barrow (1992) maintains that in certain respects our society is relaxing some ageist attitudes and is loosening its expectations for particular ages, citing examples of a twenty-three-year-old computer company owner, a thirty-six-year-old grandmother, a sixty-year-old college student, and an eighty-year-old business executive. In his view, changing marriage, career, and educational patterns now contribute to a more flexible attitude toward what people are and do at different times in life. These trends can counter some negative stereotypes of what old people are like and what they can do. Eugene Bianchi advises that the elderly reflect on the degree to which they have incorporated stereotypes about aging into the way they view themselves; they need to explore their own inner lives to determine where negative images of aging prevent them from developing their potential. He recommends that the elderly read about persons who have been models of fulfillment and accomplishment in old age in order to overcome prevalent and self-defeating stereotypes.

Bianchi emphasizes the need to face the social attitudes and evils that handicap the elderly. In his view, the competitive ethos of contemporary society militates against reforms to benefit the aged. He contrasts the way old people are treated in modern societies and in nonindustrialized societies, where older people have more political and economic power. Bianchi notes that modern societies must strive to improve economic conditions for the elderly, because old people who are financially secure manifest greater self-esteem and morale, which in turn inspires them to be more involved with others.

EMPIRICAL STUDIES

This section considers findings that show religion and spirituality have a very positive effect on the elderly. The work of Erik and Joan Erikson will also help us understand aspects of implicit religion in old age, especially the elements of identity and values. Research on religion and aging has grown rapidly in recent years, due in part to the high degree of religiosity among the current cohort of older adults. Some believe the growing research on religion and aging reflects efforts to find more positive alternatives to the biomedical views that focus chiefly on physical decline in old age. The literature on aging has now produced a large body of evidence about the effects of religion on health, showing that religious and spiritual beliefs, behaviors, and experiences contribute significantly to the well-being of the elderly; nevertheless, mainstream scientists and scholars are often unaware of this expanding empirical support of a salutary role for religion (Levin, 1994). As older adults experience declining health, they often participate less in organized religion, but their spirituality and implicit religion may continue to grow and develop.

Gerontological research has attempted to go beyond simple measures of religiosity, such as religious affiliation or attendance, to capture the deeper dimensions of religion. McFadden and Levin (1996) report that the results of more than 200 published studies of religion's impact on physical health show the positive effect of religious involvement, whether this is measured by religious attendance, belief in God, religious experience, or frequency of prayer. They suggest that religion may produce these salutary effects in a variety of ways:

- religious commitment is usually associated with lower rates of deleterious behaviors, such as smoking, drinking, and drug abuse;
- religious participation can act as a social support network;
- religious worship and prayer engender positive emotional experiences, such as relaxation, hope, forgiveness, and love;
- religious faith may lead to optimism about one's health, trusting that God looks after all aspects of life;
- religious worldviews are significantly correlated with health; and
- a combination of the aforementioned links.

McFadden and Levin note that emotional processes underlie all of these possible links between religion and health.

Harold Koenig (1992) cites growing evidence that in later life mature commitment to religious beliefs and activities help the elderly cope with their problems. Studies show that people who consider religion important in their lives have better adjustment to bereavement, lower death anxiety, fewer depressive symptoms, and lower suicide rates. Death of family and friends is a frequent experience for most old people. Studies show that religious beliefs and practices often help cushion the sometimes overwhelming pain associated with such losses (Koenig, 1994). Religion provides both a cognitive framework and emotional support for dealing with grief at the death of loved ones. Where people derive their identity and purpose primarily from religious and spiritual beliefs, the loss of a spouse may be less threatening to their sense of self than it would if their spouse was the center of their life and identity.

According to Koenig's (1994) study, even though anxiety about death diminishes in late life, 50 to 75 percent of older adults say they experience fear or anxiety about death. He cites a number of studies that indicate an inverse relationship between religiosity and fear of death. In his view, the sense that God is present and watching over the elderly gives them a certain tranquility as they face death.

Depression is the most common treatable psychiatric disorder in late life. It not only destroys satisfaction and meaning in life, but it also interferes with people's ability to comply with medical treatments and can lead to suicide. Koenig (1992) describes his large-scale mental health study of hospitalized veterans, which examines depression in 850 men aged sixty-five and older. All the patients were evaluated on self-rated and observer-rated scales of depression. Koenig reports that those who used religion to cope with their depression had significantly fewer depressive symptoms, based on both self-report and observer ratings.

Some intriguing empirical studies of aging indicate that older people pay increased attention to, and place greater value on, life's emotional facets than do younger adults. The elderly better regulate their emotions with age, and they maximize emotional satisfaction from social interactions. Gross et al. (1997) studied emotional experience and control across diverse samples from Africa, Europe, and the United States. They found that older adults had better control of their emotions and fewer negative emotions than younger adults. In their view, the control that older people have over their emotions permits them to selectively enhance positive emotions and dampen their experience of negative emotions, such as sadness, anger, and fear.

Another study supports the view that, as people age, they regulate their emotions better. Laura Carstensen et al. (1995) videotaped middle-aged and older married couples discussing emotionally charged topics of marital conflict and coded the discussions for content and emotional expression. They found that older couples showed better emotional regulation according to both the subjective reports and the observations of the discussions. The older couples exhibited less anger, disgust, belligerence, and whining, and expressed more affection to each other in the course of resolving their marital conflicts. Their research demonstrates that emotions become more salient in older couples, contrary to the popular view that emotions are dampened and flat in old age. Further, Carstensen et al. show that the frequency and duration of negative emotions decrease with age, at least until very old age, when negative emotions begin to increase. However, even among the very old, negative emotions are experienced no more frequently than in early adulthood. This research suggests that older adults' emotional experiences are more complex than those of younger adults, meaning the elderly experience more mixed positive and negative emotions at the same time (Kennedy et al., 2001).

Erikson's Eighth Age

Erik Erikson characterizes the final age of life as ego-integrity versus despair and disgust. He views late adulthood largely in terms of integrating and accepting one's unique life lived thus far, thereby contributing to their implicit religion or spirituality. The elderly person casts a backward glance as the ego strives for emotional integration of life's varied and sometimes contradictory experiences. The main achievement in this process, according to Erikson, is to accept one's life as something that had to be—even with its limitations and failures. This acceptance includes a retrospective sense of fate having guided life. If the elderly person is unable to reach a degree of emotional integration, despair develops around the realization that sufficient time and energy no longer remain for building something that seems "right."

Achieving wisdom, the virtue or ego strength appropriate to this life stage, requires the elderly to live in a larger context. Ideally, they should see their lives as part of human history, a meaningful expression of where the cycle of human generations stands at a particular time. In the Eriksons' (1997) view, the end of the life cycle turns back on the beginning. The hope engendered in the young as their first virtue or ego strength is related to the mature hope and faith of the aged as they approach the end of their lives. The Eriksons grant that this relationship between the beginning and the end of the life cycle is more evident in cultures where there is continuity of family life and where children are deeply influenced by their encounters with old people. Such cultures provide the elderly with the vital involvement they need to stay really alive; at the same time, the young learn to trust life as they experience the integrity of their elders.

The Eriksons emphasize that the individual life cycle must always be considered in relation to its social context, which includes society's images and ideals of the various stages of life. They find this relationship between individual and society especially problematic in regard to social attitudes towards late adulthood. The Eriksons (1997) observe: "Lacking a culturally viable ideal of old age, our civilization does not really harbor a concept of the whole of life" (p. 114). This lack results in a society that does not know how to integrate old people into its vital functioning. To the degree that elders are overlooked or viewed as embodiments of shame rather than bearers of wisdom, society has failed in a central task.

Facing death squarely as a necessary part of life leads the elderly to reflect on life's ultimate horizons, and how these horizons form the backdrop of the movement from one generation to the next. The Eriksons believe the life cycle is fulfilled with the development of children who do not fear life because their elders have reached a state of mind in which they do not fear death. A life review often helps older people to achieve some degree of ego integrity and some gerontologists believe that writing autobiographies can enable the elderly to capture and share with others the essence of their spiritual lives (Achenbaum, 2001). The Eriksons note that, as many older people look back over their lives, they focus on their relationships, especially their marriage, children, and grandchildren. The elderly frequently feel that they contribute to their grandchildren's development and take pride in these achievements. This connection to younger generations gives the elderly coherence and a sense of their place in the cycles of life. Reviewing their lives allows older adults to integrate rather than deny the mixed feelings that come from comparing life actually lived with the life anticipated in youthful imaginings (Erikson et al., 1986). Coming to terms with failures and missed opportunities as well as accomplishments requires the elderly to experience a wide range of positive and negative emotions on their way to ego integrity, a fundamental aspect of their spirituality and implicit religion.

A Ninth Age

Erik's longtime wife and collaborator, Joan Erikson, emphasizes the challenges of being in one's eighties and nineties. At this age, even well-cared-for bodies lose some of their autonomy. She observes that despair, which threatens the eighth stage, is a close companion in the last stage of life. Erik Erikson himself lived to the ripe age of ninety-two, allowing him to experience the extreme challenges of growing very old. This experience led him to reflect on a possible ninth stage of life. While Erik did not publish these late thoughts, Joan wrote about their views on the ninth age after his death.

The Eriksons (1997) stress the down-to-earth character of ego integrity in late adulthood, the way it promotes contact with people and the world. In their view, ego integrity heightens our experience of light, sound, smell, and touch, making everything and everybody matter more intensely. Such integrity is sturdy and reliable, they maintain, not ethereal. It requires the attentive management of everyday activities in order to achieve a day well lived. Ego integrity demands the effort to adapt to life's changes and a willingness to accept disabilities with perspective and even humor. Joan, who lived to be ninety-five years old, describes how despair is always close at hand for those in their eighties and nineties, as their bodies lose autonomy, strength, and independence. Self-esteem and self-confidence often weaken as the older person experiences declining physical and mental powers.

All of the challenges of previous stages are revisited, the Eriksons point out, but now, in old age, the "dystonic" or negative elements are more dominant.[2] They underscore this change by placing the dystonic elements first in the life-stage chart, as the elderly face their more restricted daily existence. In their view, the ninth stage now looks like this, as the achievements of earlier stages are challenged in very old age. Mistrust often becomes a more prominent factor than trust. A certain amount of mistrust protects the elderly, but as the body inevitably weakens, mistrust threatens to take over all aspects of their lives. Shame and doubt become more prominent than autonomy. The very old may experience shame and self-doubt when they lose control over their bodies and life choices. Moreover, guilt may become more prominent than initiative. A sense of inadequacy and guilt often follow close on the heals of failed initiatives. Feelings of inferiority rise as competence

---

2. See chapter two for an explanation of dystonic and syntonic elements in Erikson's theory.

wanes. When challenges press the very old to do more than they are able, their sense of inadequacy may seem overwhelming.

As old people's status and roles change, they often feel confused about who they are. The identity that was a prized achievement of adolescence and early adulthood now seems in question. The contrast between the clarity of an earlier identity and the uncertainty about their role in very old age can be disorienting. Elders in the ninth stage may feel isolated as their usual ways of relating to others are altered by new living circumstances, dependencies, and infirmities. While the elderly may not be productive in society's terms, they still want to be needed. Stagnation threatens to take over if they withdraw totally from all forms of generativity and caring for and with others.

It is clear from the Eriksons' description of the ninth stage of the life cycle that the dystonic elements inevitably dominate as time marches on. Even the virtue of wisdom is sorely tested, as the very old may no longer be able to focus much energy on the retrospective accounting of their lives to date, which is a big part of wisdom in the eighth stage. Most of the old person's attention may be caught up in the daily functions of life, so that getting through a day intact is achievement enough. People in their eighties or nineties may also be worn down by the losses they have suffered, the death of parents, partners, brothers, sisters, lifelong friends, and even children. To cope with these losses a certain basic trust is necessary, according to the Eriksons. At this point in life, the trust and hope developed in early childhood is again seen as the foundation of the human personality, allowing the very old to endure in the face of loss and death.

All of these personal challenges are exacerbated by a society that segregates the elderly from the larger community. According to the Eriksons, our society has not adequately envisioned a program to incorporate elders into modern living arrangements. This segregation of the elders diminishes the lives of both young and old people alike. They ask, "How can we learn from our elders how to prepare for the end of life . . . if our role models do not live among us?" The Eriksons (1997) distinguish between consciously chosen and forced withdrawal of the elderly. They maintain that withdrawal from the usual activities of daily life may represent a paradox of continued involvement despite disengagement, what Erik Erikson has called a "deeply involved disinvolvement." The focus here is not on letting go, so much as the development of a new self which is open to transcendence. From this perspective, withdrawal may or may not be a part of the spiritual potential of old age.

Even with the gradual disintegration occurring in very old age, the Eriksons maintain that a cosmic, transcendent perspective can emerge. This cosmic perspective, which has been labeled gerotranscendence, offers a kind of peace of mind beyond a materialistic and strictly rational perspective on life. This broadened perspective can be a major foundation of the spirituality and implicit religion of the elderly. The Eriksons playfully call this spiritual state "gerotranscen*dance*" to emphasize that play, joy, and music may be part of the self emerging in old age. In her view, the image of a dance implies contact with others and with the planet; moreover, transcen*dance* refers to the dance of life and the arts which speak deeply and meaningfully to our hearts and souls.

SPIRITUAL POTENTIAL IN LATE ADULTHOOD

In recent years a number of writers have attempted to focus on the important spiritual developments that can occur in late adulthood. Here we consider three key contributors to our awareness of the religious and spiritual opportunities in old age.

Gerotranscendence

Lars Tornstam (1994) maintains that human aging, especially when it reaches into old age, manifests a general potential toward gerotranscendence, which he defines as a shift from a materialistic and rational vision to a more cosmic and transcendent one. Gerotranscendent people feel a sense of communion with the "spirit of the universe" and have a broadened self-understanding that alters their experience of space, time, life, and death. According to Tornstam, this altered viewpoint is a significant religious and spiritual development, even though gerotranscendence is not necessarily connected with organized religion.

The theory of gerotranscendence can be understood as a way to reinterpret patterns in old age that have been previously identified as disengaging from life. Tornstam locates his theory between disengagement theory, with its emphasis on withdrawing from life in preparation for death, and activity theory, with its focus on old age as a continuation of midlife developments and values. In his view, both disengagement theory and activity theory have tended to focus on external behavior and to overlook the crucial factor of inner meaning, which is the key to gerotranscendence. As a person ages, he argues, the degree of transcendence should increase if conditions are right. Aging potentially leads to a new cosmic perspective which views individuals as interconnected with earlier generations and the cosmos. Tornstam believes that the process toward gerotranscendence can be obstructed or accelerated by social and cultural circumstances. Not everyone automatically reaches a high degree of gerotranscendence as they age; materialistic worldviews and values frequently interfere with the development of this cosmic perspective. Gerotranscendence, with its enlarged view of the self and the world, looks forward and outward, in contrast to Erikson's view of integrity and wisdom, for example, which mainly looks back on life lived, accepting both its good and bad aspects.

Gerotranscendence recognizes a contemplative quality among the elderly, a fact largely overlooked by activity theory. Eugene Thomas (2001) finds support for the gerotranscendence concept in research he carried out in Turkey. There, he conducted interviews and participant observation with both religious and nonreligious persons over the age of sixty-five. The religious group was composed of mostly male (fourteen of fifteen), devout Muslims identified with the Sufi tradition. Eight women and nine men constituted the nonreligious group. Over half of the total respondents displayed some gerotranscendence; five of the respondents exhibited the full range of gerotranscendence, including a unitive cosmology, self-understanding, decrease in self-centeredness, awareness of the mystery dimension of life, and the importance of relationships and service to others.

The five persons exhibiting the highest level of gerotranscendence also showed the highest level of life satisfaction, according to Thomas. He gives various possible explanations for this correlation: A transcendent view of life enables people to place their lives and suffering in a larger, meaningful context. A strong belief in life after death allows them to view misfortune and adversity with equanimity. Moreover, decreased competitiveness and a sense of relatedness to others, attitudes associated with gerotranscendence, contribute to people's satisfaction with their lives. Thomas adds that, although life satisfaction is positively related to gerotranscendence, some of the nontranscenders also reported satisfaction with their lives.

Aging as a Spiritual Journey

Eugene Bianchi (1993) maintains that aging is more important as a spiritual than a biological process. He interprets the conditions of old age primarily in light of their impact on spiritual development. Because the elderly are no longer hemmed in by necessities of family and work, and have more discretionary time at their disposal, they may have more occasions for reflection and growth. Even the difficult challenges of changing social roles can shake up ingrained patterns of thought and behavior, providing opportunities to adopt new values and discover new relationships and activities. In Bianchi's view, as the elderly "disidentify" with previous social roles, they surrender a less authentic identity. This disidentification with earlier roles permits them to tap into personal depths and unfulfilled aspirations as they form their unique identity in old age. Bianchi describes this process of reidentification as recovering the soul's unrealized desires and finding ways to express them in the world. He believes that art may open the elderly to their undeveloped interior resources, and religion may help them reidentify themselves. According to Bianchi, this kind of interiority in old age is not an escape from responsibility or a fearful withdrawal from the complications of modern society; it is rather a courageous attempt to reach new ways of self-understanding and action in late adulthood.

Bianchi attempts to balance this introspective project of reidentification in old age with an emphasis on social responsibility. He argues that a reorientation of identity, values, and worldview in late adulthood has a bearing on crucial social issues such as peace, justice, and the ecology. Discovering their inner connection to the divine unites the elderly with others in the struggle against social evils. Bianchi stresses the need for the elderly to recognize that their social responsibilities do not end with retirement. He criticizes the view that the elderly have already served society enough and are now entitled to withdraw into private life. In his view, older persons still have an obligation to serve others and to be stewards of the world.

This commitment to social well-being is an essential part of spirituality that is often underemphasized in favor of a private piety focused on personal salvation, according to Bianchi. At the same time, he recognizes that, even though active social involvement can increase the elderly's sense of purpose and help overcome their isolation, a certain aloneness is inevitable due to the lowering of physical energy, the death of family and friends, and a sense of time running out. In Bianchi's opinion, a fine line separates loneliness and creative aloneness. While loneliness arises from the many endings experienced in old age, aloneness is the occasion for spiritual development. He believes aloneness can allow the elderly to come to terms with emotional hurts from the past and fears about the future; it can also permit them to experience their true selves by laying aside external norms.

Bianchi underscores the importance of living in the present and making the most of the time still available to the elderly. This focus on the here and now offsets the tendency of old people to live in the past in a way that blocks out the present. On the other hand, he warns that such a present-centered attitude should not exclude an openness to the future. Bianchi believes that when old people no longer have an orientation to the future, they are conceding that life is over. He insists that the proximity of death should not obscure our connection to, and hope for, our family, friends, the wider community, and the ecological systems of the planet.

In Bianchi's view, a less self-centered commitment to the care and integration of the whole human project is the essence of wisdom in old age. He argues that the elderly, as custodians of the wisdom of the human race, should be even more directed to the future than the young or middle-aged who are usually caught up in the immediate concerns of family and career. According to Bianchi, the elderly have the special role of cherishing life for its own intrinsic meaning; this stewardship of life itself is the vital mission of old age.

Paul Tournier (1972) also recognizes the importance of the elderly's role as stewards of life. He views this broadening appreciation of life as a development of universal commitments and a search for new ways of human bonding that reach out beyond the individual to universal human concerns. Tournier stresses that when the elderly universalize their concern for life, they do not neglect individual needs, but rather recognize the transcendent dimensions of those needs. In this process, the elderly become less possessive of things and more attached to people.

Sage-ing

Zalman Schachter-Shalomi's *From Age-ing to Sage-ing* (1997) is a particularly valuable attempt to tap the positive potential of old age. This section deals with his perspective in some detail as it highlights the kind of identity, values, and worldview that are central to spirituality and implicit religion in late adulthood. Schachter-Shalomi objects to the model of the life span that sees a gradual development from childhood to the zenith of success in midlife, which gives way to decline, weakness, and impoverishment in old age. He offers *sage-ing* as an alternative to this picture of late-life diminishment. According to Schachter-Shalomi, *sage-ing* is a process that enables the elderly to develop spiritually and become socially responsible "elders of the tribe."

His work on sage-ing grew out of his own uneasiness about growing old, facing infirmity, and dying. To come to terms with his anxieties, he secluded himself in a cabin and immersed himself in Sufi, Buddhist, and Native American spiritual traditions. There, he discovered insights which give the elderly meaning in life and help them avoid becoming economic and psychological burdens on their families, friends, and society. He admits his debt to the consciousness movement of the 1960s which introduced various traditional forms of meditation to mainstream Western culture. Humanistic psychology's focus on human potential and transpersonal psychology's interest in spiritual disciplines and extraordinary states of consciousness also greatly influence his notion of spiritual elders.

For Schachter-Shalomi, late adulthood is largely unmapped country, and elders are explorers trying to penetrate beneath the cultural prejudices and stereotypes surrounding old age. He rejects Simone de Beauvoir's (1972) uniformly negative portrait of late adulthood and her sentiment that most people approach old age with sorrow or rebellion, fearing it even more than death itself. The goal is to replace these negative images of aging with the positive potential of sage-ing, according to Schachter-Shalomi. The main problem, in his view, is not aging itself but rather the cultural expectations about old age. Even the more benign images of old people as "senior citizens" playing cards, shuffleboard, and bingo in Florida sell the elderly short. The view that old people withdraw from actively participating in the world, pursue innocuous hobbies, and mainly reminisce about the past does not tap the potential of the elderly. Schachter-Shalomi (1997) recommends for old people an alternative image of the elderly as still growing and learning and connected to the future" (pp. 14–15).

Not all the elderly are elders and *sage-ing* does not automatically come with advancing age. It requires inner work that leads to expanding consciousness. Schachter-Shalomi distinguishes between "elders" and the "elderly." The former undergo a process of deliberate growth, whereas the latter are simply those in their late years of life. He believes that elderhood is a state of consciousness that can emerge around traditional retirement age, but developing this consciousness usually requires a positive vision of the elderly's potential. The *sage-ing* process revisions old age as the culmination of spiritual development, the harvesting of wisdom, and the crowning achievement of life, rather than a time of unmitigated decline.

Schachter-Shalomi criticizes the model of successful aging that dominates modern gerontology, namely, that achievement and activity are the key goals even in old age. This dominant perspective carries on into late adulthood the values that shape the early and middle years of life. He balks at this vision of "productive aging" so characteristic of our time and culture. According to Schachter-Shalomi, this emphasis on "doing" should give way to an appreciation of "being." After so many years of effort to establish and maintain a place in society, old age can offer the quietness and inwardness that enable spiritual experience and contemplation of the divine in the present moment. In old age, people are free to pursue inner fulfillment, rather than conform to external standards and goals. In this regard, aging can be seen as a kind of natural monastery that strips away earlier roles, attachments, and activities, so that new energy and a miraculous sense of discovery can emerge (Moody, 1988).

Some see increased longevity as part of the process of human evolution unfolding in world history (Heard, 1963). In Schachter-Shalomi's view, the increasing elderly population will play a major role in humanity's next evolutionary step, the emergence of people who see the world as sacred and recognize the innumerable species on this planet as a single living entity. This expansion of humanity's worldview beyond the materialism of present consumer society honors the values of cooperation over competition and responsible stewardship over acquisitiveness. Schachter-Shalomi advises the elderly to acquaint themselves with the great mystics of various religious traditions in order to develop their spiritual lives and cultivate reverence for the earth. He believes many people mistakenly search for meaning through addictions and consumerism because they are cut off from transcendent experiences. He agrees with Mathew Fox's (1988) view that mystical experience engenders feelings of awe and wonder that connect us to the world of nature, allowing elders to rediscover their rootedness in the cosmos.

Even with its emphasis on "being" over "doing," *sage-ing* includes a strong social vision. The elders' widening vision of humanity's interrelationship with the rest of the universe affects not only the elders themselves, but evokes the higher potential of society as a whole. Schachter-Shalomi refers to this social or cultural contribution as the elders' "invisible productivity" (1997, p. 215). He sees the social contribution of spiritual elderhood as an essential corrective to a destructive individualism, which has grown since the Enlightenment and the Industrial Revolution to a point where it now dominates all aspects of life in Western societies. This individualism undermines a sense of connectedness to our communities, nature, and the earth. To offset this individualism requires a broader consciousness than the personal identity usually developed in adolescence and young adulthood. This broader identity must ultimately extend to all humanity, other species, and the entire planet, says Schachter-Shalomi.

The kind of spirituality Schachter-Shalomi recommends for elders recognizes late adulthood as the culmination of a sense of connectedness to the world that began in early childhood. This spirituality is consistent with Harry Guntrip's idea that religion is all about a fundamental sense of personal connectedness to, and validation by, the universe and ultimate reality. This sense of connectedness is the emotional foundation of religion and spirituality that gives meaning to old age and allows children to move into life with trust and hope. When elders broaden their identity and worldview to acknowledge their place in the interconnected web of all things, they contribute vision and care that can sustain future generations. As elders reach the pinnacle of their own spiritual quest, they lay the foundations for the next phase in the cycle of generations. This view builds on Erikson's understanding of the movement of generations. The final stage of the life cycle includes ego integrity, but goes beyond the ego to a perspective that is transpersonal. Precisely to the degree that spiritual elders come to discover their connection to the divine in the cosmos can they represent and mediate this experience to the next generations.

EXAMPLES OF RELIGIOUS AND SPIRITUAL DEVELOPMENT IN LATE LIFE

Melvin Kimble

Kimble (2001), a Lutheran pastor, describes how the spiritual dimension is the central feature of his experience of aging. He sees this spiritual dimension as a striving for meaning and purpose. As he reviews his personal history, he highlights a number of spiritually significant milestones, including his choice of vocation and life partner. One experience in particular transformed his consciousness in old age, namely, being diagnosed with cancer. Facing major surgery and little hope for recovery, he was ready for death. After the surgery, his cancer went into remission and subsequently he was amazed by the resulting changes in his attitude toward life.

Suddenly, he felt that each day was a gift, an unexpected bonus, and he came to see every person in his life as more precious and valued than ever before. He altered his priorities and use of time. The beauty of nature was almost overwhelming: sunrise, sunset, and the full moon became extraordinary events not to be missed. The music of Bach was especially poignant and soul-stirring. Kimble describes this state of mind as his "postmortem life," recalling the term Abraham

Maslow used to characterize his own attitudinal change following his first heart attack.

Kimble observes that the meaning of time has changed for him. He values past experiences as accomplishments and finds greater meaning in his life by reflecting on this "storehouse of the past" (2001, p. 153). He also notes a melding of masculine and feminine sensitivities that has broadened his perception of life. Finally, Kimble states that he has become aware of the spiritual energy that grounds his life.

Ethel Chilvers

Phillip Wiebe (1997) relates the story of Ethel Chilvers, a ninety-three-year-old woman who had immigrated to Canada from England with her parents when she was six and had been a nurse for some sixty years. She was raised as a Methodist but attended different churches over the course of her life. When she was living in Toronto at age ninety-one, she had a religious experience that confirmed her belief in God. While she was in the kitchen washing dishes, she turned toward the table and was startled to see the profile of Jesus above the table, facing the city center. She described him as having a beard, shoulder-length hair, white skin, and was wearing a cloak. He stood still, did not speak, and had little expression on his face. She was particularly struck by the power of his presence and felt that he was capable of destroying the whole world but was restrained from doing so by his love of humanity.

While there was no particular message for her in this vision, it did cause her to reflect back on her life and to regret not having followed through on earlier plans she had when still young to work as a missionary nurse in China. It also heightened her sense of God's involvement in human affairs. Even as her health was failing, she continued to be lively and actively involved with friends. Her religious experience reinforced her belief in an underlying spiritual reality that directed the visible world and gave her life meaning.

Louise

Louise was in her late seventies when I met her twenty years ago in a continuing education course I was teaching at the University of Toronto. She took this course on dreams and human development because she wanted to meet people and learn more about the spiritual dimension of her life. I marveled at her enthusiasm and how she enjoyed sharing her life experiences and wisdom with the rest of the class. She told us about a remarkable transformation that occurred to her only a few years earlier.

After her husband died unexpectedly of heart failure, she lost all sense of enjoyment in life and sunk into a deep depression. They had been very close and shared many interests. She had no children and her circle of friends was small. When she was alone, she would become anxious and fear that she was developing cancer. Even after her doctor assured her that she had no serious illness, she continued to obsess over her health. While she was in this depressed and anxious state, she had a dream that helped change her attitude and life.

In the dream she is preparing dinner for an unknown guest. She is just going through the motions of cooking without any interest in what she is doing. When the doorbell rings, she panics because the dinner is far from ready. As she opens the door, she is shocked to see her deceased husband. She is confused because she is aware that he is dead but at the same time she is overjoyed to see him again. He embraces her and she begins to cry, and she apologizes for not having the dinner ready. He smiles at her with great understanding and motions for her to sit down. He tells her to forget about the dinner because he is not hungry. He says he is only there to remind her that he is still with her and wants her to enjoy her life and appreciate her friends. As he speaks, she cries again, feeling great relief.

Louise could not get this dream out of her mind. Throughout the next weeks, she frequently remembered the happy image of her husband in the dream and the message he communicated to her. Slowly she began to take renewed interest in the people around her and her daily activities. She developed a curiosity about the possibility of life after death and enjoyed reading about dreams, especially those which involved messages from deceased relatives and friends. Louise died a few years ago, but she maintained her interest in life and a positive attitude right to the end. Her story always reminds me of the significant changes in spirituality and implicit religion possible in late adulthood.

DEATH AND BEYOND

This section deals with death, the last stage of the life cycle. Death can be a significant occasion for spiritual and religious growth, the final chance to become more fully human. Contemplating death can enrich life by reminding us to value the time we have so that we do not put off what we mean to be and do. Elisabeth Kuebler-Ross (1986), a psychiatrist who has worked extensively with the dying, sees death as a highly creative force for personal growth. In her view, the thought and study of death can generate the highest spiritual values of life. Her attitude toward death has precedents in the world religions. For example, in Buddhism and Hinduism, thinking about death as an ever-present ingredient in the life process itself is a source of growth and enlightenment in this life (Long, 1986). In terms of spirituality and implicit religion, death can bring out the ultimate transpersonal dimensions of identity, values, and worldview that are the culmination of the developmental processes we have observed in this book moving from childhood through adulthood.

Death is one of the few certainties in the course of the life cycle, but we often deny it or at least ignore it. Our society contributes to this situation in a number of ways. Science tries to persuade us that we can postpone death indefinitely as it solves the riddles of life and increases longevity. It is only a matter of time before we conquer that last frontier, science assures us. Medicine fights for life at all costs, sometimes making the final hours of life a desperate attempt to avoid the inevitable. Frequently, hectic activity and a sea of tubes and machines surround the dying, instead of allowing them to focus their remaining consciousness on one of the major events of the life cycle. Today we are often isolated from death because we do not see people die. Many old people die in hospitals and institutions, away from home and family. Only a few generations ago, death and dying were experienced by both young and old in the home, where the body remained until people paid their respects to the dead person (Barrow, 1992).

The media also help us to maintain a distance from death and dying. For example, the numerous images of death on the television news can seem unreal as we watch thousands of people killed in endless wars from the secure comfort of our living rooms. In the movies, death is not taken seriously, even when the screen may be littered with corpses. Death is rarely portrayed as a momentous conscious process that brings us face to face with the ultimate horizon of our existence. Countless deaths in the movies are framed in a carnival-like atmosphere of violence and revenge that prevents us from experiencing the many conflicting emotions that actually surround our death and the deaths of family members and friends.

Bianchi (1993) believes that our society's extreme emphasis on physical medicine can overlook dying people's spiritual needs. He recognizes that the dying may find peace and insight in art, music, and literature, as well as in more traditional religious conventions. In his view, anything that uplifts and enobles the dying person's spirit contributes greatly to the process of dying.

Death: The End of the Life Cycle?

People have puzzled over the possibility of some kind of continued existence after death since the dawn of humankind. Life after death has been a major concern of many world religions, and some even see the experience of death as the beginning of religion and mythology (Campbell, 1988). Paleolithic graves dating back as far as 50,000 BCE indicate ideas about death and the state of the dead. Food, weapons, ornaments, and tools found in these burial sites suggest that people believed the dead continue to exist in a way that is somehow continuous with this life. Apart from theological and philosophical speculations, evidence of life after death is limited to certain nonordinary states of consciousness, such as dreams and near-death experiences (NDEs). There are also remarkable cases of young children seeming to remember previous lives.

Here we shall consider some of these hints because they encourage us to contemplate larger possible contexts of the individual life cycle that can expand a person's identity and worldview and give further meaning to life. Thinking about the possibility of life after death can be psychologically hygienic. Jung (1963) holds that it is important for people to form some kind of view about death and a possible "hereafter." As a psychotherapist, he maintains that most people live more sensibly, feel better, and experience greater peace when they assume that their lives will continue in some way beyond death. Jung sees the notion of life after death as a powerful archetype which helps to make our own individual lives whole. In his judgment, the more of this unconscious archetype we can bring to consciousness, the more of life we integrate. He considered this matter so central that he once described his life's work as an ever-renewed attempt to deal with the interplay between the "here" and the "hereafter" (p. 299). Even so, he expressly writes about life after death only in his autobiographical *Memories, Dreams, Reflections*, which is not included in his collected works. He reserves his thoughts about this important subject for a literary form in which he feels free to mythologize and tell stories, largely based on his dream experiences.

Dreams

As discussed above, Jung places great value on the intuitions and wisdom of the deep psyche, which he calls the collective unconscious. His ideas on death and a hereafter are shaped mostly by his dreams and intuitions which may provide leads, even though he grants that such dreams and ideas may ultimately prove to be false. In Jung's view, the mere fact of extraordinary dreams about death and after death sheds light on the human mind and spirit, even if they may only express ancient wishes and fears of the human race. Critical rationalism has all but eliminated mythic conceptions of life after death because it identifies human beings almost exclusively with their conscious minds, but this view simply rules out whatever transcends our present limited worldview.

Jung recounts different aspects of dreams about the dead and death which have caused him to ponder the relationship of death to the unconscious. He is particularly intrigued by certain dreams that anticipate or shed light on someone's death. In one example, a dream communicates the fact of someone's death, an experience not uncommon in the literature on dreams. Jung describes a dream in which a figure resembling his wife floats up from a bed that looks like an ancient grave. She is wearing a white gown with strange black symbols and he hears a deep sigh, like someone "giving up the ghost." When he awoke, he thought the dream might signify a death, so he told his wife the dream and checked the time, noting it was three o'clock in the morning. At seven o'clock news arrived that his wife's cousin had died at three o'clock, the time when his dream occurred.

Such remarkable dream experiences create a strong impression when they actually happen to us. I had a dream experience communicating the fact of someone's death while I was visiting my father in Florida twenty years ago. In the dream, I am walking in from a large field toward an old farm house. My mother is sitting in an old rocking chair on the porch reading the newspaper. She says to me, "Oh, look who died." I look at the paper and see a picture of two men who look like my father. When I awoke at four in the morning I was worried about what this dream might mean. Two hours later, we received a call that my father's cousin had died. I was struck by the art of this dream, showing a man's picture that resembles my father, since this cousin looked very much like my father. My mother, who had died a year before the dream, called my attention to the recent "news" of this death. In the literature on dreams, the dead are occasionally the bearers of news about a recent death.

Jung (1963) warns against overestimating the importance of dream hints and intimations. Even so, he places weight on a couple of dreams that seem to indicate that the dead are somehow dependent on the living for answers to their questions. He tells of a dream in which he is visiting a friend who died two weeks earlier. In life, this person was unreflective and conventional. But now, in the dream, he sits at a table, talking with great interest to his daughter who is a psychologist, in order to grasp the reality of his psychological and spiritual life. In another dream, Jung is with his wife (who died a year earlier) in France where she is working on studies of the Holy Grail. For Jung, this dream means that she is somehow continuing work on her further spiritual development.

One particular dream Jung finds suggestive occurred the night before his mother died. In the dream, he is in a dense forest, surrounded by gigantic boulders and junglelike trees. Suddenly he hears a piercing whistle so loud that it resounds through the universe and makes his body shake. Then he hears crashing sounds in the underbrush and a gigantic wolfhound bursts forth. As this terrifying beast tears past him, he realizes it is sent by the Wild Huntsman to carry a soul back to the ancestors. The next morning Jung received word of his mother's death. He believes the dream portrays his mother's death as her being taken by the nature god (the Wild Huntsman) into that part of the self where the wholeness of nature and spirit resolve the contradictions we struggle with in this life.

While Jung rode the night train home for his mother's funeral, he was filled with grief, yet during the entire journey he heard dance music and the sounds of laughter and a wedding celebration. He describes how he was continually thrown back and forth between contrasting emotions of grief and joy. Jung tries to make sense of these contradictory feelings by seeing death as a paradox: From the ego's point of view, death is a brutal catastrophe that tears us away from those we love, but, from the spiritual point of view, it is a wedding in which the soul achieves wholeness by being joined to its missing half. Jung notes religious beliefs that liken dying to celebrating a wedding and the custom of holding picnics on graves during All Souls' Day. These ideas express the soul's perspective that death is really a celebration of fulfillment.

Jung does not discount the possibility of reincarnation, although he claims no evidence for it. He only mentions a series of dreams which seem to portray a process of reincarnation in one of his deceased friends. While he does not describe this dream series, he confesses that these dreams allowed him to view the possibility of reincarnation more positively. According to Jung, if life continues, it is likely to do so in the realm of images, a kind of psychic existence. He imagines life in the hereafter as a logical continuation of the elderly's psychological life, which increasingly attends to inner images of past and present. From this viewpoint old age can be understood as a preparation for death, and the spirits of the dead may be indistinguishable from figures of the unconscious and located in the deep psyche which transcends space and time.

In Jung's view, if life does somehow continue in a hereafter, it is likely to follow the course of nature, in which the play of opposites defines the rules. He sees the working of opposites as an essential element of existence, with moral and physical opposites such as good/evil, love/hate, light/shadow, body/spirit, life/death, male/female, young/old, and ascent/descent structuring our entire experience. After-death existence could be both grand and terrible, like all of nature that we know. He recalls from his NDE in 1944, that he felt the deepest bliss, but darkness as well, and a cessation of human warmth. Jung imagines that the souls of the dead only gradually find the limits of their after-death state and the possibility of reincarnating. In all this speculation, he notes, we have no proof that anything continues to exist, or is conscious of itself, after death; there is only some probability of psychic existence after death.

Jung cites two further dreams that seem to illuminate the relationship of the ego, mortal, and located in time and space, and the larger self that has a timeless and eternal quality. These two dreams provide a basis for imagining the link between our conscious personality and the infinite or divine. In Jung's view, imagining and recognizing this link changes our attitudes about life and death, allowing us to experience ourselves as both limited (ego) and eternal (the self). For Jung (1963), the conscious realization of our transcendent potential is a living myth that can sustain our psychological and spiritual lives. The essential purpose of human existence is, according to this mythical vision, "to kindle a light in the darkness of mere being" (p. 326).

In the first dream he sees two lens-shaped metallic discs (unidentified flying objects or UFOs) hurtle over his house. Then another comes, shaped like a circular lens with a metallic extension leading to a magic lantern. At about seventy yards from him, it stands in midair, pointing at him. As he views the lens focusing on him, he has the feeling that his earthly existence is created as a projection of the magic lantern. This view is exactly the opposite of the usual interpretation of UFOs as projections of our minds. The magic lantern here is mysterious and represents the creative force or divinity that creates our ego's body-based existence.

In the second dream, Jung is hiking through hilly landscape. The sun is shining and he has a wide view in every direction. Then he comes to a small chapel with the door ajar. As he enters the chapel, he is surprised to see no crucifix or statue of the Virgin Mary on the altar, but rather a magnificent flower arrangement. Then he notices that on the floor in front of the altar, a yogi sits facing him in lotus posture in deep meditation. As he looks more closely, he sees that the yogi looks just like himself. Jung is shocked and frightened to realize that the yogi is creating him by meditating and dreaming. He also knows that when the yogi is no longer meditating or dreaming, the person Carl Jung will no longer exist.

He interprets this dream as a parable. The yogi represents his unconscious prenatal wholeness, his larger self. His self retires into meditation and thereby creates his earthly form. Jung likens this creative process to someone putting on a diving suit to dive deep into the sea. Here, the sea is a metaphor for the unconscious depths of our human existence. According to Jung, both dreams reverse the usual relationship between the ego and the unconscious. Normally, we think of our conscious personality as solid reality and the unconscious as a not very substantial, shadowy reality. The yogi's meditation, like the magic lantern in the first dream, projects the person's physical existence. This perspective makes the unconscious the "real" existence, and the source of the conscious personality, which is now viewed as a kind of projected, illusory reality. From this vantage point, our conscious reality seems to be like a dream experience, real only so long as we are in it.

Near-Death Experiences (NDEs)

Another possible source of insight about death comes from those who have been at death's door and have even been declared clinically dead. Millions of people of all ages have had NDEs. Though people were once reluctant to talk about these experiences, they are now more willing to discuss them after Raymond Moody opened the subject for scientific research. Researchers have observed similar traits among these experiences regardless of the cause of near fatality. While many report pleasant and positively transforming NDEs, others tell of horrendous experiences (Rawlings, 1987). Not all people experiencing NDEs have all of the common elements reported; most have only one or two of the following traits. First, there is often a sense of being dead. Some experience peace and painlessness even as their bodies undergo severe trauma. Others have out-of-body experiences (OBEs) in which they see themselves from a point above them. Many feel they are moving through a tunnel and see relatives or people filled with light at the end of the tunnel's darkness. People often reexperience many aspects of their lives in a kind of life review. Some people report that they were reluctant to return to their body, but someone tells them there are still tasks for them to do in their life, so they must return. Finally, some people undergo a complete personality transformation, with a different worldview and sense of self. A number of people studied state that, as a result of their NDE, they now have a greater zest for life and no longer fear death (Morse & Perry, 1992).

Many NDEs clearly have a dramatic effect on the spirituality and religiosity of those who have experienced them. Individuals often return to their lives with a new sense of meaning, altered priorities, and an awareness of the interconnectedness of all things. As noted researcher Ken Ring (1984) has stated, NDEs are essentially catalysts for spiritual awakening and development. Furthermore, the visions that accompany NDEs not only imply some kind of personal after-death existence, they also seem to represent an evolutionary development of higher consciousness for the human race as a whole. Ring believes that the millions of reported NDEs are already unlocking previously dormant spiritual potentials that are a further development of conscious life on this planet (p. 256).

According to Ring (1984), the collective importance of NDEs is suggested by the visionary experiences that occasionally accompany NDEs. Although each of these planetary visions is slightly different, he discerns the following general pattern of elements. There is a sense of total knowledge, seeing the earth's evolution and history from beginning to end. There are many reports of earthquakes, volcanic activity, and major geophysical changes. People see weather patterns, food supplies, and the world economic system severely disturbed. Respondents do not agree on whether a nuclear catastrophe will occur. These trying events are seen as a transition to a more ultimately peaceful and cooperative era in human history. While such visions may well reflect the psychological and physical trauma of the individual undergoing the NDE, the number of such accounts of observing these future planetary events suggests to Ring that at the point of death one may be able to see things from a wider cosmic viewpoint that might even continue after death.

Cases Suggestive of Reincarnation

Reincarnation studies offer further possible clues about death and a hereafter. According to Christopher Bache (1991), reincarnation expands the idea of the life cycle beyond the individual's lifetime, stretching

across centuries. Reincarnation emphasizes the remarkable connectedness of various individual life cycles in the overall web of life. Because
Judaism and Christianity, foundations of Western civilization, do not
include a concept of postmortem transmigration of souls into other
bodies, many in the West consider reincarnation a fringe idea, yet those
who believe in reincarnation may outnumber those who have never
heard of the idea or reject it (Stevenson, 1987). The belief in reincarnation in India extends all the way back to the period of the later
Vedas, about 1000 BCE.

There have been various types of evidence put forward to support
the case for reincarnation, such as past-life readings, hypnotic regression, déjà vu experiences, dreams, and meditation experiences. While
such experiences may be powerful and convincing to the adults having
them, they are generally difficult to verify. However, there is another
way of investigating reincarnation that may be more promising. Over
the past forty years, Ian Stevenson (1974, 1987) has collected from
around the world cases of young children who spontaneously begin to
speak about previous lives. He maintains that at the young age when
these children first speak about a previous life, they have not yet
received through normal channels much information about death and
the dead. Stevenson (1987) identifies a number of recurrent characteristics of the cases he has studied: Someone dreams about a deceased
person coming to a particular family; a baby has birth marks or birth
defects corresponding to wounds or other marks on the body of the
deceased person; soon after learning to speak, the child makes statements about a deceased person's life; and the child behaves in ways
that are unusual for his or her family, but which match the deceased
person's behavior as reported by informants.

Only a few of Stevenson's hundreds of cases show all of these characteristics. The children's memories generally center around the last
year, month, and days of the life remembered, and they remember
more details about the death when it was violent rather than natural.
The children usually forget the previous-life memories sometime between
the ages of five and eight, so the window of opportunity to investigate
such cases is relatively small. Such cases are significant because they are
not so easily dismissed or explained away as adults' memories of previous lives. The uncanny details described by children who are too young
to really understand death or the lives they speak about are hard to
account for outside of some actual continuity between the children
and the experiences of previous lives they relate.

SUMMARY

Late adulthood is often a time of difficult challenges as well as opportunities for religious and spiritual developments. The elderly require vital involvement in meaningful relationships and activities in order to feel good about themselves and to contribute the wisdom of their experience to their families and the larger community.

Many elderly also desire to explore their inner lives and contemplate the profound mysteries of life and death. A combination of active participation and reflective withdrawal allow for a complete and fulfilling experience in late adulthood.

Negative images and stereotypes of aging sometimes make it difficult to appreciate the positive potential of this time in life; nevertheless, late adulthood can represent the culmination of a lifetime of religious and spiritual development. An ageless self often endures in late adulthood, even through the physical, psychological, and social changes of aging.

Empirical studies indicate a high degree of religiosity among the current cohort of older adults, and a large body of research shows the positive effects of religion and spirituality on health. The religious and spiritual beliefs, behaviors, and experiences of the elderly contribute significantly to their well-being and their ability to cope with problems. Even when their participation in organized religion decreases due to declining health, their spirituality and implicit religion may continue to grow.

Important studies have emphasized the possibilities for spiritual development in old age. Tornstam's theory of gerotranscendence focuses on this positive potential. His theory holds that, as people age, they tend to shift from a materialistic and highly rational vision of life to a more cosmic and transcendent one. This altered viewpoint is a central spiritual development in which people feel a sense of communion with the universe and gain a broadened identity that affects their experience of time, space, life, and death.

Bianchi highlights the spiritual dimensions of aging. He sees late adulthood as a prime time for reflection and growth when people are less preoccupied with the necessities of family and work. Shedding earlier social roles can provide opportunities to discover new values, relationships, and activities. He characterizes this change as recovering the soul's unrealized desires. At the same time, he emphasizes that a reorientation of identity, values, and worldview in late adulthood can inspire a new commitment to social issues such as peace, justice, and the ecology. Such a concern for the social well-being helps to balance a private piety focused exclusively on personal salvation.

Schachter-Shalomi also underscores the elderly's social responsibility in his notion of "spiritual eldering," which envisions spiritual elders both as custodians of past wisdom and as agents of future evolution. He believes that the increasing elderly population will play a significant role in broadening humanity's worldview, so that the world is seen as sacred and the various species on this planet are viewed as a single living entity. Such an enlarged worldview is at the heart of spirituality and implicit religion in late adulthood.

Death represents the end of the observable life cycle and challenges the core spiritual elements of identity, values, and worldview. Paleolithic grave sites indicate that ideas about death and the state of the dead are among the oldest concerns of humankind and the beginning of religious consciousness. Jung believed it to be psychologically and spiritually healthful to form some kind of view about death and a possible hereafter. Over the centuries, religious and philosophical traditions have offered various images for understanding death and a possible after-death existence. These traditions consider thinking about death as a source of spiritual growth and enlightenment.

Certain nonordinary states of consciousness, such as dreams and NDEs, may provide further hints about the events at the end of the life cycle. Jung's dream experiences suggest that we may remain in contact with the dead and that there is some probability of individual psychic existence after death. Certain reincarnation studies also imply that the life cycle extends beyond the individual's lifetime. Stevenson's cases of young children who spontaneously speak about previous lives are impressive and challenge the core assumptions of the modern Western philosophical worldview that the mind is reducible to brain activity and death is the absolute end of the human life cycle.

Many NDEs have had a transforming effect on the spirituality of those who have experienced them, giving people a heightened sense of meaning, a feeling that death is not the end, and an awareness of the hidden order and interconnectedness of all things. Ring maintains that NDEs imply some kind of personal after-death existence and may even represent an evolutionary development of higher consciousness for the human race as a whole.

Returning to Table 10 of the movement of spiritual development, we see that major changes in late adulthood continue the transpersonal developments that may occur in the midlife passage. The spiritual developments characterized by Tornstam, Bianchi, and Shachter-Shalomi are seen in the table as an expanded sense of self, commitment to universal principles and values that reach beyond the individual, and a worldview that sees the unity and sacred dimension of all things.

Table 10: Movement of Spiritual Development and Implicit Religion in Late Adulthood

	Self-Stream	Values Stream	Worldview Stream
Transpersonal Level	A. Identity begins to include the next generations and a possible relation to the divine	B. Values broaden toward universal principles, the well-being of society and health of the planet	C. Worldview recognizes the sacredness and interconnectedness of all things
Personal Level			
Prepersonal Level			

Late adulthood continues the transpersonal development in all aspects of spirituality and implicit religion that frequently begin in the midlife transformation. The sense of self (A) expands to include a connection to, and vital concern with, the next generations and the possible continuation of life in a spiritual dimension or in relation to the divine. The values stream (B) may broaden toward a commitment to justice, peace, the well-being of society, and the health of the planet. Worldview (C) may come to recognize the sacredness of the world and the interconnectedness of all species on the earth.

Throughout this book we have seen that as people age they can learn to transcend the ego, adopt transpersonal values, and universalize their worldview. Late adulthood can be seen as the culmination of this process of development in spirituality and implicit religion that begins in childhood and proceeds throughout the life cycle. This development is often uneven over the course of life and there are frequent reversals along the way. However, even in the final stages of the individual life cycle, the possibilities of growth in spirituality and implicit religion remain.

CONCLUSION

———————— ❧ ————————

> Most people go on living their everyday life: half frightened,
> half indifferent, they behold the ghostly tragi-comedy that
> is being performed on the international stage before the eyes
> and ears of the world. . . . We scientists believe that what we
> and our fellow men do or fail to do within the next few
> years will determine the fate of our civilization.
>   — Albert Einstein, *Out of My Later Years*

Just as the life-cycle concept provides a context for understanding people's religious and spiritual developments, so the physical, social, and political state of the world can be seen as the larger context in which the individual life cycle operates. We have seen that, as people enter midlife and late adulthood, their attention is often directed more toward future generations and the human species itself. Erikson's "care" as the central virtue of middle adulthood looks to the well-being of the next generations. The future orientation of the elderly as they see their lives in a larger and possibly cosmic context often gives them a deep concern for humanity as a whole. A number of observers have called attention to the precarious state of our world which gives an urgency to our interest in the future of the human life cycle.

STATE OF THE WORLD

Roger Walsh (1993) cites developments from 1968 to 1993 that indicate the precarious state of the world at the end of the twentieth century. In that twenty-five-year period, the world's population increased by two billion people despite the death of approximately half a billion people from malnutrition and starvation, or about 50,000 deaths each day. During those same twenty-five years, the world spent over ten trillion U.S. dollars on arms, with expenditures increasing to over one trillion U.S. dollars in 1993 alone. To emphasize the absurdity of this trend, Walsh notes that if one spent a million dollars a day since the birth of Christ, one would still not have spent a trillion dollars. At the same time, he points out that a Presidential Commission on World Hunger has estimated that about six billion dollars a year, less than one week's armament expenditures, could eradicate worldwide starvation.

This situation represents insanity and immorality on a scale unmatched in human history and has brought human development to a new and terrifying stage, says Walsh (1996). Formerly, human beings have inflicted suffering and premature death on countless individuals, but now they threaten our entire species and planet. Unless we radically reduce the root causes of greed, hatred, and delusion, says Walsh, we are unlikely to survive this dangerous world situation. He looks to the contemplative practices and wisdom of both Eastern and Western religions to help bring about the necessary change in consciousness.

The so-called Club of Rome, a group of international researchers working in conjunction with the Sloan School of Management at M.I.T. to generate a computer model for understanding the dynamic behavior of complex systems, called attention to the dangers of exponential growth in world population and industrialization. They published a controversial study, *The Limits to Growth* (Meadows et al., 1972), in which they examined the web of contemporary issues they called "the world problematique": overpopulation, food production, consumption of non-renewable natural resources, industrialization, and pollution. Their computer model predicted that at the current rate of growth, humanity would reach planetary limits within a hundred years. The few computer scenarios that avoided total economic collapse required a global decision to limit family size to two surviving children and to voluntarily reduce consumption to a simple but adequate standard of living. Twenty years later, their follow-up study maintained that many of the warnings in the first report were still valid, yet resistance to their concept of "organic growth" remains strong despite warning signs (Pestel, 1989).

Christopher Bache (2000) maintains that we are entering a critical stage in the collective evolution of the human species. He argues that our industrial culture is the greatest threat to the survival of the human species in the last two centuries. At the same time, he observes that public confidence in the power of scientific technology to solve our major problems has been seriously eroded by environmental and industrial disasters. Contaminating our planet's air, water, and soil, depleting its irreplaceable natural resources, altering the earth's baseline temperature, erasing one species per hour, and creating weapons of such power that they can destroy the planet are symptoms of a disturbed and pathological culture, according to Bache.

Bache (2000) describes the present global situation as a crisis of sustainability. He maintains that our current industrial and social trends are driving us toward a devastating ecological and economic collapse. In his view, our goal of continuous economic expansion is suicidal, and the only question is how long it will take at the current rate before we exceed planetary limits. Based on analyses of global industrial, social, and environmental trends, Bache believes that the current pace of population growth, industrial production, and material consumption are on a disastrous trajectory. He notes that, in 1992, over 1,600 scientists issued a clarion call entitled *Warning to Humanity*, which stressed the fact that humankind and the natural world were on a collision course and that major changes in our stewardship of the earth would be required to avoid vast human misery and the irretrievable mutilation of the planet. A majority of the living Nobel laureates in the sciences were among the signatories of this urgent call for change.

While this forecast is bleak, Bache believes that dawn will follow the dark-night phase of humanity's present crisis. The spiritual transformation he envisages will require a strong, well-developed, though not isolated, individuality that can withstand the meltdown of civilization as we know it. In his view, the last four thousand years have been preparing the human being for this next evolutionary phase. Bache maintains that the looming planetary crisis will push humanity toward a spiritual transformation unthinkable at an earlier stage of evolutionary development. He sees this spiritual dawn as a divine marriage of Individuality and Essential Ground and the birth of a renewed humanity rising out of the chaos of near-extinction.

The planetary visions that are part of some NDEs also seem directed toward the future of the human species. Michael Grosso (1997) sees the planetary visions in NDEs as part of a significant change occurring in the collective unconscious. In his view, these NDE visions, along with other phenomena, such as Marian visions, angelic apparitions, UFO sightings, and abductions, are psychological and spiritual reactions to the emerging crisis of global survival under the threat of weapons of mass destruction and ecological collapse; these visionary experiences are signs that the human species is subliminally aware that it has entered an unprecedented phase in its approximately million-year existence. According to Grosso, just as NDEs often precipitate precognitive and telepathic experiences in individuals, so the specter of the end of humanity may be calling forth visions of the planet's future. In the best-case scenario, the global crisis may fuel a psychic transformation of our species.

Stan Grof (1985) summarizes various ways of describing the underlying problems causing the catastrophic situation in the world today: an imbalance between the intellectual and emotional maturation of humanity, a disproportionate evolution of the neocortex in relation to archaic areas of the brain, or an interference of unconscious instinctual forces with conscious processes. He believes that modern science and technology could solve most of the world's urgent problems of disease, starvation, poverty, and energy production, but forces within the human personality stand in the way. The main alternatives he sees are either to continue to externalize and act out our aggression and greed, or to turn within and undergo transformation to a new level of consciousness. In this book, we have seen the individual's religious and spiritual development through the human life cycle as a movement from prepersonal to personal to transpersonal levels of identity, values, and worldview. From this vantage point, it appears that spiritual growth in the course of the life cycle is directed toward that change in consciousness which will be required to avoid disaster.

EVOLUTIONARY DEVELOPMENT

Most observers of human evolution see a major development of species consciousness in the very distant future. These estimates of a continuing slow pace of the evolution of consciousness are based on the long view of past developments. For example, Teilhard de Chardin (1964) maintains that it may take several million years for humanity to reach a psychically centered consciousness; Ken Wilber (1981) believes that it may require thousands or even millions of years for humanity as a whole to achieve a transpersonal superconsciousness; and Arnold Toynbee (1948) suggests that it will take roughly three thousand years for humanity to develop a kind of higher consciousness after the old civilizations crumble.

Duane Elgin (1993) finds these predictions way off the mark, arguing that students of evolution seriously underestimate the accelerating pace of change. He states that we should not be entirely surprised if the human species moves very rapidly toward higher stages of consciousness. Elgin believes that the exponential growth in electronic communications is promoting a reflective consciousness on a planetary scale and global crises are pushing human beings to evolve more rapidly than we would expect judging solely from the pace of past evolutionary developments. Although he does not consider humanity's ascent to a new level of consciousness as inevitable or automatic, he maintains that when communication systems reach a certain level of development and integration, they will lead to our maturity as a planetary civilization. Elgin describes eight stages of human evolution, each marked by a distinct type of consciousness. Our present mode of collective consciousness, which gave birth to the scientific, industrial age, is seriously fragmented, resulting in our short-sighted abuse of the planet that sustains us. Although it has taken humanity about a million years to reach this present level of consciousness, the accelerating pace of cultural evolution may allow us to make the transition to a more integrated and holistic state of consciousness in a relatively short time.

Peter Russell, in *The Awakening Earth: Our Next Evolutionary Leap*, addresses the global crisis, stressing the ambiguity of humanity's role in the evolutionary process. He reminds us that the Chinese word for crisis indicates both danger and the opportunity to change. In his view, technological, cultural, and psychological pressures are forcing the human species to expand its current state of ego consciousness toward a more transpersonal consciousness. These forces press harder as the tempo of evolution continues to speed up.

Russell (1982) paints a breathtaking picture of how the tempo of change has accelerated incredibly in the last two hundred years. He observes that if we begin our reckoning from current estimates of the origin of the universe and compress the fifteen billion years of cosmic existence into a year-long film, we can gain a heightened sense of how rapidly the human dimension of evolution has been accelerating. From this broad perspective of the ultimate year-long "epic" of cosmic existence, the show begins on January first with the Big Bang; the galaxies and stars begin to form by March, and new stars condense from the debris of exploding stars in the next months. After eight months of film, by early September, our own sun and solar system take form. Things speed up considerably then, and by the beginning of October early forms of life, algae and bacteria, appear.

An oxygen atmosphere develops through the process of photosynthesis by early November. In late November, complex cells with well-defined nuclei evolve to enable sexual reproduction. With the evolution of life just beginning, most of the film is over, though now evolution accelerates rapidly. By early December, multicellular organisms emerge and shortly thereafter vertebrates crawl onto land from out of the sea.

Dinosaurs appear around Christmas and dominate the earth during most of the last week of the film. Our apelike ancestors enter about noon of the last day of the film, and by eleven o'clock at night they begin to walk upright. Now, with only one-and-a-half minutes before midnight, human language emerges, and farming begins in the last half-minute.

The Buddha reaches enlightenment five-and-a-half seconds before the film ends, with Christ appearing a second later. The Industrial Revolution happens with half a second left and World War II occurs in the last tenth of a second. The rest of modern history, with all its remarkable technological and cultural developments, is in the last frame of the one hundred thousand miles of film required for this "epic." As the film comes to an end, we see the pace of evolution continuing to accelerate even more rapidly.

Russell highlights the dramatic leaps that punctuate this film of cosmic evolution. He notes that the accelerating changes have not occurred smoothly, but rather in a series of sudden steps, for example, the sudden formation of hydrogen, the transition from matter to life, and the appearance of consciousness. Self-reflective consciousness represents a huge leap forward, allowing human beings to anticipate the results of their actions and actively participate in directing the evolutionary process. Humanity has the potential of spearheading evolution and allowing the universe to evolve through us, but at the same time humankind threatens the process of evolution on this planet. Thomas Berry (1988) underlines the tragic irony in the way our efforts to improve the human condition have resulted in creating a wasteland of the earth instead of the sought-after wonderland. Russell describes a parallel between the way cancer develops and destroys the body on which it is dependent and the way humanity has eaten its way indiscriminately across the earth and is now in danger of destroying its planetary host. Continuing the parallel, he notes that in the case of the cancerous cell some information is missing that would link it with the system as a whole and regulate its growth; in the human species, an egocentric consciousness that is cut off from the rest of the cosmos is a prime factor in humanity's threat to the earth's future evolutionary development.

To reverse this malignant trend of human evolution, maintains Russell, humanity must reach a state of consciousness that ties it back to the system of the whole. He notes that the word *religion* (from Latin *religare*) means to tie us again to our common source, to experience our oneness with the world. In Russell's view, the next leap in evolution will have to incorporate such a broad worldview and sense of human identity if the human dimension of evolution is to carry forward at all. In this regard, he believes that only a widespread spiritual renewal and shift in consciousness as traditionally described by the mystics can control the lethal tendency of humanity that currently endangers all species and the planet. For Russell, the key question facing humankind is whether or not we can facilitate this inner evolution in time.

Given the slow pace of spiritual development up to this point in history, we may well wonder whether there is time to turn things around. The age-old quest for spiritual transformation has been part of humanity's religious concerns for thousands of years, and yet we have not been able to achieve on a broad scale a state of consciousness that can adequately cope with rapid social and technological changes. Spiritual development has not been able to keep up with technological innovations and manage the harmful effects of human beings on this planet. The title of Hillman and Ventura's (1992) book, *We've Had a Hundred Years of Psychotherapy, and the World's Getting Worse,* captures the frustration with humanity's slow rate of spiritual development as compared with the accelerating pace of technological and cultural change.

Despite the dismal record of human consciousness in guiding behavior and technology, Russell believes there is still reason for hope. He applies biologist Rupert Sheldrake's theory of morphic resonance to the development of higher states of consciousness to suggest that humanity could gather sufficient momentum in the direction of enlightenment to offset humanity's harmful tendencies. According to Sheldrake's (1987) theory, if one member of a biological species learns a new behavior, the morphogenetic field that organizes the whole species changes to some degree, and in time the novel behavior becomes easier for others to learn. For example, as more mice learn a particular task, the more easily and quickly other mice learn that task.

Applying this theory to spiritual development, Russell maintains that the more individuals raise their own level of consciousness, the easier it will be for others to reach that level of consciousness. Because the rate of growth depends on others' achievements, he argues, momentum will build until it reaches a critical mass of consciousness, a threshold beyond which it will spread as a chain reaction throughout society. This theory supports Maharishi's view that even if just 1 percent of the world population were to practice transcendental meditation, humanity would be significantly transformed.

Cultural historian William Irwin Thompson (1978) characterizes the next step in evolution as a transformation from a materialistic industrial society to a planetary culture based on unitive consciousness and ecological symbiosis. However, in his view, the transition will be difficult. At the same time the multinational corporations are creating structures for planetization, they also accelerate the ecological death of the planet and increase the gap between rich and poor worldwide. Thompson sees the struggle for a higher level of consciousness as an initiation experience for the entire human race, a rite of passage accompanied by terrifying images of nuclear war, widespread famine and starvation, and ecological catastrophes.

In this process of initiation, our civilization will be forced to recognize its dark side, namely, the greed and lust for power that now threaten the whole planet. Thompson argues that our civilization's self-image and view of reality are breaking down. This collapse represents the defeat of civilization's ego which hitherto rested on the belief that we were becoming better and better, and that all we needed was to expand industrial society so as to extend greater opportunities for material consumption to everyone. Although this blow to civilization's ego is painful and disorienting, Thompson sees it as a necessary stage in the birth of a new planetary identity which will call for a revisioning of nature, self, and society.

THE INDIVIDUAL'S LIFE CYCLE AND HUMANITY'S FUTURE

Thompson addresses the larger contexts of historical, cultural, and social change that will be involved in the future evolution of humanity. In his view, we stand at the edge of history, where precedents of the past are no longer adequate guides for our future. He believes that only myths emerging from the depths of the collective unconscious are equal to the enormous task of shaping the newly emerging planetary culture. Now, with increased longevity and the accelerating pace of change, the life cycle is long enough and cultural transformation swift enough that individuals and society are becoming conscious of cultural evolution as it occurs. For Thompson (1974), the macrocosm of human evolution is playing itself out in the microcosm of individual lives. This view of the relationship between the individual and the species as microcosm to macrocosm adds to the main argument of this book, which can be simply formulated: As people age, they can learn to transcend the ego, adopt transpersonal values, and universalize their worldview. Thompson's perspective allows us to see the microcosm of individual development contributing to the macrocosm of species development, ultimately leading to a species consciousness that may permit the course of earth's evolution to continue.

Throughout this book we have examined the role of religion (both implicit and explicit) and spirituality in the life cycle, observing an overall movement toward transpersonal levels of development. This kind of religious and spiritual development through the life cycle represents the kind of change in the microcosm that Thompson believes can reflect and support the current planetary shift in the macrocosm. We have traced three fundamental streams of development that are at the heart of implicit religion and spirituality, namely, identity (the sense of self), values, and worldview, and have noted that each tends to move from an initially unconscious, prepersonal level in childhood, through an increasingly conscious personal level in adolescence and early adulthood, to a more transpersonal level in midlife and late adulthood. This primary thesis is illustrated in our exploration of spirituality and religion from childhood through old age.

The understanding of childhood provided by the psychologists we have examined is that parents, caretakers, siblings, and early experiences largely shape the child's sense of self, values, and worldview. Many psychological approaches have contributed to our understanding of these unconscious and emotional roots of religion and spirituality in childhood. We have seen that Freud called attention to the unconscious dynamics at work in the processes of internalization and projection that form the early sense of self, values, and worldview. The object-relations theorists have highlighted the important influence of parental love on childhood religion and spirituality, especially as it connects the child to other human beings and the universe. Erikson underlined the central role of trust in the religious and spiritual foundations of personality. Finally, developmental psychologists have revealed how growing cognitive capabilities influence the child's religious and spiritual ideas, values, and practices.

At this prepersonal stage, the sense of self is very fluid. Imitation and the desire to please and avoid punishment play a major role in guiding a child's behavior. The young child's worldview is magical and greatly influenced by family and early experiences. In exceptional cases, children may have extraordinary experiences that expand their sense of identity, values, and worldview, as seen in a number of examples in chapter two. These examples of spiritual experience in childhood show that childhood spirituality and implicit religion are located primarily in a sense of wonder at the mysteries of life and in the feeling of trust and connection to other human beings and the world. Such childhood experiences and insight into the nature of the self and the world may anticipate some aspects of the consciousness achieved toward the end of the life cycle, but they are usually fleeting and may take years to be integrated into personal identity.

In adolescence individuals begin to form their identities, a main task at the personal level of development. They build on the prior, largely unconscious prepersonal level, consciously sorting out their identities, values, and worldviews as they gradually become more independent of their families. While young people often doubt and criticize organized religion at this stage in life, religion and spirituality, along with family and peers, often play a significant role in shaping their identities. Even when young people may not articulate aspects of their spirituality and religion, their life stories express these features in a way that gives unity and meaning to their personalities. In adolescence as in childhood, individuals may glimpse a larger spiritual identity and worldview, as suggested by the frequency of religious conversion in adolescence. Generally, though, the personal story that embodies adolescents' implicit religion and spirituality is directed toward the more immediate challenges they will face in young adulthood.

In young adulthood, people solidify identities, values, and worldviews established in adolescence. These main elements of young adult spirituality and implicit religion are typically expressed in their occupations, relationships, and family lives. Young adults tend to emphasize their control over the forces of life and personal boundaries of identity and worldview that distinguish them from others. Focusing on current life tasks, they often believe they can manage the world by rational means and ignore transcendent dimensions of this complex and mysterious world. Frequently, a painful clash with life's polarities and unbending realities forces young adults to recognize the limitations of their spirituality and implicit religion which is so closely tied to demands of work and family. At that point, psychotherapy may help them reframe their life stories and adjust their identity, values, and worldview in a transpersonal direction.

Although aspects of religion and spirituality prior to middle age may foreshadow a transpersonal expansion of identity, values, and worldview, the midlife passage is increasingly recognized as the period when such developments typically occur. Midlife is often a time when people review and modify their lives, and wrestle with the major polarities of life, such as feminine/masculine, young/old, and life/death. During this period, people frequently explore their inner worlds and discover previously unknown, transpersonal dimensions of spirituality and implicit religion. Their identities may extend beyond the personal level to include a sense of participation in a divine drama or a connection to the divine as traditionally expressed in religion and mythology. Their values may reach beyond personal concerns with self-preservation, family needs, and national ideals toward universal principles such as compassion, justice, peace, and life. Their worldviews may enlarge to envision the sacredness and interconnectedness of all things.

Finally, as people approach the end of the life cycle, they often contemplate the meaning of their lives in relation to their children and grandchildren. Late adulthood poses difficult challenges as well as opportunities for religious and spiritual changes at the transpersonal level. Discarding earlier roles can allow the elderly to discover new values, relationships, and activities. Religious and spiritual beliefs and experiences may help them cope with their problems and contribute to their sense of well-being. Many elderly explore their inner lives and contemplate the mysteries of life, death, and the cycle of generations. This reflective mode may allow them to shift from a materialistic and highly rational view of life to a more transcendent and cosmic perspective. Such a reorientation of their identity, values, and worldview can inspire a new commitment to issues of peace, justice, and the health of the planet.

The shift in midlife and late adulthood to transpersonal levels of identity, values, and worldview may be seen as an important step toward broadening humanity's perspective so that we can see the complex issues facing the future of the earth and its inhabitants in a different light. While individuals at any age can have transforming religious and spiritual experiences, the overall movement of the life cycle from prepersonal to personal to transpersonal structures leads us to hope and imagine that all the troubles and efforts of individuals and previous generations will have a positive cumulative effect on the state of the world and the way we approach it.

THE GREAT WORK

Throughout this book, we have focused primarily on the spiritual and religious developments within the individual's life cycle, even though we recognize that society, culture, and history always influence such individual transformations of consciousness. Given the enormous role that social, economic, and technological forces play in human life, we need to relate at least briefly the spiritual and religious developments we have described throughout this book to certain dominant aspects of our society that influence the life cycle. We require a theoretical and practical framework to help us connect the unfolding of spirituality and religion through the life cycle with changes occurring in our society and the world. Thomas Berry's *The Great Work: Our Way into the Future* offers one such framework to understand some of the forces currently at work in our industrial civilization.

Berry (1999) analyzes the social forces that are pushing humanity relentlessly toward ecological collapse. In his view, the fundamental attitude endorsed and reinforced by the religious, political, intellectual, and economic establishment is at the heart of the present crisis. This problematic attitude can be summarized as a failure to recognize the inherent rights and values of the other-than-human world. He sees the mechanistic worldview put forward in Descartes' radical separation between the material and spiritual world and Newton's mechanics as major sources of our current problem. Another source of this difficulty is the religious and humanistic exaltation of the human at the expense of the nonhuman world. These attitudes have encouraged the ruthless domination of nature and the industrial plundering that have already degraded the planet beyond any acceptable limits, according to Berry.

This problem is particularly difficult to overcome because of the overwhelming power of the financial and industrial forces that control the planet. Berry observes that the inherent rights of the natural world are given no legal status in today's industrial-commercial world. Further, he maintains that we must adopt a more comprehensive perspective than the traditional ethical focus on the rights and duties of individuals, which ignores the rights of the plant and animal world and the planet itself. According to Berry, even education has reinforced this trend with its emphasis on training people to be productive in industrial society rather than helping them discover their place in the universe.

In Berry's view, education should focus on the universe story, for only in that context can the human project come to an integral understanding of itself. This epic story must characterize the universe as an intellect-producing, aesthetic-producing, and intimacy-producing process, rather than a mechanistic and random series of physical events. According to Berry, modern science reveals the following essential elements in the epic story of the universe:

1. the unity of the universe, such that each component of the universe is immediately in contact with each of the other components of the universe;

2. the emergent nature of the universe, which means that not only the earth but the entire universe has come into being through a

sequence of evolutionary changes over an immense period of time; and

3. human intelligence as an integral component of the universe, which implies that the universe from the beginning must be a psychic- and intelligence-producing process.

The story of the universe is essentially the journey of each individual being within the irreversible journey of the universe itself. This story, argues Berry, provides a deep sense of personal identity that is grounded in the universe. This larger sense of personal identity in relation to the universe is consistent with the spiritual and religious developments we have studied in the life cycle as the broadening of identity, values, and worldview in a transpersonal direction.

Berry's analysis extends to the industrial, commercial, and financial corporations that now dominate the international scene. These corporations organize and direct the discovery and use of modern science and technology. He notes their fundamental ambivalence as they seek both financial profit and human benefit. While corporations have alleviated human misery in some ways, they have also disrupted the human community and severely damaged the planet. In his view, to seek human benefit by devastating the planet is not an acceptable project. Though there is competition and tension among the corporations, they are committed to the same market economy and oppose national or international restraints on their activities based on protection of the environment.

Berry argues that corporate influence, especially through advertising, has invaded human consciousness and evoked a psychic compulsion toward limitless consumption. He adds that the corporations control our minds through their influence over the public media, and dominate governments through financial support of selected political candidates and immense lobbying efforts to oppose restrictive environmental legislation and to back subsidies for corporations. Transnational corporations have become the dominant powers on a global scale and now directly or indirectly control the natural resources of the entire planet. Berry maintains that, in the United States, corporations largely escape governmental control over their activities and are responsible only to themselves and their stockholders.

Even though the tide of corporate and economic globalization seems overwhelming, Berry states that corporations are entering a new phase in their history as they begin to recognize that a human economy can only exist as a subsystem of the earth economy and that they can only survive within the limited natural resources of the planet. But this dawning realization will have to penetrate the many layers of corporate life and be given expression in political, intellectual, and ethical institutions throughout our society. In Berry's judgment, we shall need to restructure all areas of life, including religion and spirituality, in a way that brings humans into a more integral relationship with the world of nature and the planet.

Berry describes this restructuring in radical terms: "The historical mission of our times is to reinvent the human—at the species level, with critical reflection, within the community of life-systems ... " (1999, p. 159). His phrase "reinventing the human" emphasizes the degree to which human beings are malleable and create their own world as compared with other species which receive their basic life patterns at the time of their birth through instincts. The relatively long period of childhood in humans allows them to learn about many aspects of their existence through teaching and creative adaptation to their environment.

Berry acknowledges that our cultural traditions do not seem adequate to deal with the present threat to the life systems of the planet. The new cultural forms required must place the human within the dynamics of the planet, rather than seeing the planet and its various life forms within the dynamics of the human. Berry looks to certain energy constellations in the depths of the human unconscious to give some guidance as humans face one of the major challenges in the history of their evolutionary development. He sees the Heroic Journey, Death-Rebirth, the Sacred Center, the Great Mother, and the Tree of Life as transformation archetypes that may see humans through this enormous transition we face in the years ahead.

Each of these archetypal themes are embedded in the human psyche and have been given a variety of expressions in the art and literature of societies throughout the world. In Berry's view, all of these archetypal patterns can deepen our sense of relationship with the earth and its inhabitants, and provide a new revelatory experience. Such an experience must offset the myth now supporting industrial civilization, the myth of continuing and inevitable progress through domination of the natural world, which, according to Berry, manifests Western society's deep inner rage against its earthly condition as a part of the total life community.

If the social commentators considered here are correct, we are at an unprecedented stage in history and culture. Adopting a transpersonal perspective allows us to make sense of the spiritual and religious changes that psychologists and psychotherapists have observed, and tracking the streams of self, values, and worldview, elements essential to spirituality and implicit religion, helps to illuminate individual developments. I have tried to suggest how these spiritual developments in the individual's life cycle might contribute to the evolution of human consciousness and the way we handle the threats to our planet and future. This perspective recognizes the influence of society, culture, and history on the development of the individual's spirituality and implicit religion, even though that has not been a primary focus of this book. If individual developments of spirituality and religion are to affect species consciousness, they will do so through cultural channels.

This book has attempted to trace this development of religion and spirituality in a way that allows us to see how spiritual potential unfolds in the life cycle. Whether such growth in consciousness throughout the life cycle is sufficient to offset the destructive tendencies of humanity remains to be seen. Although religious and spiritual beliefs are easily distorted and put in the service of hatred, revenge, intolerance, and greed, they also inspire images of a sacred earth and the hope that individuals and human society can reach a higher, unified state of consciousness that can fulfill their promise as integral parts of our unfolding universe.

REFERENCES

Abraham, K. 1924. The influence of oral erotism on character formation. In K. Abraham, *Selected Papers.* London: Hogarth Press. Pp. 393–406.

Achenbaum, W. 2001. The flow of spiritual time amid the tides of life. In *Aging and the meaning of time,* ed. S. McFadden & R. Atchley. New York: Springer Publishing. Pp. 3–19.

Adler, A. 1964. *Social interest: Challenge to mankind.* New York: Capricorn Books.

Allport, G. 1960. *The individual and his religion.* New York: Macmillan.

———. 1966. The religious context of prejudice. *Journal for the Scientific Study of Religion,* 5, 447–457.

Alpert, R. 1971. *Remember be here now.* San Cristobal, NM: Lama Foundation.

Applebaum, S. 1985. The rediscovery of spirituality through psychotherapy. In *Psychotherapy of the Religious patient,* ed. M. Spero. Springfield, IL: Thomas Books. Pp. 140–153.

Armstrong, T. 1984. Transpersonal experience in childhood. *Journal of Transpersonal Psychology,* 162, 207–230.

Ashley, M. 2000. Secular spirituality and implicit religion: The realization of human potential. *Implicit Religion,* 31, 31–49.

Ashmore, R., & Jussim, L. 1997. Introduction: Toward a second century of the scientific analysis of self and identity. In *Self and identity: Fundamental issues,* ed. R. Ashmore & L. Jussim. New York: Oxford University Press. Pp. 3–19.

Atchley, R. 1971. Disengagement among professors. *Journal of Gerontology,* 26, 476–480.

———. 1991. *Social forces and aging: An introduction to social gerontology.* Belmont, CA: Wadsworth Publishing.

Bache, C. 1991. *Lifecycles: Reincarnation and the web of life.* New York: Paragon House.

———. 2000. *Dark night, early dawn: Steps to a deep ecology of mind.* Albany: State University of New York Press.

Bailey, E. I. 1990. Implicit religion: A bibliographical introduction. *Social Compass,* 37(4), 499–509.

———. 1997. *Implicit religion in contemporary society.* Weinheim: Deutscher Studien Verlag.

———. 1998. *Implicit religion: An introduction.* London: Middlesex University Press.

———. 2000. Introduction. *Implicit Religion,* 41, 3–4.

Barrow, G. 1992. *Aging, the individual, and society.* St. Paul, MN: West Publishing.

Bateson, M. C. 1989. *Composing a life.* New York: Atlantic Monthly Press.

Batson, C., Schoenrade, P., & Ventis, W. 1993. *Religion and the individual: A social-psychological perspective.* New York: Oxford University Press.

Baumeister, R., & Newman, L. 1994. How stories make sense of personal experiences: Motives that shape autobiographical narratives. *Personality and Sociology Bulletin,* 20, 676–690.

Beit-Hallahmi, B. 1989. *Prolegomena to the psychological study of religion.* Lewisburg, PA: Bucknell University Press.

Bellah, R. 1985. *Habits of the heart.* Berkeley, CA: University of California Press.

Benson, P. 1992. Patterns of religious development in adolescence and adulthood. *Psychology of Religion Newsletter,* 172, 2–9.

Berger, P. 1974. Some second thoughts on substantive versus functional definitions of religion. *Journal for the Scientific Study of Religion,* 13, 125–134.

Bergin, A. 1980. Psychotherapy and religious values. *Journal of Consulting and Clinical Psychology,* 481, 95–105.

Bergin, A., & Jensen, J. 1990. Religiosity of psychotherapists: A national survey. *Psychotherapy,* 271, 3–7.

Berry, T. 1988. *The dream of the earth.* San Francisco: Sierra Club Books.

———. 1999. *The great work: Our way into the future.* New York: Bell Tower.

Beutler, L. 1981. Convergence in counseling and psychotherapy: A current look. *Clinical Psychology Review,* 1, 79–101.

Bianchi, E. 1993. *Aging as a spiritual journey.* New York: Crossroad Publishing.

Bibby, R. 1987. *Fragmented gods: The poverty and potential of religion in Canada.* Toronto: Irwin.

———. 1993. *Unknown gods: The ongoing story of religion in Canada.* Toronto: Stoddart.

———. 2002. *Restless gods: The renaissance of religion in Canada.* Toronto: Stoddart.

Biggs, D., Pulvino, C., & Beck, C. 1976. *Counseling and values.* Washington, DC: APGA Press.

Blazer, D. 1998. Religion and academia in mental health. In *Handbook of religion and mental health,* ed. H. Koenig. San Diego, CA: Academic Press. Pp. 379–389.

Blos, P. 1979. *The adolescent passage: Developmental issues.* New York: International Universities Press.

Bly, J. 1990. *Iron John: A book about men.* Reading, MA: Addison-Wesley.

Bohm, D. 1980. *Wholeness and the implicate order.* London: ARK Paperbacks.

Bohr, N. 1958. *Atomic physics and human knowledge.* New York: Wiley.

Bolen, J. 1984. *Goddesses in everywoman: A new psychology of women.* San Francisco: Harper & Row.

———. 1994. *Crossing to Avalon: A woman's midlife pilgrimage.* San Francisco: Harper Collins.

Borysenko, J. 1996. *A woman's book of life: The biology, psychology, and spirituality of the feminine life cycle.* New York: Riverhead Books.

Brinthaupt, T., & Lipka, R. 2002. *Understanding early adolescent self and identity: Applications and interventions.* Albany: State University of New York Press.

Campbell, J. 1973. *The hero with a thousand faces.* Princeton, NJ: Princeton University Press.

———. 1988. *The power of myth.* New York: Doubleday.

Campbell, R. 2001. When implicit religion becomes explicit: The case of the Boy Scouts in Canada. *Implicit Religion,* 41, 15–25.

Carp, F. 1968. Some components of disengagement. *Journal of Gerontology,* 23, 382–386.

Carstensen, L. 1992. Social and emotional patterns in adulthood: Support for socio-emotional selectivity theory. *Psychology and Aging*, 7(3), 331–338.

Carstensen, L., Gottman, J., & Levenson, R. 1995. Emotional behavior in long-term marriage. *Psychology and Aging*, 10, 140–149.

Chodorow, N. 1978. *The reproduction of mothering: Psychoanalysis and the sociology of gender.* Berkeley: University of California Press.

Clark, W. H. 1958. *The psychology of religion: An introduction to religious experience and behavior.* New York: Macmillan.

Coles, R. 1990. *The spiritual life of children.* Boston: Houghton Mifflin.

Connell, J. 1996. *Meetings with Mary: Visions of the Blessed Mother.* New York: Ballantine Books.

———. 1998. *The visions of the children: The apparitions of the Blessed Mother at Medjugorje.* New York: St. Martin's Press.

Copley, T. 2000. *Spiritual development in the state school: A perspective on worship and spirituality in the educational system of England and Wales.* Exeter, UK: University of Exeter Press.

Cortright, B. 1997. *Psychotherapy and spirit: Theory and practice in transpersonal psychotherapy.* Albany: State University of New York Press.

Coupland, N., Nussbaum, J., & Grossman, A. 1993. Introduction: Discourse, selfhood and the lifespan. In *Discourse and lifespan identity*, ed. N. Coupland & J. Nussbaum. London: Sage Publications. Pp. x–xxviii.

Cumming, E., & Henry, W. 1961. *Growing old: The process of disengagement.* New York: Basic Books.

Dalai Lama & Cutler, H. 1998. *The art of happiness: A handbook for living.* New York: Riverhead Books.

Dante Alighieri. 1971. *The divine comedy.* Vol. 1. *Hell.* Harmondsworth, UK: Penguin Classics.

Dayringer, R. 2000. *Life cycle: Psychological and theological perceptions.* New York: Haworth Press.

de Beauvoir, S. 1972. *Old age.* Translated by P. O'Brian. London: Cox and Wyman.

Dittes, J. 1969. Psychology of religion. In *Handbook of social psychology* (vol. 5, 2nd ed.), ed. G. Lindzey & E. Aronson. Reading, MA: Addison-Wesley. Pp. 602–659.

Donaldson, M. 1992. *Human minds: An exploration.* New York: Penguin Books.

Elder, G. Jr., & Kirkpatrick Johnson, M. 2003. The life course and aging: Challenges, lessons, and new directions. In *Invitation to the life course: Toward new understandings of later life*, ed. R. Settersten Jr. Amityville, NY: Baywood Publishing. Pp. 49–81.

Elgin, D. 1993. *Awakening earth: Exploring the evolution of human culture and consciousness.* New York: William Morrow.

Elkind, D. 1996. David Elkind. In *A history of developmental psychology in autobiography*, ed. D. Thompson & J. Hogan. Boulder, CO: Westview Press. Pp. 71–83.

Elkins, D. 1995. Psychotherapy and spirituality: Toward a theory of the soul. *Journal of Humanistic Psychology*, 35, 78–98.

———. 1998. *Beyond religion.* Wheaton, IL: Quest Books.

Elkins, D., Hedstrom, L., Hughes, L., Leaf, J., & Saunders, C. 1988. Toward a humanistic-phenomenological spirituality: Definition, description, and measurement. *Journal of Humanistic Psychology*, 28, 5–18.

Ellis, A. 1980. Psychotherapy and atheistic values: A response to A. E. Bergin's "Psychotherapy and religious values." *Journal of Consulting and Clinical Psychology*, 48, 635–639.

————. 2000. Can rational emotive behavior therapy (REBT) be effectively used with people who have devout beliefs in God and religion? *Professional Psychology: Research and Practice* 311, 29–33.

Emerson, R. W. 1941. *Essays, poems, addresses.* Roslyn, NY: Walter J. Black.

Emmons, R. 1986. Personal strivings: An approach to personality and subjective well-being. *Journal of Personality and Social Psychology* 51, 1058–1068.

————. 1998. Religion and personality. In *Handbook of religion and mental health,* ed. H. Koenig. San Diego, CA: Academic Press. Pp. 63–74.

————. 1999. *The psychology of ultimate concerns: Motivation and spirituality in personality.* New York: Guilford Press.

Erikson, E. 1950/63. *Childhood and society.* New York: W. W. Norton.

————. 1968. *Identity, youth, and crisis.* New York: W. W. Norton.

————. 1977. *Toys and reasons: Stages in the ritualization of experience.* New York: W. W. Norton.

————. 1985. Life cycle. In *Life span development: Bases for preventive and interventive helping,* ed. M. Bloom. New York: Macmillan. Pp. 35–44.

————. 1995. *A way of looking at things: Selected papers from 1930–1980.* Ed. S. Schlein. New York: W. W. Norton.

Erikson, E., & Erikson, J. 1997. *The life cycle completed: Extended version.* New York: W. W. Norton.

Erikson, E., Erikson, J., & Kivnick, H. 1986. *Vital involvement in old age: The experience of old age in our time.* New York: Norton.

Erricker, C., & Erricker, J., eds. 2001. *Contemporary spiritualities: Social and religious contexts.* London: Continuum.

Fairbairn, R. 1943. The repression and the return of bad objects. *British Journal of Medical Psychology,* 19, 327–341.

————. 1955. Observations in defence of the object-relations theory of personality. *British Journal of Medical Psychology,* 28, 144–156.

Fallot, R. 1998a. Spiritual and religious demensions of mental illness recovery narratives. *New Directions for Mental Health Services,* 80, 35–44.

————. 1998b. *Spirituality and religion in recovery from mental illness.* San Francisco: Jossey-Bass Publishers.

Feifel, H. 1958. Symposium on the relationship between religion and mental health. *American Psychologist,* 13, 555–556.

Feinstein, D. 1979. Personal mythology as a paradigm for a holistic public psychology. *American Journal of Orthopsychiatry,* 49, 198–217.

Feinstein, D., Krippner, S., & Granger, D. 1988. Mythmaking and human development. *Journal of Humanistic Psychology,* 28(3), 23–50.

Feldman, D. 1986. *Nature's gambit: Child prodigies and the development of human potential.* New York: Basic Books.

Ferrer, J. 2002. *Revisioning transpersonal theory: A participatory vision of human spirituality.* Albany: State University of New York Press.

Finkenauer, C., Engels, R., Meeus, W., and Oosterwegel, A. 2002. Self and identity in early adolescence: The pains and gains of knowing who and what you are. In *Understanding early adolescent self and identity: Applications and interventions,* ed. T. Brinthaupt & R. Lipka. Albany: State University of New York Press.

Fitzgerald, J. 1986. *Lifespan human development.* Belmont, CA: Wadsworth Publishing.

Flanagan, O. 1991. *The science of the mind.* Cambridge, MA: Massachusetts Institute of Technology Press.

Fowler, J. 1981. *The stages of faith: The psychology of human development and the quest for meaning.* San Francisco: Harper & Row.

Fox, M. 1988. *The coming of the cosmic Christ: The healing of Mother Earth and the birth of a global renaissance.* San Francisco: Harper & Row.

Frank, J. 1977. Nature and functions of belief systems: Humanism and transcendental religion. *American Psychologist,* 32, 555–559.

Frankl, V. 1962. *Man's search for meaning.* Boston: Beacon Press.

———. 1975. *The unconscious God.* New York: Simon & Schuster.

———. 1986. *The doctor and the soul.* New York: Vintage.

Franz, C., and Stewart, A., eds. 1994. *Women creating lives: Identities, resilience, and resistance.* Boulder, CO: Westview Press.

Freud, S. 1953–1974. *The standard edition of the complete psychological works of Sigmund Freud.* 24 vols. Translated under the general editorship of J. Strachey. London: Hogarth Press and the Institute of Psychoanalysis.

———. 1905. Three essays on the theory of sexuality. In *Standard Edition,* vol. 7, 1961, pp. 125–245.

———. 1908. Character and anal erotism. In *Standard Edition,* vol. 9, 1959, pp. 167–175.

———. 1916. *Introductory lectures on psychoanalysis.* In *Standard Edition,* vol. 15, 1961, and vol. 16, 1961.

———. 1923a. The ego and the id. In *Standard Edition,* vol. 19, 1961, pp. 1–66.

———. 1923b. A seventeenth-century demonological neurosis. In *Standard Edition,* vol. 19, 1961, pp. 67–105.

———. 1925. Some psychical consequences of the anatomical distinction between the sexes. In *Standard Edition,* vol. 19, 1961, pp. 241–258.

———. 1927. *The future of an illusion.* In *Standard Edition,* vol. 21, 1961, pp. 1–56.

———. 1930. *Civilization and its discontents.* In *Standard Edition,* vol. 21, 1961, pp. 57–145.

———. 1933. *New introductory lectures on psychoanalysis.* In *Standard Edition,* vol. 22, 1961, pp. 1–182.

Fromm, E. 1950. *Psychoanalysis and religion.* New Haven, CT: Yale University Press.

Fuller, R. 1988. *Religion and the life cycle.* Philadelphia: Fortress Press.

———. 2001. *Spiritual but not religious: Understanding unchurched America.* New York: Oxford University Press.

Gadamer, H. 1989. *Truth and method.* New York: Crossroad.

Gaeffke, P. 1987. Hindu mandalas. In *The encyclopedia of religion,* vol. 9, ed. M. Eliade. New York: Macmillan. Pp. 153–155.

Gardner, H. 1983. *Frames of mind: The theory of multiple intelligences.* New York: Basic Books.

Gartner, J., Larson, D., & Allan, G. 1991. Religious commitment and mental health: A review of the empirical literature. *Journal of Psychology and Theology,* 191, 6–25.

Giddens, A. 1991. *Modernity and self-identity: Self and society in the late modern age.* Cambridge, UK: Polity Press.

Gilligan, C. 1982. *In a different voice: Psychological theory and women's development.* Cambridge, MA: Harvard University Press.

Goldman, R. 1965. *Readiness for religion: A basis for developmental religious education.* London: Routledge & Kegan Paul.

Goldsmith, M. 2000. Spirituality: Blowin' in the wind. www.caps.net/CAPS-West/newsletter.

Goldstein, J. 1998. Neither this way nor that way: Developmental models as skillful means. In *Ken Wilber in dialogue: Conversations with leading transpersonal thinkers,* ed. D. Rothberg & S. Kelley. Wheaton, IL: Theosophical Publishing House. Pp. 147–154.

Goleman, D. 1995. *Emotional intelligence.* New York: Bantam Books.

Gollnick, J. 1987. *Dreams in the psychology of religion.* Lewiston, NY: Edwin Mellen Press.

———. 1992. *Love and the soul: Psychological interpretations of the Eros and Psyche myth.* Waterloo, ON: Wilfrid Laurier University Press.

———. 1999. *The religious dreamworld of Apuleius' Metamorphoses.* Waterloo, ON: Wilfrid Laurier University Press.

———. 2002. Implicit religion in the psychology of religion. *Implicit Religion,* 52, 81–92.

Gorsuch, R., & Miller, W. 1999. Assessing spirituality. In *Integrating spirituality into treatment,* ed. W. Miller. Washington, DC: American Psychological Association. Pp. 47–64.

Gould, R. 1978. *Transformations: Growth and change in adult life.* New York: Simon & Schuster.

Gregg, G. 1991. *Self-representation: Life narrative studies in identity and ideology.* New York: Greenwood Press.

Grof, S. 1975. *Realms of the human unconscious: Observations from LSD research.* London: Souvenir Press.

———. 1985. *Beyond the brain: Birth, death, and transcendence in psychotherapy.* Albany: State University of New York Press.

———. 1988. *The Adventure of Self-Discovery.* Albany: State University of New York Press.

———. 1993. Spiritual emergency: The understanding and treatment of transpersonal crises. In *Paths beyond ego: The transpersonal vision,* ed. R. Walsh & F. Vaughn. Los Angeles: Tarcher. Pp. 137–144.

Gross, J., Carstensen, L., Pasupathi, M., Tsai, J., Skorpen, C., & Hsu, A. 1997. Emotion and aging: Experience, expression and control. *Psychology and Aging,* 12(4), 590–599.

Grosso, M. 1997. *Millennium myth.* New York: Quest Books.

Guntrip, H. 1969. Religion in relation to personal integration. *British Journal of Medical Psychology,* 42, 323–333.

———. 1971. *Psychoanalytic theory, therapy, and the self.* New York: Basic Books.

Hall, S. 1904. *Adolescence: Its psychology and its relations to physiology, anthropology, sociology, sex, crime, religion, and education* (2 vols.). New York: D. Appleton.

Hamilton, M. 2001. Implicit religion and related concepts: Seeking precision. *Implicit Religion,* 41, 5–13.

Hardy, A. 1979. *The spiritual nature of man: A study of contemporary religious experience.* New York: Oxford University Press.

Harter, S. 1997. The personal self in social context: Barriers to authenticity. In *Self and identity: Fundamental issues,* ed. R. Ashmore & L. Jussim. New York: Oxford University Press. Pp. 81–105.

Havighurst, R., & Albrecht, R. 1980. *Older people.* New York: Arno Press.

Havighurst, R., Neugarten, B., & Tobin, S. 1996. Disengagement, personality, and life satisfaction in the later years. In *The meanings of age: Selected papers of Bernice L. Neugarten,* ed. D. Neugarten. Chicago: University of Chicago Press. Pp. 281–287.

Hay, D. 1982. *Exploring inner space: Is God still possible in the twentieth century?* Harmondsworth, UK: Penguin Books.

———. 1990. *Religious experience today: Studying the facts.* London: Mowbray.

Hay, D., and Nye, R. 1996. Identifying children's spirituality: How do you start without a starting point? *British Journal of Religious Education,* 18(3), 144–154.

Hay, D., and Nye, R. 1998. *The spirit of the child.* London: Fount.

Heard, G. 1963. *The five ages of man.* New York: Julian Press.

Helfaer, P. 1972. *The psychology of religious doubt.* Boston: Beacon Press.

Helminiak, D. 1996. *The human core of spirituality: Mind as psyche and spirit.* Albany: State University of New York Press.

Hendricks, J. 2001. It's about time. In *Aging and the meaning of time,* ed. S. McFadden & R. Atchley. New York: Springer Publishing. Pp. 21–50.

Hill, P., Pargament, K., Hood, R., Mccullough, M., Swyers, J., Larson, D., & Zinnbauer, J. 2000. Conceptualizing religion and spirituality: Points of commonality, points of departure. *Journal for the Theory of Social Behaviour* 30, 51–77.

Hillman, J. 1975. *Re-visioning psychology.* New York: Harper & Row.

———. 1979. *The dream and the underworld.* New York: Harper & Row.

Hillman, J., & Ventura, M. 1992. *We've had a hundred years of psychotherapy, and the world's getting worse.* San Francisco: Harper Collins Publishers.

Hoffman, E. 1998. Peak experiences in childhood: An exploratory study. *Journal of Humanistic Psychology,* 381, 109–120.

Hood, R. 2000. The relationship between religion and spirituality. Paper presented at the Society for the Scientific Study of Religion annual conference, Houston, Texas.

Hood, R., Spilka, B., Hunsberger, B., & Gorsuch, R. 1996. *The psychology of religion: An empirical approach.* New York: Guilford Press.

Horder, D. 1973. Religious education in a pluralistic society. *Religious Education,* 68(4s), 7–20.

Horney, K. 1939. *New ways in psychoanalysis.* New York: Norton.

Horton, P. 1974. The mystical experience: Substance of an illusion. *Journal of the American Psychoanalytic Association,* 222, 364–380.

Houston, J. 1987. Psyche and Eros. In *The search for the beloved.* Los Angeles: J. P. Tarcher. Pp. 151–188.

Hyde, K. 1990. *Religion in childhood and adolescence: A comprehensive review of the research.* Birmingham, AL: Religious Education Press.

James, W. 1961. *The varieties of religious experience.* New York: Collier Books. (Originally published in 1902.)

———. 1981. *The principles of psychology* (3 vols.). Cambridge, MA: Harvard University Press.

Johnson, R. 1976. *She: Understanding feminine psychology.* New York: Perennial Library.

Jones, S. 1994. A constructive relationship for religion with science and the profession of psychology: Perhaps the boldest model yet. *American Psychologist,* 49(3), 184–199.

Jung, C. G. 1953-1979. *The collected works of C. G. Jung* (20 vols.). ed. H. Read, M. Fordham, & G. Adler, trans. R. F. C. Hull. Princeton, NJ: Princeton University Press.

———. 1912. *Symbols of transformation.* In *Collected works,* vol. 5.

———. 1921. *Psychological types.* In *Collected works,* vol. 6.

———. 1928. Child development and education. In *Collected works,* vol. 17, pp. 47–62.

——. 1930. The stages of life. In *Collected works*, vol. 8, pp. 387–403.

——. 1931. The aims of psychotherapy. In *Collected works*, vol. 16, pp. 36–52.

——. 1934. The archetypes of the collective unconscious. In *Collected works*, vol. 9i, pp. 3–41.

——. 1935a. The Tavistock lectures. In *Collected works*, vol. 18, pp. 5–182.

——. 1935b. Psychological commentary on the *Tibetan Book of the Dead*. In *Collected works*, vol. 11, pp. 509–526.

——. 1936a. The concept of the collective unconscious. In *Collected works*, vol. 9i, pp. 42–53.

——. 1936b. Individual dream symbolism in relation to alchemy. In *Collected works*, vol. 12, pp. 39–223.

——. 1938. *Psychology and religion*. New Haven, CT: Yale University Press.

——. 1944. *Psychology and alchemy*. In *Collected works*, vol. 12.

——. 1950. Concerning mandala symbolism. In *Collected works*, vol. 9i, pp. 355–384.

——. 1952. *Answer to Job*. In *Collected works*, vol. 11, pp. 355–470.

——. 1955. Mandalas. In *Collected works*, vol. 9i, pp. 387–390.

——. 1958. A psychological view of conscience. In *Collected works*, vol. 10, pp. 437–455.

——. 1961. Symbols and the interpretation of dreams. In *Collected works*, vol. 18, pp. 183–264.

——. 1963. *Memories, dreams, reflections*. Recorded and edited by A. Jaffe and translated by R. and C. Winston. New York: Pantheon.

Kaufman, S. 1986. *The ageless self: Sources of meaning in late life*. Madison: University of Wisconsin Press.

Keen, S. 1978. Body/faith: Trust, dissolution, and grace. In *Life maps: Conversations on the journey of faith*, ed. J. Berryman. Oak Grove, MN: Winston Press. Pp. 102–129.

Kelly, S. 1998. Revisioning the mandala of consciousness: A critical appraisal of Wilber's holarchical paradigm. In *Ken Wilber in dialogue: Conversations with leading transpersonal thinkers*, ed. D. Rothberg & S. Kelly. Wheaton, IL: Theosophical Publishing House. Pp. 117–130.

Kennedy, Q., Fung, H., & Carstensen, L. 2001. Aging, time estimation, and emotion. In *Aging and the meaning of time*, ed. S. McFadden & R. Atchley. New York: Spring Publishing. Pp. 51–73.

Kimble, M. 2001. A personal journey of aging: The spiritual dimension. In *Aging and the meaning of time*, ed. S. McFadden & R. Atchley. New York: Springer Publishing. Pp. 151–154.

Koenig, H. 1992. Religion and mental health in later life. In *Religion and mental health*, ed. J. Schumaker. New York: Oxford University Press. Pp. 177–188.

——. 1994. *Aging and God: Spiritual pathways to mental health in midlife and later years*. Binghamton, NY: Haworth Pastoral Press.

Koenig, H., & Pritchett, J. 1998. Religion and psychotherapy. In *Handbook of religion and mental health*, ed. H. Koenig. San Diego, CA: Academic Press. Pp. 323–336.

Kohlberg, L. 1984. *The psychology of moral development: The nature and validity of moral stages*. San Francisco: Harper & Row.

——. 1987. *Child psychology and childhood education: A cognitive-developmental view*. New York: Longman.

Kohut, H. 1971. *The analysis of the self*. New York: International Universities Press.

Kornfield, J. 1998. The mandala of awakening. In *Ken Wilber in dialogue: Conversations with leading transpersonal thinkers*, ed. D. Rothberg & S. Kelley. Wheaton, IL: Theosophical Publishing House. Pp. 156–164.

Kris, E. 1956. The personal myth: A problem in psychoanalytic technique. *Journal of the American Psychoanalytic Association*, 4, 653–681.

Kroger, J. 1989. *Identity in adolescence: The balance between self and other*. London: Routledge.

Kuebler-Ross, E. 1986. *Death: The final stage of growth*. New York: Touchstone Books.

Kung, H. 1990. *Freud and the problem of God*. New Haven, CT: Yale University Press.

Kurtz, E. 1999. The historical context. In *Integrating spirituality into treatment*, ed. W. Miller. Washington, DC: American Psychological Association, pp. 19–46.

Langbaum, R. 1977. *The mystery of identity: A theme in modern literature*. New York: Oxford University Press.

Lannert, J. 1991. Countertransference and spirituality. *Journal of Humanistic Psychology*, 31(4), 68–76.

Levin, J. 1994. Introduction: Religion in aging and health. In *Religion in aging and health*, ed. J. Levin. Thousand Oaks, CA: Sage Publications. Pp. xv–xxiv.

Levinson, D. 1996. *The seasons of a woman's life*. New York: Alfred Knopf.

Levinson, D., Darrow, C., Klein, E., Levinson, M., & McKee, B. 1978. *The seasons of a man's life*. New York: Alfred Knopf.

Lewis, C. S. 1955. *Surprised by joy: The shape of my early life*. London: G. Bles.

Loevinger, J. 1976. *Ego development: Conceptions and theories*. San Francisco: Jossey-Bass Publications.

Long, J. 1986. The death that ends death in Hinduism and Buddhism. In *Death: The final stage of growth*, ed. E. Kuebler-Ross. New York: Touchstone Books. Pp. 52–57.

Loukes, H. 1965. *New ground in Christian education*. London: SCM Press.

Lukoff, D. 1985. The diagnosis of mystical experiences with psychotic features. *Journal of Transpersonal Psychology*, 17, 155–181.

Lukoff, D., Lu, F., & Turner, R. 1992a. Toward a more culturally sensitive *DSM-IV*: Psychoreligious and psychospiritual problems. *The Journal of Nervous and Mental Disease*, 180, 673–682.

Lukoff, D., Turner, R., & Lu, F. 1992b. Transpersonal psychology research review: Psychoreligious dimensions of healing. *Journal of Transpersonal Psychology*, 241, 41–60.

Lukoff, D., Turner, R., & Lu, F. 1993. Transpersonal psychology research review: Psychospiritual dimensions of healing. *Journal of Transpersonal Psychology*, 251, 11–28.

Maharishi. 1963. *The science of being and art of living*. New York: Signet Books.

Mahler, M. 1968. *On human symbiosis and the vicissitudes of individuation*. New York: International Universities Press.

Maslow, A. 1964. *Religions, values, and peak experiences*. New York: Viking Press.

———. 1969. The farther reaches of human nature. *Journal of Transpersonal Psychology*, 11, 1–10.

Masters, K., & Bergin, A. 1992. Religious orientation and mental health. In *Religion and mental health*, ed. J. Schumaker. New York: Oxford University Press. Pp. 221–232.

May, R. 1991. *The cry for myth*. New York: W. W. Norton.

McAdams, D. 1995. What do we know when we know a person? *Journal of Personality*, 63, 365–396.

————. 1996. Alternative futures for the study of human individuality. *Journal of Research in Personality*, 30, 374–388.

————. 1997. The case for unity in the (post)modern self: A modest proposal. In *Self and identity: Fundamental issues*, ed. R. Ashmore & L. Jussim. New York: Oxford University Press. Pp. 46–78.

McFadden, S., & Levin, J. 1996. Religion, emotion, and health. In *Handbook of emotion, adult development, and aging*, ed. C. Magai & S. McFadden. San Diego, CA: Academic Press. Pp. 349–365.

McNeill, J. 1951. *A history of the cure of souls*. New York: Harper & Row.

Mead, G. H. 1967. *Mind, self and society: From the standpoint of a social behaviorist*. Chicago: University of Chicago Press.

Meadows, D. H., Meadows, D., & Randers, J. 1972. *The limits to growth: A report for the Club of Rome's project on the predicament of mankind*. New York: Universe Books.

Meehl, P. 1959. Some technical and axiological problems in the therapeutic handling of religious and valuational material. *Journal of Counseling Psychology*, 6(4), 255–259.

Midgley, M. 1994. *Science as salvation: A modern myth and its meaning*. London: Routledge.

Miller, J. 1976. *Toward a new psychology of women*. Boston: Beacon Press.

Miller, W. 1999. Diversity training in spiritual and religious issues. In *Integrating spirituality into treatment*, ed. W. Miller. Washington, DC: American Psychological Association. Pp. 253–263.

Miller, W., & Thorensen, C. 1999. Spirituality and health. In *Integrating spirituality into treatment*, ed. W. Miller. Washington, DC: American Psychological Association. Pp. 3–18.

Moody, H. 1988. *Abundance of life: Human development policies for an aging society*. New York: Columbia University Press.

Moore, T. 1992. *Care of the soul: A guide for cultivating depth and sacredness in everyday life*. New York: HarperCollins Publishers.

Morse, M., & Perry, P. 1992. *Transformed by the light: The powerful effect of near-death experiences on people's lives*. New York: Ivy Books.

Murphy, M. 1992. *The future of the body: Explorations into the further evolution of human nature*. New York: Tarcher/Putnam.

Mussen, P., Congar, J., Kagan, J., & Geiwitz, J. 1979. *Psychological development: A life-span approach*. New York: Harper & Row.

Naisbitt, J. 1990. *Megatrends 2000*. New York: W. Morrow.

Nesti, A. 1990. Implicit religion: The issues and dynamics of a phenomenon. *Social Compass*, 37(4), 423–438.

Neugarten, B. 1985. Time, age and the life cycle. In *Life span development: Bases for preventive and interventive helping*, ed. M. Bloom. New York: Macmillan Publishing. Pp. 360–369.

————. 1996a. Age groups in American society and the rise of the young-old. In *The meanings of age: Selected papers of Bernice L. Neugarten*, ed. D. Neugarten. Chicago: University of Chicago Press. Pp. 34–46.

————. 1996b. Personality and the aging process. In *The meanings of age: Selected papers of Bernice L. Neugarten*, ed. D. Neugarten. Chicago: University of Chicago Press. Pp. 270–280.

Neugarten, B., & Havighurst, R. 1996. Disengagement reconsidered in a cross-national context. In *The meanings of age: Selected papers of Bernice L. Neugarten*, ed. D. Neugarten. Chicago: University of Chicago Press. Pp. 288–295.

Neumann, E. 1954. *The origins and history of consciousness*, trans. R. Hull. New York: Pantheon Books.

———. 1956. *Amor and Psyche: The psychic development of the feminine*. New York: Pantheon Books.

Novak, M. 1971. *Ascent of the mountain, flight of the dove*. New York: Harper & Row.

Nouwen, H., & Gaffney, W. 1974. *Aging*. New York: Doubleday.

Nuessel, F. 1982. The language of ageism. *The Gerontologist*, 22(3), 273–276.

Odell, M. 2003. Intersecting worldviews: Including vs. imposing spirituality in therapy. *Family Therapy Magazine*, 26–30.

O'Donohue, W. 1989. The (even) bolder model: The clinical psychologist as metaphysician-scientist-practitioner. *American Psychologist*, 4412, 146–168.

Oser, F. 1991. The development of religious judgment. In *Religious development in childhood and adolescence*, ed. F. Oser & W. Scarlett. San Francisco: Jossey-Bass.

Oser, F., & Gmuender, P. 1991. *Religious judgment: A developmental perspective*. Birmingham, AL: Religious Education Press.

Otto, R. 1958. *The idea of the holy: An inquiry into the non-rational factor in the idea of the divine and its relation to the rational*, trans. J. Harvey. New York: Oxford University Press.

Paffard, M. 1973. *Inglorious Wordsworths: A study of some transcendental experiences in childhood and adolescence*. London: Hodder & Stoughton.

Palmore, E. 1990. *Ageism: Negative and positive*. New York: Springer Publishing.

Paloutzian, R. 1996. *Invitation to the psychology of religion*. Needham Heights, MA: Allyn & Bacon.

Papadopoulos, I. 1999. Spirituality and holistic caring: An exploration of the literature. *Implicit Religion*, 22, 101–107.

Pargament, K. 1997. *The psychology of religion and coping*. New York: Guilford Press.

Pearce, J. 1992. *Evolution's end: Claiming the potential of our intelligence*. New York: HarperCollins.

Peck, S. 1978. *The road less traveled*. New York: Touchstone Books.

Pestel, E. 1989. *Beyond the limits to growth: A report of the Club of Rome*. New York: Universe Books.

Piaget, J. 1969. *The child's conception of the world*. Totowa, NJ: Littlefield, Adams.

Piechowski, M. 2001. Childhood spirituality. *Journal of Transpersonal Psychology*, 331, 1–15.

Porter, N., & Taylor, N. 1972. *How to assess the moral reasoning of students: A teachers' guide to the use of Lawrence Kohlberg's stage-developmental method*. Toronto: Ontario Institute for Studies in Education.

Pribram, K. 1988. The implicate brain. In *Quantum implications: Essays in honour of David Bohm*, ed. B. Hiley & D. Peat. London: Routledge & Kegan Paul. Pp. 365–385.

Principe, W. 1983. Towards defining spirituality. *Studies in Religion/Sciences Religieuses* 12(2), 127–141.

Quinnan, E. 1994. Life narrative and spiritual journey of elderly male religious. In *Aging and the religious dimension*, ed. L. Thomas & S. Einhandler. Westport, CT: Auburn House. Pp. 147–165.

Rabuzzi, K. 1988. *Motherself: A mythic analysis of motherhood*. Bloomington: Indiana University Press.

Ram Dass, B. 2000. *Still here: Embracing aging, changing, and dying.* New York: Riverhead Books.

Rawlings, M. 1987. *Beyond death's door.* New York: Bantam Books.

Richards, P., Rector, J., & Tjeltveit, A. 1999. Values, spirituality, and psychotherapy. In *Integrating spirituality into treatment,* ed. W. Miller. Washington, DC: American Psychological Association. Pp. 133–160.

Richards, P., & Bergin, A. 2000. Religious diversity and psychotherapy: Conclusions, recommendations, and future directions. In *Handbook of psychotherapy and religious diversity,* ed. P. Richards & A. Bergin. Washington, DC: American Psychological Association. Pp. 469–489.

Ricoeur, P. 1978. The hermeneutics of symbols and philosophical reflection. In *The philosophy of Paul Ricoeur,* ed. C. Reajan and D. Stewart. Boston: Beacon Press. Pp. 36–58.

Rieff, P. 1966. *The triumph of the therapeutic: Uses of faith after Freud.* New York: Harper & Row.

Ring, K. 1984. *Heading toward omega: In search of the meaning of the near-death experience.* New York: William & Marrow.

Rizzuto, A.-M. 1979. *The birth of the living god: A psychoanalytic study.* Chicago: University of Chicago Press.

Robinson, E. 1983. *The original vision: A study of the religious experience of childhood.* New York: Seabury Press.

Rokeach, M. 1960. *The open and closed mind.* New York: Basic Books.

Roof, W. 1993. *A generation of seekers: The spiritual journeys of the baby boom generation.* San Francisco: Harper.

———. 1999. *Spiritual marketplace: Baby boomers and the remaking of American religion.* Princeton, NJ: Princeton University Press.

Rosenthal, D. 1955. Changes in some moral values following psychotherapy. *Journal of Consulting Psychology,* 19(6), 431–436.

Rosow, I. 1974. *Socialization to old age.* Berkeley, CA: University of California Press.

Rothberg, D. 1998a. How straight is the spiritual path? Conversations with three Buddhist teachers. In *Ken Wilber in dialogue: Conversations with leading transpersonal thinkers,* ed. D. Rothberg & S. Kelly. Wheaton, IL: Theosophical Publishing House. Pp. 133–147.

———. 1998b. Ken Wilber and the future of transpersonal inquiry: An introduction to the conversation. In *Ken Wilber in dialogue: Conversations with leading transpersonal thinkers,* ed. D. Rothberg & S. Kelly. Wheaton, IL: Theosophical Publishing House. Pp. 1–27.

———. 1999. Transpersonal issues at the millennium. *Journal of Transpersonal Psychology,* 31, 41–67.

Rowse, A. L. 1947. *A Cornish childhood: Autobiography of a Cornishman.* New York: Macmillan.

Rubinstein, R. 1994. Generativity as pragmatic spirituality. In *Aging and the religious dimension,* ed. L. Thomas & S. Einhandler. Westport, CN: Auburn House. Pp. 169–181.

Russell, P. 1982. *The awakening earth: Our next evolutionary leap.* London: Routledge & Kegan Paul.

Ryff, C. 1985. The subjective experience of life-span transitions. In *Gender and the life course,* ed. A. Rossi. New York: Aldine Publishing. Pp. 97–113.

Samler, J. 1960. Change in values: A goal of counseling. *Journal of Counseling Psychology,* 7(1), 32–39.

Sarbin, T., ed. 1986. *Narrative psychology: The storied nature of human conduct.* New York: Praeger.

Saunders, E. 1987. Buddhist mandalas. In *The encyclopedia of religion,* vol. 9, ed. M. Eliade. New York: Macmillan. Pp. 155–158.

Schachter-Shalomi, Z. 1997. *From age-ing to sage-ing: A profound new vision of growing older.* New York: Warner Books.

Schafer, R. 1980. Narration in the psychoanalytic dialogue. *Critical Inquiry* 7, 29–53.

Segal, S. 1959. The role of the counselor's religious values in counseling. *Journal of Counseling Psychology,* 6(4), 270–274.

Settersten, R. Jr. 2003. Propositions and controversies in life-course scholarship. In *Invitation to the life course: Toward new understandings of later life,* ed. R. Settersten Jr. Amityville, NY: Baywood Publishing. Pp. 15–445.

Shafranske, E., & Gorsuch, R. 1984. Factors associated with the perception of spirituality in psychotherapy. *Journal of Transpersonal Psychology,* 162, 231–241.

Shafranske, E., & Malony, N. 1990. Clinical psychologists' religious and spiritual orientations and their practice of psychotherapy. *Psychotherapy,* 271, 72–78.

Shakespeare, W. 1937. *The complete works.* Roslyn, NY: Walter J. Black.

Sheehy, G. 1978. *Passages: Predictable crises of adult life.* New York: Bantam Books.

———. 1996. *New passages: Mapping your life across time.* New York: Ballantine Books.

Sheldrake, P. 1991. *Spirituality and history.* London: SPCK Press.

Sheldrake, R. 1987. *A new science of life: The hypothesis of formative causation.* Glasgow: Paladin Books.

Shotter, J. 1993. Becoming someone: Identity and belonging. In *Discourse and lifespan identity,* ed. N. Coupland & J. Nussbaum. London: Sage Publications. Pp. 5–27.

Smith, M. B. 1961. Mental health reconsidered: A special case of the problem of values in psychology. *American Psychologist,* 16, 299–306.

Smith, W. C. 1963. *The meaning and end of religion.* New York: Mentor Books.

Spence, D. 1982. *Narrative Truth and Historical Truth: Meaning and Interpretation in Psychoanalysis.* New York: W. W. Norton.

Spero, M., Ed. 1985. *Psychotherapy of the religious patient.* Springfield, IL: Thomas Books.

Spilka, B. 1993. Spirituality: Problems and directions in operationalizing a fuzzy concept. Paper presented at the American Psychological Association annual conference, Toronto, ON.

Stahl, W. 1999. *God and the chip.* Waterloo, ON: Wilfrid Laurier University Press.

Starbuck, E. 1899. *The psychology of religion.* New York: Scribner.

Stark, R. 1971. Psychopathology and religious commitment. *Review of Religious Research,* 12, 165–176.

Stevenson, I. 1974. *Twenty cases suggestive of reincarnation.* Charlottesville: University Press of Virginia.

———. 1987. *Children who remember previous lives: A question of reincarnation.* Charlottesville: University Press of Virginia.

Stoeber, M. 1994. *Theo-monistic mysticism: A Hindu-Christian comparison.* New York: St. Martin's Press.

Sutich, A. 1969. Some considerations regarding transpersonal psychology. *Journal of Transpersonal Psychology,* 11, 11–20.

Suttie, I. 1935. *The origins of love and hate.* New York: Julian Press.

Swatos, W. 1997. Implicit religion, http://www.adelphi.edu/ci/ARTICLES/SWATOS97.HTM.

———. 1999. Revisiting the sacred. *Implicit Religion,* 21, 33–38.

Tarnas, R. 2001. A new birth in freedom: A (p)review of Jorge Ferrer's *Revisioning transpersonal theory: A participatory vision of human spirituality. Journal of Transpersonal Psychology,* 33, 64–71.

Tart, C. 1975. Science, states of consciousness and spiritual experiences: The need for state-specific sciences. In *Transpersonal psychologies,* ed. C. Tart. New York: Harper & Row. Pp. 9–58.

Taylor, C. 1989. *Sources of the self: The making of the modern identity.* Cambridge, MA: Harvard University Press.

Teilhard de Chardin, P. 1964. *The future of man,* trans. N. Denny. London: Collins.

Thomas, L. E. 2001. The Job hypothesis. Gerotranscendence and life satisfaction among elderly Turkish Muslims. In *Aging and the meaning of time,* ed. S. McFadden & R. Atchley. New York: Springer Publishing. Pp. 207–227.

Thompson, W. I. 1974. *Passages about earth: An exploration of the new planetary culture.* New York: Harper & Row.

———. 1978. *Darkness and scattered light: Speculations on the future.* Garden City, NY: Anchor Books.

Thorne, B. 1998. *Person-centered counseling and Christian spirituality: The secular and the holy.* London: Whurr Publishers.

Tillich, P. 1957. *Dynamics of Faith.* New York: Harper & Row.

Tonigan, J., Toscova, R., & Connors, G. 1999. Spirituality and the 12-step programs: A guide for clinicians. In *Integrating spirituality into treatment,* ed. W. Miller. Washington, DC: American Psychological Association.

Tornstam, L. 1994. Gero-transcendence: A theoretical and empirical exploration. In *Aging and the religious dimension,* ed. L. Thomas & S. Einhandler. Westport, CT: Auburn House. Pp. 203–225.

Tournier, P. 1972. *Learn to grow old.* New York: Harper & Row.

Toynbee, A. 1948. *Civilization on trial.* New York: Oxford University Press.

Tuckman, J., & Lorge, I. 1953. Attitudes toward old people. *Journal of Gerontology,* 32, 227–232.

Turner, R., Lukoff, D., Barnhouse, R., & Lu, F. 1995. Religious or spiritual problem: A culturally sensitive diagnostic category in the *DSM-IV. Journal of Nervous and Mental Disease,* 183, 435–444.

Ulanov, A. 1971. *The feminine in Jungian psychology and Christian theology.* Evanston, IL: Northwestern University Press.

Underhill, E. 1922. *The life of the spirit and the life of today.* London: Methuen.

Vaughan, F. 1991. Spiritual issues in psychotherapy. *Journal of Transpersonal Psychology,* 23, 105–119.

Ventis, L. 1995. The relationships between religion and mental health. *Journal of Social Issues,* 512, 33–48.

Von Franz, M. 1970. *A psychological interpretation of the Golden Ass of Apuleius.* Zurich: Spring Publications.

Walsh, R. 1993. The transpersonal movement: A history and state of the art. *Journal of Transpersonal Psychology,* 252, 123–139.

———. 1996. Toward a synthesis of Eastern and Western psychologies. In *Healing East and West: Ancient wisdom and modern psychology*, ed. A. & K. Sheikh. New York: John Wiley & Sons. Pp. 542–555.

Walsh, R., & Vaughn, F. 1993. Introduction. In *Paths beyond ego: The transpersonal vision*, ed. R. Walsh & F. Vaughn. Los Angeles: Tarcher. Pp. 1–10.

Washburn, M. 1988. *The ego and the dynamic ground: Transpersonal theory of human development*. Albany: State University of New York Press.

———. 1994. *Transpersonal psychology in psychoanalytic perspective*. Albany: State University of New York Press.

———. 1998. The pre-trans fallacy reconsidered. In *Ken Wilber in dialogue: Conversations with leading transpersonal thinkers*, ed. D. Rothberg & S. Kelly. Wheaton, IL: Theosophical Publishing House. Pp. 64–83.

Watts, F., Nye, R., & Savage, S. 2002. *Psychology for Christian ministry*. London: Routledge.

Westbrooks, K. 2003. Spirituality and therapy: Insights from intimate conversations. *Family Therapy Magazine*, 20–25.

White, H. 1978. *Tropics of discourse: Essays in cultural criticism*. Baltimore: Johns Hopkins University Press.

Wicklund, R., & Gollwitzer, P. 1982. *Symbolic self-completion*. Hillsdale, NJ: L. Erlbaum Associates.

Wiebe, P. 1997. *Visions of Jesus: Direct encounters from the New Testament and today*. New York: Oxford University Press.

Wilber, K. 1977. *The spectrum of consciousness*. Wheaton, IL: Quest.

———. 1981. *Up from Eden*. New York: Doubleday.

———. 1982. *The Atman project: A transpersonal view of human development*. Wheaton, IL: Quest Books.

———. 1990. *Eye to eye: The quest for the new paradigm*. Boston: Shambhala Press.

———. 1993a. The pre/trans fallacy. In *Paths beyond ego: The transpersonal vision*, ed. R. Walsh & F. Vaughn. Los Angeles: Tarcher. Pp. 124–129.

———. 1993b. Psychologia perennis: The spectrum of consciousness. In *Paths beyond ego: The transpersonal vision*, ed. R. Walsh & F. Vaughn. Los Angeles: Tarcher. Pp. 21–33.

———. 1993c. The spectrum of transpersonal development. In *Paths beyond ego: The transpersonal vision*, ed. R. Walsh & F. Vaughn. Los Angeles: Tarcher. Pp. 116–117.

———. 1995. *Sex, ecology, spirituality: The spirit of evolution*. Boston: Shambhala Press.

———. 1996. *A brief history of everything*. Boston: Shambhala Press.

———. 1997. *The eye of the spirit: An integral vision for a world gone slightly mad*. Boston: Shambhala Press.

———. 1998. *The marriage of sense and soul: Integrating science and religion*. New York: Random House.

———. 1999. Spiritual and developmental lines: Are there stages? *Journal of Transpersonal Psychology*, 31, 1–10.

———. 2000. *Integral Psychology*. Boston: Shambhala Press.

Winnicott, D. 1965. Morals and education. In *The Maturational Processes and the Facilitating Environment: Studies in the Theory of Emotional Development*, ed. M. Khan. New York: International Universities Press. Pp. 90–107.

———. 1971. *Playing and reality*. London: Tavistock.

Woodman, M. 1985. *The pregnant virgin.* Toronto: Inner City Books.

Woolfolk, R. 1998. *The cure of souls: Science, values, and psychotherapy.* San Francisco: Jossey-Bass Publishers.

Wordsworth, W. 1963. Intimations of immortality from recollections of early childhood. In *Immortal poems of the English language,* ed. O. Williams. New York: Washington Square Press. Pp. 260–266.

Worthington, E. Jr., Kurusu, T., McCullough, M., & Sandage, S. 1996. Empirical research on religion and psychotherapeutic processes and outcomes: A ten-year review and research prospectus. *Psychological Bulletin,* 119, 448–487.

Wright, P. 1998. Gender issues in Ken Wilber's transpersonal theory. In *Ken Wilber in dialogue: Conversations with leading transpersonal thinkers,* ed. D. Rothberg & S. Kelly. Wheaton, IL: Theosophical Publishing House. Pp. 209–236.

Wulff, D. 1996. *Psychology of religion: Classic and contemporary.* New York: John Wiley & Sons.

Wuthnow, R. 1998. *After heaven: Spirituality in America since the 1950s.* Berkeley: University of California Press.

Yogananda, P. 1971. *Autobiography of a yogi.* Los Angeles: Self-Realization Fellowship.

Youngman, D. 1999. Introduction: An historical perspective of life span development. In *Human development across the life span: Educatinal and psychological applications,* ed. R. Mosher, D. Youngman, & J. Day. Westport, CT: Praeger. Pp. 1–5.

Zinnbauer, B., Pargament, K., Cole, B., Rye, M., Butter, E., Belavich, T., Hipp, K., Scott, A., & Dadar, J. 1997. Religion and spirituality: Unfuzzying the fuzzy. *Journal for the Scientific Study of Religion,* 36, 549–564.

Zinnbauer, B., Pargament, K., & Scott, A. 1999. The emerging meanings of religiousness and spirituality: Problems and prospects. *Journal of Personality* 67(6), 889–919.

INDEX

Peter L. Laurence &
Victor H. Kazanjian, Jr.
General Editors

Studies in Education and Spirituality presents the reader with the most recent thinking about the role of religion and spirituality in higher education. It includes a wide variety of perspectives, including students, faculty, administrators, religious life and student life professionals, and representatives of related educational and religious institutions. These are people who have thought deeply about the topic and share their insights and experiences through this series. These works address the questions: What is the impact of religious diversity on higher education? What is the potential of religious pluralism as a strategy to address the dramatic growth of religious diversity in American colleges and universities? To what extent do institutions of higher learning desire to prepare their students for life and work in a religiously pluralistic world? What is the role of spirituality at colleges and universities,
particularly in relationship to teaching and learning pedagogy, the cultivation of values, moral and ethical development, and the fostering of global learning communities and responsible global citizens?

For additional information about this series or for the submission of manuscripts, please contact:

> Peter L. Laurence
> 5 Trading Post Lane
> Putnam Valley, NY 10579

To order other books in this series, please contact our Customer Service Department:

> (800) 770-LANG (within the U.S.)
> (212) 647-7706 (outside the U.S.)
> (212) 647-7707 FAX

Or browse online by series:

> www.peterlangusa.com